THE DEVELOPMENT
OF NORTH AMERICAN
ARCHAEOLOGY

ESSAYS IN THE HISTORY OF
REGIONAL TRADITIONS

Edited by JAMES E. FITTING

THE PENNSYLVANIA STATE
UNIVERSITY PRESS
UNIVERSITY PARK AND LONDON

Published simultaneously in paperback by Anchor Books,
Anchor Press/Doubleday, Garden City, New York.

ISBN: 0-271-01161-0
Library of Congress Catalog Card Number 73-5862
Copyright © 1973 by James E. Fitting
All Rights Reserved
Printed in the United States of America

CONTENTS

PREFACE

The primary purpose of this volume is to serve as a supplemental reader in North American archaeology courses. It may have a use beyond the classroom as a source book for regional archaeological bibliography and interpretation for amateur and professional archaeologists alike. It appears at a time when it may make a contribution to archaeology in a topical rather than a regional sense. The exact goals, both planned and unplanned, are spelled out in Chapter 1 with the account of how this book came to be written. Only time will tell how it came to be used.

The authors of the various chapters in this volume do not represent a research group or even a single intellectual tradition. They obtained their training at a number of schools. Although we do converse at meetings, in only one instance have contributors participated in a joint writing project prior to this volume. I have, however, enjoyed the cooperation and enthusiastic spirit with which their chapters were prepared and am impressed by the unanimity of style and expression that has been reached.

Contributors were given only the vaguest definition of areas, and often marginal literature for one area is essential to another. This was done on purpose, as it was hoped that the archaeological literature for the regions would define the regions themselves. It was originally planned to combine the bibliographies of the various authors to eliminate overlap in sources, but this idea was abandoned when I came to realize the significance of each author's bibliography as an entry into the regional research of his area.

My personal thanks goes to all of the contributors to this volume, particularly Al Dekin, who joined the project later than most but was one of the first to complete his contribution. Mrs Annie Wade at the Case Western Reserve University Department of Anthropology typed both draft and final copies of this volume. A final note of thanks needs to be voiced for Kate Brown and Toni Werbel, our editors at Doubleday. They have had faith in this project for several years now and have waited with great patience through the procrastinations and peregrinations of the authors and the editor. Finally, I would like to thank my wife, Molly, for her support throughout the project and in particular for her efforts during the summer of 1972 when she coordinated the final editing while all authors and the editor were engaged in field work in widely scattered and often unaccessible parts of North America.

THE DEVELOPMENT
OF NORTH AMERICAN ARCHAEOLOGY

1 HISTORY AND CRISIS IN ARCHAEOLOGY

James E. Fitting

Why write a book about the history of archaeology? Is it not enough just to teach archaeology as fact and let it go at that? Within the sphere of normal science it would be enough to write a book of facts but, in times of scientific crisis, facts themselves can vanish. There are many indications that American archaeology is at such a crisis stage at this moment. A volume such as this is another indication of the crisis, although none of us viewed it as such in the planning stages and some may not view it as such at the moment.

The contributors to this volume all received their graduate training within the past decade while the crisis was emerging. All are North Americanists strongly identified with the traditions of the areas about which they write. They are all productive scholars who have contributed to the literatures of the regions about which they write. No single school or academic tradition is represented, and even those with degrees from the same schools often represent different traditions within these schools. Although many of the contributors are associated with analytical and interpretive innovations, none can be considered as intellectual radicals within the profession. In fact, we may be a fairly conservative group; so conservative that in spite of our collective academic youth, over half of the group has served, or is serving, as department chairman or head.

I would suspect that a common concern is to do good archaeology; work that is useful to, and wins the approbation of, our peers. I am certain that we are all concerned with teaching in archaeology, and all of us teach courses in North American archaeology. Our concern for teaching in North American archaeology is what initially led to the planning for this volume.

There has long been a call for textbooks in North American archaeology, and several interesting and excellent textbooks, prepared by senior members of our profession, have appeared in the past decade. The most notable of these are the books by Jennings (1968) and Willey (1966). All of us teach courses in North American archaeology at several levels and can attest to the need for such books. We called for them, and now that they are available, we use them in our teaching.

However, after waiting for such texts, we use them with some apprehension. As several reviewers have noted, summaries of areas other than our own seem excellent, but as we approach those portions of our courses that deal with our own research regions, we become increasingly apprehensive. The more we know of the history of ideas and events in our own area, the more difficult it becomes to stick to the "facts" as they are presented in the introductory text. A common experience was that of letting students read the textbook for the facts while we spent our lecture time explaining how these facts came into existence. The next step was to wonder if the same thing was not true for other areas as well.

Most of us have used the books of Glyn Daniel in interpreting and teaching European archaeology. Aside from a few scattered papers, nothing similar is available for North American archaeology. What we needed was a history of North American archaeology that could help us to see the development of archaeology in other regions in the same way that we could see it in our own region. We would all like to see a volume on the history of North American archaeology similar to Daniel's *A Hundred Years of Archaeology*. There would be much merit in such a volume, and although we agree that it needs to be written, none of us was prepared to write it. Furthermore, if we were to prepare such a volume for ourselves, it would be of little direct use to students in undergraduate North

American archaeology courses. These are usually large heterogeneous groups containing relatively few potential professional anthropologists. Although anthropologists read volumes like Harris's *The Rise of Anthropological Theory,* we seldom assign it to introductory anthropology classes.

The model that was selected was a much more compact one, essentially that of a series of essays similar to those presented in Glyn Daniel's *The Idea of Prehistory,* although it was obvious that there would be many differences between it and our book. We were interested in a much larger geographical area with a more diffuse, and quite probably larger, literature. The introductory North American archaeology textbooks, following the historical development of regional archaeological literature, were arranged on a culture area pattern. Our goal was to provide a compact historical survey of the archaeological development in each of these regions. The major problem was one of concentrating information, and the initial contributions of almost all authors were far longer than the space we had allotted for each. Where each contributor wished to read only thirty manuscript pages on other areas, most felt that it would take at least one hundred pages to outline adequately their own. There are two results of this tendency: One is a rather heavy editing of many of the contributions. This would be expected in a situation where a two-thirds reduction in manuscript size was often required. The second tendency has been for spinoff publications of the larger summaries as separate monographs. Three such longer regional monographs are now in preparation, and I suspect that several more will appear over the next few years as well. The research done for these chapters has provided more depth than can be used for such a summary volume, but this in-depth coverage will be of immense interest to other specialists within our particular geographical regions.

But what does our preparation of this volume, a pedagogical device and a paean to the regional tradition, have to do with a crisis in archaeology? In fact, does a crisis exist and, if so, how is it manifest and what is its significance?

An impressive analysis of scientific change is to be found in Thomas S. Kuhn's *The Structure of Scientific Revolutions,* which appeared in 1962 and again, in an enlarged edition, in 1970. This volume has engendered much debate in many fields, and its concepts have been increasingly applicable to American archaeology over the past few years. This was pointed out several years ago in a *Science* article by Robert McC. Adams (1968), but has not, to my knowledge, been further developed in printed sources in archaeology. Kuhn has created an underground classic, and I am still not sure whether everyone reads this book or no one does. Apparently it is appropriate to invoke his work as common knowledge at the beginning of an essay, as Adams did in his *Science* article, or to use an example from another field, as Berry and Marble (1968:5) do in their introduction to *Spatial Analysis: A Reader in Statistical Geography.* A delightful little parody of the pomposity of some contemporary archaeology that was circulated in ditto form in 1972 was replete with a token reference to Kuhn (Kehoe n.d.). Still, few of my colleagues, and certainly fewer of the students for whom this volume is intended, seem that familiar with this work on scientific revolutions and paradigmatic change. These concepts seem so topical that the following regional summaries must be read in the light of them.

It is certainly clear that some sort of change is going on in American archaeology. It is the keynote of Adams' 1968 paper, "Archaeological Research Strategies: Past and Present." The spirit of change is discussed in the preface to the second edition of Hole and Heizer's *An Introduction to Prehistoric Archaeology,* an edition that appeared only four years after the first. In this second-edition preface they write:

> The spirit of these times has been principally to devise new and better ways of recovering and analyzing data, but as we

write the second edition the spirit is changing. The new emphasis is on methods and theories of interpreting archaeological data in cultural terms. A much more rigorous application of scientific method is now being made in the selecting of problems for investigation, in the posing of meaningful hypotheses about these problems, and in the testing of the hypotheses with data deliberately obtained for that purpose.

We may be wrong in some of our guesses, but we shall probably be correct in saying that the next decade will bring conceptual changes of magnitude equal to Libby's invention of the Carbon-14 dating method which gave impetus to the extensive development of the technical applications in the previous decade [Hole and Heizer 1969:vi–vii].

The entire mode of communication in archaeology is changing as well. When the long-called-for and -awaited textbooks on North American archaeology appeared, we were a little embarrassed about them and had to spend our time justifying them to our students. We could not accept archaeology as fact, a certain sign of crisis, and sought to explain it in a history of ideas.

Newer books are on archaeology as a study rather than on the archaeology of places, and even these are being replaced by monographs, journal articles, and even book reviews as modes of communication. A decade ago direct citation to book reviews was rare. Today Kent Flannery's (1967) review of *An Introduction to North American Archaeology: Volume I* still stands as the most fluent statement on processual archaeology, and Mark Leone's (1971) review of *New Perspectives in Archaeology* (Binford and Binford 1968) may be more memorable than the volume itself. It is not necessary to agree with these reviews but only to recognize them as forces shaping the literature of American archaeology.

Hole and Heizer predicted a revolution. To Leone, this revolution is already over:

The period of rapid change in American Archaeology began ten years ago. The bulk of research reported in *New*

Perspectives was done during the first half of the last decade. It is research that represents the thorough revitalization of anthropological archaeology. The work done by these men and their colleagues offered enticing and exciting problems to students and to many who felt that archaeology was becoming moribund. The battles and confrontations that the work in *New Perspectives* provoked have died down and these men, their colleagues and the problems they attend represent the undisputed frontier in archaeology. If anyone thinks a revolution did occur, the same must think that the revolution is over. Suddenly the new archaeology is everybody's archaeology. The rhetorical scene is quiet [Leone 1971:222].

The beginning of a revolution in science is to be found in its antithesis, normal science. Within the framework of normal science there is a set of rules, a body of theory, upon which all practitioners agree. This is a paradigm. Science is carried out like a game of chess. The combination of moves may be viewed as infinite, but they all take place within the squares of the chessboard.

It is possible to deal with preparadigmatic stages in many fields. At this stage, there are many competing theories with no common sets of problems, no common measurement, and no recognition of what constitutes a solution to any of these problems. Such a stage is prescientific, although the methods of science may be carried out by the individual practitioners of the time. It could be argued, I suppose, that American archaeology is at this stage now. I think not, for, as will be seen in later chapters, there have been paradigms, periods with common goals and purposes in American archaeology when American archaeology has had all the attributes of normal science. In fact, the denial of such past paradigms is, as we shall see, to be expected from those who advance new paradigms. Yesterday's science can no longer be viewed as scientific after a scientific revolution.

The establishment of a paradigm is marked by the formation of professional societies and the publication of journals in a particular field. The literature of normal science is the textbook and the often esoteric journal article dealing with the solution of minor problems within a paradigm. Arguments are inner-directed, and the general public finds it difficult or impossible to judge the results of professional debates which, because of a common set of symbols furnished by the paradigm, often appear as an abbreviated form or shorthand.

The major goal of normal science is problem solving. Although the major outlines of a field may be known, it is important to fill in gaps in knowledge and explain minor anomalies, and this, like the chess game, can be an almost infinite process. Normal science, however, restricts the world view of its practitioners. It sets boundaries on what it considers to be legitimate problems. Realities that do not conform to the expected paradigm are simply ignored. "Normal science does not aim at anomaly in facts and theories and when successful, does not find them" (Kuhn 1970:52).

Even as normal science does normal research, it does encounter anomalies. Indeed, one of the goals of normal sciences is to explain and fit such anomalies into its paradigm. Anomalies are to be found in the discovery of things that do not exist within the normal paradigm. In the early 1960s archaeologists in a number of places and situations began to see properties in archaeological materials that had not been noticed, or at least not emphasized, before. It is when such anomalies come to occupy the entire research aims of at least a small group of practitioners that a crisis situation develops.

Some of Kuhn's recent research has dealt with the sociology of scientific crises. It is possible for a crisis to arise and be solved by a small group of practitioners concentrating on a single problem before the profession, as a whole, is even aware that there is a crisis. The debate that follows is then after the fact and may center on simple understanding of what the crisis was that already has been met.

It is also the case that the crisis is unanticipated. The scientists who find the anomalies usually start their work with the goals of normal science, of perfecting the existing paradigm and creating a more perfect set of rules with which to work. The histories of science that are written in the postrevolutionary period, however, invariably and inevitably find, or read into, the literature, anticipators and ancestors that justify their own existence.

When a crisis occurs, there are usually many attempts to explain anomalies in terms of the existing paradigms. This leads to a blurring of the paradigm, and rules of normal science are also blurred until few can tell exactly what the paradigms or the rules of normal science are. I would interpret a series of recent books in archaeology, particularly *Rethinking Archaeology* (Chang 1967), as attempts to get a hold of traditional theory that is in the process of becoming difficult to define.

New theory during the crisis develops from the concentration on the anomalies that bring about the crisis. Very often, there is a direct borrowing of theories from other fields to explain these anomalies. Within American archaeology, locational analysis has proven to be a major source for new theories and methods (Gumerman 1971), but even locational analysis admits to a borrowing from other fields (Haggett 1963:281). New theory for explaining anomalies can also be developed internally, that is, in the imagination of the theoretician. I suspect that nothing is as repugnant to normal science as the spectacle of internally developed theory, the mystic speculations of the individual, accepted by younger members of the profession. It appears as though the world has gone mad and reverted to a nonscientific, preparadigmatic condition.

There are other aspects of scientific revolutions that make them repugnant to normal science. In their earlier stages, new paradigms often explain less to normal science than the traditional paradigms that they purport to replace. Their acceptance seems, and is, irrational and done as an article of faith. The revolutionary scientist acts like the political or religious zealot, and there is a clear parallel between scientific and political revolutions. Both are initiated by small, dedicated, and sometimes even ruthless groups, often competing with one another. If the revolution is successful, the competing groups achieve a unity and rewrite history to show that they have always had such unity and that they have always had mass support for the revolution. After the revolution, the new archaeology is everybody's archaeology.

With the revolution, old problems become "unscientific." This clearly seems to be the case with American archaeology. A traditional goal of archaeology, as explicitly stated by Robert Braidwood in the 1971 American Anthropological Association Lecture, has been simple discovery, to find out what is there. Today, this end is viewed as unscientific. To test this point one has only to submit a research proposal for simple discovery to a peer panel review and see how fast the expected funding is declined.

In fact, the problems that were trivial to normal science become the archetypes of the new science. Individuals who were yesterday's madmen become today's heroes as the revolutionary paradigm seeks its history and vindication.

New paradigms do not find immediate universal acceptance, and this leads to many personal tragedies in science. Indeed, Kuhn has suggested that countless people have left science, or moved to new fields, simply to avoid a scientific crisis and the inevitable purge that follows a revolution. Debate continues after a revolution, but it is a hollow debate. Holders of the old and new paradigms use the same words but in different ways; ways that make communication impossible. It has become a traditional spectacle in recent meetings for normal science archaeologists to try to explain new paradigms in old terms to uncomprehending, or even hostile, holders of these paradigms. Communication is made possible only through agreement on a common set of premises—in effect, a return to a common paradigm.

Change in paradigms alter the nature of reality itself, or at least our ability to comprehend reality. People see new things. It has been suggested that a new paradigm creates an entirely new physical universe, a point that the synthesizers cannot comprehend. Since facts are seen only through theories, the nature of facts themselves changes.

What comes after the revolution? The revolution itself disappears after it is complete. It justifies its own existence and becomes normal, traditional science in its own right. It may take time for the revolution to be complete, but there is no way of preventing this from happening. As we indicated, there is no middle ground, and failure to accept a new paradigm is to be passed by, to become unscientific.

New paradigms are most readily accepted by the younger scientists who grow up, intellectually at least, with the new language and the new paradigms. They understand the new paradigm and are impatient with older models. It is also these new students who normalize revolutionary science by again regularizing and perfecting the predictive aspects of their paradigms. Opposition to the new paradigm quite literally dies away with the older generation of scientists who had been trained in the old normal science.

Prerevolutionary scientists are left with outdated concepts, and if they are not inclined to fight the new paradigm or to synthesize the new and old paradigms (both shown to be disastrous courses) they are still left with several alternative courses of action. It is possible to immerse themselves totally in the new paradigm. In such a situation, they cannot actually make contributions to it, but often they will be canonized by the revolutionaries as "anticipators." Anticipators are those whose good work has led to the final overthrow of the old normal science. I would suspect that a person's primary productive career would virtually cease with such canonization. It would be limited to writing favorable reviews of works created with the new paradigm.

There are older scientists who partially accept the new paradigm in middle years. Kuhn expresses sympathy for them. They try to rephrase their normal science to the new expectations but find that they no longer have a primary role. Their studies are usually derivative and devoted to amplification of revolutionary models rather than the creation of them. It is significant that the revolution that Hole and Heizer see as imminent is, to Leone, already over.

The structure of a scientific revolution has a haunting familiarity to anyone who has followed the course of American archaeology over the past ten years. There can be no question about the occurrence of revolution. The question that can then be asked is what role this particular volume plays in such a revolution?

The planning of this volume grew out of a pedagogical crisis brought about by a lack of faith in at least one aspect of existing textbooks in North American archaeology. This volume was planned as a straightforward historical presentation, with a discussion of history as fact. Individual chapters were solicited from recognized younger regional specialists. The format for each paper was left open, but an independent and surprising uniformity developed among the contributors. No author was asked to develop a model of revolutions, and at that point I had no intention of pursuing it in the introduction to such a volume.

At the planning stage, my introductory chapter was intended to have been a statement on the cumulative nature of archaeological knowledge and why it is important to study the history of a field in order to tell where it is and where it is going at a particular time. My original introduction would have drawn more heavily on *Ecclesiastes* than the *Structure of Scientific Revolutions,* and I do not even know how many of the contributors to this volume are familiar with the work. Certainly none of the following chapters makes explicit reference to it, and several consciously take the traditional position of cumulative development of knowledge. However, all contain implicit recognition of situations of past and present paradigmatic change.

It is interesting to note that although all of the chapters

mention current trends, none takes the extreme position of the "new archaeology" and references to the better-known practitioners of the "new archaeology," while present, are comparatively rare.

This might mean one of two things. If Leone is correct and this revolution is over, we must have lived through it and have been a part of it. If this is the case, then we will have prepared a postrevolutionary benediction to the revolution without knowing it. What will be included is the canonization of the anticipators and heroes of the revolution. We will have unconsciously prepared a piece of propaganda.

On the other hand, Hole and Heizer may be correct, and the real revolution is yet to come. In this case, this volume will stand as a benchmark of what the history of North American archaeology used to be before it was rewritten to conform to new interpretive modes. In this case, it might prove useful to some future historian of science who, like Kuhn, is convinced that subjective truth is relative and science basically irrational.

There is a possibility that this volume will fulfill neither of these roles, which would not be disappointing, since it was not originally conceived as either. It was conceived as something to be used by people teaching North American archaeology courses; a series of short essays on how the various chapters of Willey and Jennings came to be written as they are. We will have succeeded if this goal is reached.

Finally, I ask forgiveness from my collaborators in this effort for using their presentation as a proving ground for theory of scientific change. This was not my original intention, but the development of North American archaeology is relentless and demands its due.

REFERENCES

ADAMS, ROBERT McC.
    1968   "Archaeological Research Strategies: Past and Present." *Science* 160:1187–92.

BERRY, BRIAN J. L., and MARBLE, DUANE F. (eds.)
    1968   *Spatial Analysis: A Reader in Statistical Geography.* Englewood Cliffs, New Jersey: Prentice-Hall.

BINFORD, SALLY R., and BINFORD, LEWIS R. (eds.)
    1968   *New Perspectives in Archaeology.* Chicago: Aldine-Atherton.

DANIEL, GLYN
    1950   *A Hundred Years of Archaeology.* London: Duckworth.
    1954   *The Idea of Prehistory.* Baltimore, Maryland: Pelican.

FLANNERY, KENT V.
    1967   Review of G. R. Willey, *An Introduction to American Archaeology,* Vol. I. *Sci. Am.* 217:117–21.

GUMERMAN, GEORGE J. (ed.)
    1971   "The Distribution of Prehistoric Population Aggregates." *Prescott College Anthropological Report* 1.

HAGGET, PETER
    1963   *Locational Analysis in Human Geography.* New York: St. Martin's Press.

HOLE, FRANK, and HEIZER, ROBERT F.
    1969   *An Introduction to Prehistoric Archeology.* New York: Holt, Rinehart & Winston.

JENNINGS, JESSE D.
    1968   *Prehistory of North America.* New York: McGraw-Hill Book Company.

KEHOE, ALICE B.
    n.d.   "A Laboratory Contribution to the 'New Archaeology': Systematic Testing of a Multivariate Regressive Analysis in a Structured Case." Unpublished manuscript.

KUHN, THOMAS S.
    1970   *The Structure of Scientific Revolutions.* Enlarged Edition. Chicago: University of Chicago Press.

LEONE, MARK
    1971   Review of S. R. Binford and L. R. Binford (eds.), *New Perspectives in Archaeology.* *Am. Ant.* 36:220–22.

WILLEY, GORDON R.
    1966   *An Introduction to American Archaeology,* Vol. 1. Englewood Cliffs, New Jersey: Prentice-Hall.

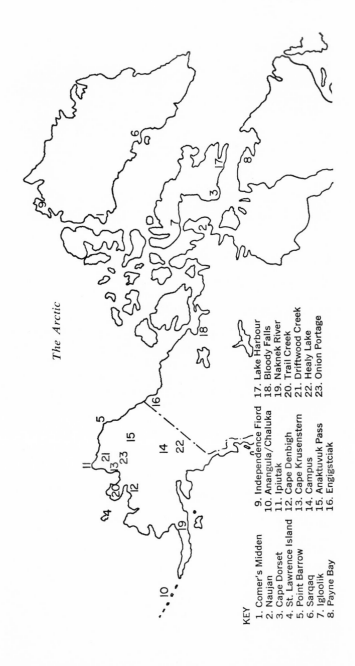

The Arctic

KEY

1. Comer's Midden
2. Naujan
3. Cape Dorset
4. St. Lawrence Island
5. Point Barrow
6. Sarqaq
7. Igloolik
8. Payne Bay
9. Independence Fiord
10. Anangula/Chaluka
11. Ipiutak
12. Cape Denbigh
13. Cape Krusenstern
14. Campus
15. Anaktuvuk Pass
16. Engigstciak
17. Lake Harbour
18. Bloody Falls
19. Naknek River
20. Trail Creek
21. Driftwood Creek
22. Healy Lake
23. Onion Portage

2 THE ARCTIC

Albert A. Dekin, Jr.

INTRODUCTION

I see four stages in the development of Arctic archaeology, paralleling the development of the rest of anthropological archaeology in North America. Early archaeological work was based on data gleaned from what was basically ethnographic research (Stage I). With the realization that problems of ethnic origins and prehistory could not really be answered by ethnology and trait distribution studies alone, archaeologists undertook systematic field excavations and expeditions (Stage II). This was the pioneering era of archaeological research, when each spade or trowel thrust revealed exciting and often unexpected artifacts and cultures. From about 1935–40 to about 1960 (Stage III), there was an expansion in the number of Arctic investigators and in the number of sites excavated, as well as an increase in the number of archaeologically known cultures. There was a corresponding increase in the number of research problems. Much of the archaeologists' interpretive energies were expended on problems of general chronology, utilizing new dating techniques that were developed during this period, and on problems of the general relationships among cultures. Since about 1960 (Stage IV) our knowledge of Arctic archaeological data has increased dramatically. We have escalated both the number and the complexity of archaeological problems. The increased emphasis on the anthropological aspects of archaeology has resulted in an increase of cultural-ecological studies. However, many Arctic archaeologists have been slow to approach the analysis of social change and cultural processes involving prehistoric Arctic cultures. We are presently in the adolescence of anthropological archaeology in the Arctic.

Archaeological sites in the Arctic are widely scattered, transportation and logistic problems are endemic (and expensive), living conditions are generally rustic, insects are voracious, cold rains and summer snows are not uncommon in certain areas, the excavating season is short, the land area to be covered is vast, and the investigators are comparatively few. In spite of, or because of, these factors, Arctic archaeology is one of the most fascinating and dynamic areas of American archaeology, and the story of its development follows.

EXPLORERS AND ETHNOGRAPHERS

Arctic archaeology began as the incidental by-product of exploring, whaling, and ethnographic research. As early as 1765 historians had begun speculating on the Siberian origin of Eskimos and their culture. In the 1880s, ethnographic data were used to try to solve this problem (which has continued as a major problem in Arctic archaeology to the present day). Thalbitzer, a linguist, suggested in 1904 that the Bering Sea region was the Eskimo homeland. Steensby (1917) proposed in his classic "An Anthropo-geographical Study of the Origin of Eskimo Culture" (published and translated into English, like so many important papers of this period, in the Danish journal *Meddelelser om Grønland*) that there were two cultural strata of Eskimos: the Paleoeskimo and the Neoeskimo.

Small archaeological collections from Greenland were obtained in the 1800s by several Danish ethnographers and explorers, but the artifacts were believed to be of no great age. Solberg (1907) attempted to justify a stone age of some antiquity in West Greenland using data collected from what we now know as sites of Sarqaq and Dorset cultures, but the antiquity of these finds was disputed, and as late as 1931, Mathiassen still considered these finds to date after Norse contact with the Greenland Eskimos (1931:196).

In the Central Arctic, the explorer and whaling captain George Comer returned to the United States with artifacts found in 1900 on Southampton Island in western Hudson Bay, which were described by Boas (1907) and thought to relate to recent Eskimo populations.

The French ethnologist Alphonse Pinart excavated in the Aleutians, recovering several relatively recent Aleut skeletons and grave goods in 1871 from a cave on Unga Island (Pinart 1875). From 1871–74, the geographer and naturalist William Dall undertook excavations of supposed Aleut village sites and burial caves during his spare time from his U. S. Coast and Geodetic Survey activities. Dall's 1873 excavations of the Amaknak cave and other sites were the earliest excavations in Alaska to take careful note of location and relationships among artifacts and to note and record evidence of stratification (Dall 1875).

Aleut origins were also considered at this stage. Jochelson reviewed the literature in 1925, noting that the Russian Veniaminoff as early as 1840 suggested a theory of Mongolian origin of Aleuts that was supported by other explorers (Jochelson 1925:111). Dall in 1877 pointed out that great sea distances and poor transportation potentials of the Japanese and Ainu mitigated against an Aleut migration from the west.

EXPEDITIONS AND PIONEERS

In the Eastern Arctic, ship captain George Comer, who was taking supplies north to the Crocker-Land Expedition of The American Museum of Natural History, was iced in and forced to winter in Northwest Greenland from 1915–17. He took advantage of this opportunity to conduct archaeological studies, and excavated fifty-three sites around Smith Sound. Comer observed a dichotomy between recent

sites and some earlier sites that Wissler, who reported
these finds in 1918, attributed to precontact ancestors of
the Polar Eskimos. There was no clear evidence of stratigraphy, so that stages in the development of Polar Eskimo
culture could not be defined, but the lower levels were
recognized as important and different.

The years 1921–24 saw perhaps the most important ar-
chaeological expedition in the history of the Eastern Arctic.
Knud Rasmussen's Fifth Thule Expedition, with Therkel
Mathiassen as archaeologist, excavated extensively ". . . at
Repulse Bay, on the mainland, N.W. of Hudson Bay, at
Ponds Inlet in northern Baffinland and in *Duke of York
Bay* on Southampton Island" (Mathiassen 1925:206). The
most important site was at Naujan on Repulse Bay. Considerable age was almost immediately attributed to this site
because of the location of the house ruins ". . . at an ele-
vation of from 12 to 20 m above the sea, at a distance of
100–150 m from the shoreline; from some of the houses,
it is not possible to see the sea now" (Mathiassen
1925:206) because of the isostatic rising of the land.
Mathiassen named this the Thule culture and cited widespread occurrences. Mathiassen concluded that the Thule
culture was ancestral to Polar Eskimo and Central Eskimo
but that *"The Thule-culture is much more closely related
to the recent-Point-Barrow-culture than to that of the recent Central Eskimos,* and there is some reason for the
theory that its home is to be found in Alaska" (Mathiassen
1925:215).

The earliest occupation of Greenland was felt by Mathiassen and others to be the Thule culture, which was
subsequently modified by Norse acculturation as documented by sites excavated at Inugsuk. This Inugsuk culture
then evolved through several minor stages to become the
Eskimo culture found by whalers, but it also survived in
isolated regions of East Greenland until the late nineteenth
century.

Perhaps the most important interpretive progress in the
Eastern Arctic during this period was the isolation of the

Cape Dorset culture by Diamond Jenness (1925). A rather extensive collection from southwestern Baffin Island was presented to the National Museum of Canada. Having little provenience data, Jenness was forced to rely exclusively on the morphological attributes of the artifacts in the collection. Many of the bone and ivory artifacts fit Mathiassen's typology of Thule harpoons, but a large segment of the collection had much darker patination, holes that had been incised and not drilled, or were previously unknown forms of chipped flint. Jenness suggested that this Cape Dorset culture preceded Thule culture, but he still felt that an earlier culture in this region was yet to be found.

Dorset was not immediately accepted as a valid culture, and Mathiassen considered it to be merely a peculiar local variant of Thule. In 1927 and 1929, Jenness and W. J. Wintemberg discovered pure Dorset sites in Newfoundland. In 1935 Henry Collins cautiously endorsed Dorset as pre-Thule Eskimo, but Mathiassen continued to be skeptical of the Eskimo nature of Dorset: ". . . But are these people who left their traces on the coast of Newfoundland Eskimos at all? The culture seems to have a strong Indian connection" (1935:422).

Between 1900 and 1925 several expeditions to the Western Arctic (Jesup North Pacific Expedition; Stefansson-Anderson Arctic Expedition with Diamond Jenness; Fifth Thule Expedition with Knud Rasmussen) purchased and excavated collections from apparently recent Eskimo and Thule-related sites from Victoria Island to the Aleutians. Some unusual chipped stone artifacts hinted at mixed samples and future complexities.

The first good systematic excavation in the Bering Strait area was done by Diamond Jenness of the National Museum of Canada at Cape Prince of Wales, Alaska, and on the Diomede Islands in 1926. The upper levels at Diomede contained cultures bracketing Russian contact in the area (including a Thule variant) but the lower levels, called Old Bering Sea culture, contained ivory objects inscribed with fine scroll artwork unlike any previously found in the

Arctic. Jenness thought that these were considerably older
than the overlying Thule culture (1929:86), but Mathiassen attempted to derive the complex Old Bering Sea dec-
orated harpoons from the simpler Thule harpoons. Collins'
evidence from stratigraphy and beach ridge sequences
(their first use in relative dating) on St. Lawrence Island
in 1929 and 1930 confirmed that Thule was later.

Collins' 1937 report, *Archaeology of Saint Lawrence Island*, is an important landmark in Arctic archaeology. This
monograph was awarded the gold medal of the Royal
Academy of Sciences and Letters of Denmark in 1936,
winning the competition for papers on Eskimo origins. Otto
Geist, Froelich Rainey, and Ivar Skarland excavated on
several islands in the Bering Strait between 1926 and 1935.
The stratigraphy and seriation of these important series of
Bering Strait excavations established an eight-stage continuum (Ackerman 1962:34) from Okvik and Old Bering
Sea through Birnirk, Punuk, Thule, and on to Prehistoric,
Recent, and Modern Eskimo cultures. The most important
criterion for distinguishing the early stages of this Eskimo
development was stylistic change in art and decoration.
The Asian affinities of Okvik and Old Bering Sea rein-
forced the hypothesis that the Eskimo way of life was a
product of the Old World (Collins 1954:297).

James Ford, sponsored by the Smithsonian Institution,
undertook excavations in the Point Barrow area in 1931,
1932, 1936, and later in 1953 (Ford 1959). A lack of funds
delayed final analysis and publication until 1959, when
Ford reported evidence of a developmental sequence from
Old Bering Sea through Nunagiak to Birnirk and Thule,
with some evidence of a later return migration of Thule
culture from the east.

Frederica de Laguna excavated sites at Cook Inlet in
1930 and at Prince William Sound with Kaj Birket-Smith
in 1933, establishing three stages of Eskimo culture
(Kachemak Bay I, II, III), which led up to a late phase
of Chugach Eskimo in Prince William Sound (de Laguna
1934). In this sequence, chipped stone gave way to ground

stone (slate) and "eastern" cultural influences became more important. This prehistoric Eskimo (Collins 1964: 102) sequence seemed to have more in common with Aleutian sites than with those in the Bering Strait region.

CHRONOLOGISTS AND PREHISTORIANS

This period began with a continuation of archaeological surveys and scattered research reports and ended in the middle of several extensive and fruitful projects. Excavations early in this period confirmed the presence of three cultural strata in the eastern Canadian Arctic: Dorset; Thule; and Recent Eskimo. Dorset culture came to be considered a culture of some antiquity in the Northeast. Speculators suggested similarities between the Dorset culture and the early prepottery Indian cultures of the Maritime Provinces of Canada, New England, and New York.

Ground slate, harpoons, and red ocher were "Indian" traits that some archaeologists suggested could have come from Dorset. William Ritchie took advantage of the new technique of radiocarbon dating to reverse the temporal positions of Dorset (by crossdating from the Western Arctic) and the New York Archaic, concluding that circumboreal contacts and cultural developments probably influenced both Dorset and Laurentian cultures (1951:50). After an excellent summation of our knowledge of Dorset culture in 1951, Elmer Harp, Jr., also denied Dorset Laurentian cultural exchanges, pointing out the more important trait linkages with Alaska, at the same time suggesting the possibility of Dorset-Beothuk contacts (1964:165— written in 1951) and circumpolar drifts from an unnamed and undiscovered ancient cultural stratum in the Old World.

In Greenland, one of the most important excavations of this period was by an amateur, Hans Mosegaard, in 1948. He excavated at Sarqaq in Disko Bay, West Greenland, and his collection documented the existence of a "stone age" culture. Meldgaard suggested that this Paleo-Eskimo culture (following Steensby) was pre-Thule and perhaps lasted to influence Inugsuk cultures (1952:230). Meldgaard saw Sarqaq origins in Alaska with influences from Dorset. These excavations demonstrated the existence of both Dorset and Sarqaq sites but did not demonstrate any great affinity or continuity between Dorset, Sarqaq, or any later cultures.

Eigil Knuth began excavating in Northeast Greenland in 1948. Initially he lumped all of his "paleoeskimo" remains as remains of the Dorset culture. Subsequent excavations led to Knuth's establishment of the Independence culture, whose closest affinities were with the Dorset culture and with its possible antecedents in Alaska. Knuth suggested that the Independence culture might represent the culture stratum ancestral to subsequent Eskimo cultures in Greenland (1954:378). His excavations in 1955 led to his distinction between a later Dorset-like phase called Independence II and the earlier more exotic Independence I.

From 1948, Henry Collins conducted an extensive series of excavations in the Canadian Arctic islands, digging at Frobisher Bay on Baffin Island, and later at Resolute Bay on Cornwallis Island and Southampton, Coats, Walrus, and Mansel Islands in Hudson Bay. His work has provided much of the substantive data on Thule and Dorset occupations in the Canadian Arctic. In 1954, Henry Collins was the first to use the term "Pre-Dorset" referring to the Sarqaq and Independence cultures as intermediate between Denbigh and Dorset (1954:304).

Jorgen Meldgaard excavated on a remarkable series of raised beaches in the Igloolik region of central Canada in 1954 and 1957 with joint Danish-American support. Here the horizontal and vertical raised-beach seriation contained remains of three cultural periods: Thule, Dorset, and Pre-Dorset. Meldgaard emphasized the distinction between Pre-Dorset and Dorset at Igloolik and demonstrated a major break in artifact typologies, although housing styles were relatively unchanged. Meldgaard pointed out that attempts to derive Dorset from Pre-Dorset were not in accord with his data from Igloolik, and he suggested that "The basic sources of the Dorset culture, however, must be searched far to the south" (1960a:593), specifically suggesting ". . . a possible source about 1000 B.C. somewhere in the triangle between the Great Lakes, James Bay, and Newfoundland" (1962:95).

Elmer Harp and Robert McKennan in 1958 concluded an archaeological reconnaissance along the interior Lakes of the Thelon River, and Harp distinguished five occupations of the central "barren grounds." Harp also excavated on the Coronation Gulf littoral in 1955, finding sites of the Arctic Small-Tool Tradition and typologically separating out a large flake-biface industry from the Kamut Lake site, which he felt was related typologically to cultures considered much earlier in the south.

Moreau Maxwell marshaled available evidence of changing ecological conditions in the Eastern Arctic, concluding that Pre- and Proto-Dorset peoples moved through the warmer phases of the waning climatic optimum, traveling by boat. He also pointed out correlations of the distribution of cultures with present January mean isotherms, suggesting that with reductions of annual or seasonal temperatures ". . . there was a retrenchment of Eskimo settlements and a notable diminution of culture contact across the Arctic" (1960).

In 1957 at Payne Bay on the Ungava Peninsula, William Taylor discovered the first human skeletal material from a presumed Dorset context. The individual was morphologically Eskimo (Laughlin and Taylor 1960). In 1958, at the western end of Hudson Strait, Taylor found another human mandible on Sugluk Island and another on Mansel Island in Hudson Bay, both in Dorset cultural contexts. The morphology of the mandibles suggests that these too were Eskimo, representing the closest connection of Dorset culture to anything conceptually Eskimo. Taylor's investigations at the Pre-Dorset Arnapik site on Mansel Island and at Dorset Tyara site on Sugluk Island led to his conclusion that Dorset developed rather directly from Pre-Dorset in the Eastern Canadian Arctic, with only superficial influences, if any, from any contemporary cultures outside of this area (1968).

In southwestern Alaska, Ales Hrdlicka, of the Smithsonian Institution, conducted excavations in the 1930s on Kodiak Island and the Aleutians as a part of his continued interest in the skeletal remains of Bering Strait populations. His analyses of the Uyak site on Kodiak Island indicated two cultural periods—Koniag and Pre-Koniag (1944)—which seemed to relate to Kachemak Bay III of de Laguna. Unfortunately, Hrdlicka's poor provenience data for both archaeological and skeletal material have destroyed much of their usefulness.

Archaeological research in the Aleutians must all be referred to the continued research results of William Laughlin. Starting in 1938 he worked with Ales Hrdlicka for the Smithsonian Institution, collecting artifacts from Anangula Island (Laughlin 1951), and from the Chaluka midden on Umnak Island. Laughlin and his students have continued their investigations with support from various universities and foundations. Laughlin's studies of the physical anthropology of Aleutian populations corroborated Hrdlicka's dual division of Aleut and pre-Aleut, suggesting that the Aleuts were firmly established in the Aleutians by the second millennium B.C. He saw a general cultural continuity throughout this physical change that may have taken place by A.D. 1000 in the eastern Aleutians, with a Paleo-Aleut refugium in the western Aleutians lasting much later. Laughlin and Marsh saw some lithic identity between the lower layers at Chaluka and the earlier Anangula site, although subsequent excavations at both sites have not demonstrated this.

Theodore Bank undertook a series of Aleutian excavations for the University of Michigan in 1949, 1950, and 1952 with Albert Spaulding excavating a site at Krugloi Point on Agattu Island (in 1949). Spaulding suggested that this site was a refugium of some of the earliest Aleuts, al-

though he could make no definitive statement of Krugloi
Point cultural affinities (Spaulding 1962:42–44). Allen
McCartney has recently reviewed several collections from
the Near Islands (including Krugloi Point). He suggested
that they form a "cultural phase whose particular stylistic
development took place in relative isolation from the remaining Aleutian populations" (1971:92). Excavating on
Unalaska Island at the Amaknak-D site in 1950 and 1951,
Bank concluded, ". . . despite the diversity and numerous
changes of types of artifacts throughout the occupation,
there is no level at which several changes of types occur
simultaneously in a number of different artifacts" (Bank
1953:45).

Helge Larsen, in 1950, noted the extreme inadequacy of
our knowledge of southwestern Alaska and pointed out
the "striking difference between later cultures with ground
slate implements and rather crude pottery and earlier cultures with chipped stone implements and finer pottery or
without pottery" (1950:186). He suggested that we tighten
our definitions of Paleo-Eskimo and Neo-Eskimo so that
"A Paleo-Eskimo culture would thus be a culture in which
chipped flint implements are preferably used, and a Neo-
Eskimo culture one in which ground slate implements are
predominant" (1950:186).

Catherine McClellan and Frederica de Laguna collected
ethnographic data, while Francis Riddell, Donald Mc-
Geein, Kenneth Lane, and Arthur Freed were principally
responsible for the archaeological work around Yakutat
Bay (de Laguna et al. 1964), which salvaged a great deal
of ethnographic data (Tlingit) tied in to local historic and
protohistoric sites. De Laguna's conclusions regarding the
ethnographic identification of the protohistoric sites and
of their relationships with other areas in southern Alaska
"have been hampered . . . by the fact that so little is
known about the archeology of the northern and central
Northwest Coast" (1964:207). Because we do not understand the near-historic archaeology of this region, it is no
wonder that our understanding of the much longer and

more complex prehistoric period is so often confused and incomplete.

One of the most significant excavations in Arctic archaeology was begun at Point Hope in 1939. Helge Larsen and Froelich Rainey, assisted by J. Louis Giddings, excavated at Jabbertown and at the point itself, but the more spectacular finds were at the site they named Ipiutak, which differed drastically from any "Eskimo" site previously known. The Ipiutak skeletal material was studied by George Debetz, who noted that the population was morphologically Eskimo but was somewhat different from the typologically advanced Eskimo population represented at the Old Bering Sea culture site at Uellen on the Chukchee Peninsula and at the Birnirk-related sites at Point Barrow (Debetz 1959:61).

Larsen and Rainey also grappled with the problem of what is "Eskimo," disagreeing with Birket-Smith's contention that the outstanding characteristic of Eskimos is their ability to live divorced from the forest with a rather unique adaptation to the sea (1929:pt. 2:222). "A prerequisite to the formulation of a definition of Eskimo culture is that the bearers of that culture are Eskimo in physical type or, even better, speak an Eskimo language. Then we must extend its boundaries to include all variations of Eskimo culture. This cannot be done until we are positive that we have discovered all the variants, and of that we cannot be certain until all the Eskimo territory has been thoroughly investigated archaeologically" (Larsen and Rainey 1948:150), thus leaving the "Eskimo question" as boggled as before.

Louis Giddings from 1939 to 1964 was one of the most productive of Arctic archaeologists. In 1948, 1949, and 1952 he excavated at Cape Denbigh on Norton Sound in a stratified site called Iyatayet. Iyatayet contained a layer of recent Eskimo remains over a layer of Ipiutak-related culture called Norton containing stone lamps and pottery (like Near-Ipiutak—see Larsen 1961:10). Under Norton was a thin convoluted deposit containing what Giddings called the Denbigh Flint complex, after its most distinctive lithic technology. Because of the absence of nonlithic remains and the presence of diagonally fine-flaked end blades and one "fluted point," Giddings considered the Denbigh finds to relate to "Early Man" in the Arctic (1950, 1951), estimating its age at a minimum of six thousand years. The word "Eskimo" appears twice in Giddings' 1951 article on the Denbigh Flint complex, once in a context that reinforces the interpretation that Giddings was thinking of much earlier cultures: "Permanently frozen deposits in Alaska should soon begin to give us a fuller picture of the culture that enabled man to establish himself on both sides of the Bering Strait before the elaboration of specialized Eskimo culture" (1951: 202). Subsequent geological work and radiocarbon dating suggest a more recent date of ca. 2000–3000 B.C. for the Iyatayet occupation of the Denbigh Flint complex.

In 1952, using his dendrochronological series, Giddings summarized his research on recent Eskimo occupations along the Kobuk River within the forest zone, suggesting a distinctive Eskimo culture, which he called Arctic Woodland, dated to A.D. 1200.

Giddings surveyed the region around Choris Peninsula in 1956. The peninsula consisted of eight parallel strand lines all at about the same height above the sea. On the fourth and fifth ridge were artifacts of the Norton culture, and the oldest ridge contained a new culture, which Giddings named Choris. Giddings was impressed by the chronological possibilities of beach ridges, and in 1958 he began a search for long series of beach ridges in the Kotzebue Sound region. At Cape Espenberg, he found an occupation sequence from Ipiutak to Denbigh. At nearby Cape Krusenstern were a hundred ridges capped with sod and gravel (stabilizing the ridges and the sites) preserving a relative chronology unsurpassed in previous Arctic archaeology. During four seasons, from 1958 to 1961, Giddings (with various assistants) defined the following sequence of cultures: Western Thule; Birnirk; Ipiutak;

Choris-Trail Creek; Old Whaling; and Denbigh Flint complex (Giddings 1961, 1966). In addition, he found a Battle Rock phase apparently intermediate between Denbigh and Ipiutak and, on the mainland "Palisades" behind the beaches, two phases of culture (Palisades I and II) reminiscent of presumed early cultures of the interior. This series provided a framework for Giddings to summarize his views on Alaskan Eskimo archaeology in 1960 and 1961, suggesting that the Bering Strait region was a center of circumpolar ideas and not merely a junction of people merely passing through (1960:121), thus arguing against those who seemed to seek Asian origins for anything archaeologically new in Alaska.

One of the early landmarks in the archaeology of interior Alaska was Nels Nelson's 1937 report on artifacts from the campus of the University of Alaska. Nelson illustrated small polyhedral cores and blades derived from them, pointing out that the artifacts ". . . appear to suggest definite cultural relations between Alaska and Mongolia" (Nelson 1937:267).

Scattered surface evidence of early man in Alaska (fluted points, etc.) was obtained by Frank Hibben in 1941 and Raymond Thompson and Ralph Solecki on U. S. Geological Survey field parties north of the Brooks Range between 1947 and 1950, but no absolute assessment of their age could be made.

At Anaktuvuk Pass in the Brooks Range, Robert Hackman and William Irving (in separate parties) discovered sites related to the Denbigh Flint complex. Irving returned in 1951, excavating at the Imaigenik site and other sites and blowouts that seemed to trace a typological continuum from Denbigh to other Paleo-Eskimo cultures in the western and eastern Arctic (Irving 1953:71–72).

Irving (1955) compared burins and blade cores from Alaska and the Yukon, distinguishing between Denbigh-like burins and polyhedral cores, and the flake burins and tongue-shaped cores found at the Campus site and at Pointed Mountain and Fort Liard in the Yukon.

In 1953, Irving conducted a salvage survey of the Susitna Valley for the National Park Service. In discussing
the predominantly historic and proto-historic Athabascan
sites found, he related several artifacts to what he proposed
as the "Arctic Small-Tool tradition" (1957:47), formaliz-
ing his earlier distinction between coastal-tundra Denbigh-
like burin-blade-core industries and boreal Campus-Fort
Liard burin-blade-core industries (Irving 1955). Irving
suggested that these traditions had diverged from a common ancestor, with the Arctic Small-Tool tradition having
formed in Alaska, thus opposing Collins' suggestion of its
Eurasian Mesolithic origin (Collins 1954b).

John Campbell summarized the results of his four field
seasons at Anaktuvuk Pass (1956–59) in 1962, describing
twenty-eight sites and six archaeological complexes. Campbell excavated the Kayuk site in 1957, whose projectile
points are described as Angostura-like, reminiscent of the
high plains. Campbell saw similarities with several lithic
industries in the Arctic and was "presently inclined to
consider the Kayuk complex as belonging somewhere in
time [and cultural affinity?] between the Denbigh Flint
complex and Ipiutak" (Campbell 1959:104), even though
he suspected that the sample might contain a purer Ipiutak
admixture. Later, Campbell typologically separated an
Ipiutak component from this site, and considered the remaining artifacts to represent a five-thousand-to-seven-
thousand-year-old plano complex (1962b:44).

In 1959, Campbell discovered the Tuktu complex in
Anaktuvuk Pass, which he related to Palisades II on Cape
Krusenstern and to other sites belonging to the Northwest
Microblade tradition (Campbell 1961:75).

The Denbigh Flint complex was represented at Anaktuvuk by the Natvakruak complex from two sites originally discovered by Hackman and described by Solecki
(1951). Campbell believed Natvakruak to be four thousand to six thousand years old, thus older than Tuktu
and the Northwest Microblade tradition (Campbell 1962b:
44–46).

Richard MacNeish, expanding his Yukon investigations, investigated sites on the Firth River and the Arctic coast in 1954, 1955, and 1956. His huge Engigstciak site, sixteen miles from the present coast, is one of the most extensive sites in the Arctic, although the soil processes have made stratigraphic interpretation and cultural separation problematical. In spite of these problems, MacNeish defined nine sequential cultures. The British Mountain flake industry was the earliest at Engigstciak, and MacNeish tentatively correlated it with Campbell's Kogruk complex at Anaktuvuk and at some Asian paleolithic sites. Giddings (1961:159) considered his Palisades I at Cape Krusenstern to be related to British Mountain, but MacNeish did not consider the relation to be a strong one (MacNeish 1963:99).

MacNeish's next phase is called Flint Creek, which he related to the late paleolithic in the trans-Baikal of Asia, suggesting Flint Creek as partially ancestral to the Northwest Microblade tradition (1959b:48). Later, he recognized correspondences between it and Campbell's Kayuk complex, other sites in the Yukon, and early sites in British Columbia, suggesting that all of these were part of a Cordilleran tradition (1962:25).

The Arctic small-tool tradition was represented by the next phase, called New Mountain. MacNeish noted that Asian affinities were strong. "In fact the main difference between the early Neolithic of Siberia and these New Mountain-like remains are that those in Siberia have pottery, usually net impressed, which as yet has not been found in the New World Arctic" (MacNeish 1959b:48).

The Firth River phase seemed to be a development out of New Mountain, with the principal addition of fabric impressed and cord-marked pottery (MacNeish 1962:22; 1959b:50). The next phase was Buckland Hills, which seemed to continue this developmental sequence from New Mountain and was distinguished principally by the addition of dentate stamping and the increase of drilling tools (1959b:50). The Joe Creek phase followed as a continuation of Buckland Hills. The closer similarities were with Giddings' Choris horizon on the Bering Coast.

MacNeish guardedly suggested that the above cultural sequence was pre-Eskimo and that the three final phases were related to Eskimo horizons of Alaska (1959b:52). His Cliff phase was related to Norton and Near Ipiutak, Whitefish Station related possibly to Birnirk, and the Herschel Island phase related to typical Thule (1959b:52; 1962:23).

MacNeish concurred with Giddings' statements on the steady flow of people and ideas back and forth across the Bering Strait over a long period of time, suggesting that they varied because of ecological and cultural (adaptational?) limitations (1959a; 1959b:53).

In interpreting the relationships among archaeologically known cultures in the Arctic, we must keep in mind that the small size of many archaeological samples can produce analytical differences between cultures and complexes that are artifacts of the data, their procurement and analyses, and are not representative of actual behavioral differences between these cultures. This problem and the problem of archaeological "splitters" have made the archaeological picture painted by many Arctic archaeologists tremendously complex (and often idiosyncratic). Thus, the number of different "cultures" roaming the Arctic literature is very large. Again, much of this comes as a result of data gathering and data gatherers, who are often reluctant to "lump" and synthesize. MacNeish is a notable exception, and his chronological syntheses and highly speculative hypotheses demonstrate his command of Arctic and sub-Arctic data and his ability to make splinters into boards, albeit rough ones.

ARCHAEOLOGISTS AND ANTHROPOLOGISTS

Since 1960, publication of research results has not kept pace with the rate of discovery, and this entire chapter could easily be devoted to this period alone. In the following discussion, information not specifically cited to the investigator comes from the excellent "Current Research: Arctic" reports in *American Antiquity,* compiled by John Campbell. Unfortunately, many of the finds of the last dozen years are reported only there.

In the eastern Arctic since 1960, several surveys and continued excavations have increased our knowledge of Dorset and Pre-Dorset cultures and of their distribution. One of the most important series of excavations has been that of Moreau Maxwell near Lake Harbour on the south coast of Baffin Island. Five sites were excavated in 1960, all of which were early in the Dorset period (Maxwell 1962:21) and demonstrated a continuum of development from Pre-Dorset, as Taylor had suggested (Taylor 1959: 18). Maxwell continued his research in this area in 1962, 1963, 1966, and 1967 (directed by Albert Dekin in 1967). Maxwell has suggested that Meldgaard's smell of the forest may be the result of the development of a specialized woodworking kit in southern Baffin Island and vicinity, which then spread to other areas of the Eastern Arctic, causing the rather abrupt change to Dorset that other investigators have noted elsewhere (Maxwell 1967). Albert Dekin, in preliminary papers, has suggested that climatic changes in the Eastern Arctic have contributed to cultural drift and isolation by altering local ecological conditions, forcing, facilitating, or forbidding population (and thus cultural) movements.

Additional information on the distribution of Pre-Dorset and Dorset cultures in the Eastern Arctic has been obtained by Ronald Nash in northern Manitoba, Patrick Plumet, Elmer Harp, Jr., and Georges Barre in northern Quebec, and William Fitzhugh, James Tuck, and Helen Devereux in Labrador and Newfoundland. Preliminary studies of climatic change in the Eastern Arctic indicate that fluctuations in the distribution of Pre-Dorset and Dorset cultures may well be caused by climatic changes, and associated shifts in biotic distributions (see Dekin 1969; Fitzhugh 1970).

William Taylor in 1963 inaugurated a profitable series of National Museum of Canada excavations in the Central Arctic by surveying between Cape Parry and Cambridge Bay on Victoria Island (1964). The Pre-Dorset Buchanan site (ca. 1000 B.C.) on Ekalluk River contained large quartzite bifaces and scrapers (1964:54–55) thought by Taylor to be a part of the Pre-Dorset technology at Buchanan and not representative of Archaic Indian contaminations. He suggested that they were added to the Pre-Dorset industry by "stimulus diffusion" (Taylor 1967:221, 228).

Robert McGhee conducted excavations in 1968 near Bloody Falls on the Coppermine River. His Pre-Dorset component at Bloody Falls contained a small amount of ground slate and copper pins, dated at ca. 1350 B.C. (McGhee 1970:58). McGhee considered the affinities of this site to be with those from Ekalluk River (Taylor 1964, 1967), rather than with Harp's Dismal-2 sites to the south (McGhee 1970:58–59; Harp 1958).

William Noble has discovered large bifaces on sites that he feels are Arctic Small Tool tradition but not ancestral to Dorset on Great Slave Lake, with an estimated age between 1200 and 200 B.C. (his Canadian Tundra tradition) in the middle of a long sequence of Northern Plano and Taltheli Shale cultures. Later complexes of this tradition are syncretisms demonstrating a blending of small-tool and Proto-Athapascan tool industries of an inland-oriented and forest-adapted people. Noble believes his Canadian Tundra tradition to have arisen from Taylor's Buchanan complex and to have expanded southward and eastward, penetrating the forest and giving rise to Nash's Twin Lakes complex in northern Manitoba (Noble n.d.: 28).

McGhee's 1968 survey also found some rather remarkable archaic or northern plano artifacts in the Sandwillow site on Bloody Falls that were similar to southern artifacts believed to be as old as six thousand years. Parallels were suggested with MacNeish's Taltheilei complex on Great Slave Lake (as yet undated) and with other presumably old barren grounds sites of Harp (Harp 1958, 1961a; McGhee 1970:60; see Noble n.d.).

It should be obvious that we cannot arbitrarily separate the Arctic from the sub-Arctic in the barren grounds, partly because the ecological zones have shifted and partly because the tree line may never have prevented and may have facilitated (as an ecotonal effect) crosscultural contacts. Any further discussion of relationships between the Arctic Small Tool tradition or Dorset peoples and Archaic or Northern Plano peoples awaits Noble's publication.

In general, recent excavations in the Aleutians have done little to alter the general picture of Aleutian archaeology that emerged from the 1960s. William Laughlin and his students at the University of Wisconsin continued their active investigations, producing a number of site reports and a volume of Aleutian-Koniag Prehistory in *Arctic Anthropology,* which now carries the bulk of research reports on Aleutian archaeology. Unfortunately, we have never received a synthesis of Aleutian prehistory or a cohesive anthropological monograph on the Chaluka site and its cultural affinities. The published preliminary reports on Chaluka often seem stratigraphically incompatible due to the incompleteness of the excavation, the complexity of the strata, and the lack of abrupt cultural change and corresponding artifactual horizon markers throughout the midden (compare Aigner 1966:57, 68 with Dennison 1966:85, 110–12).

Laughlin's Introduction to "Aleutian Studies" in the volume on Aleutian Kodiak prehistory, ecology, and anthropology discussed the general intent of their analysis at Anangula and its general cultural relationships, suggesting the probability that the Anangula people were ancestors of later Aleuts (see McCartney n.d.:13) and that they are dealing with an eight-thousand-year record of Aleut evolution, both physical and cultural (Laughlin 1966:24).

Donald Clark saw the latest Koniag phases on Kodiak Island as receiving different influences from the Northwest Coast and from the Bering Sea cultures (1966:173) and judged the present state of our knowledge inadequate to make further analyses or syntheses, suggesting that we need much more data from this rather cosmopolitan region (1966:175).

William Workman's comments on suggested field work also emphasize the tremendous cultural complexity of this region through time, and it seems that much work establishing chronologies and contemporaneous horizons remains to be done before we can attack more sophisticated anthropological problems in this region. There is a need for complete publication of the data from the southwest Alaskan and Aleutian sites so that previous preliminary reports and syntheses may be evaluated.

Don Dumond of the University of Oregon conducted extensive excavations on the Alaska Peninsula from 1960 to 1968 with various assistants. The presence of small-tool, Norton-related, and Western Thule sites in the Naknek drainage indicated that the cultural affinities of the Alaska Peninsula through time were generally with the Bering Strait region, and that this Eskimo cultural tradition did not generally extend south of the peninsula. Only after A.D. 1000 did Eskimo cultures exert much influence south of the peninsula, demonstrated by the southern spread of Thule pottery, the near identity of cultures across the Alaska Peninsula, and by the inferred change in Pacific Eskimo language believed to date ca. A.D. 1200 (Dumond 1964:42). This evidence suggests that Eskimo and Aleut had a long period of separate development in southwestern Alaska, leading Dumond to suggest that the Takli Alder phase might represent a cultural phase ancestral to the prehistoric occupants of the Aleutian Islands, documenting similarities with Spaulding's Krugloi Point and Clark's Ocean Bay I sites. Allen McCartney, in a recent re-examination of the archaeology of the Near Islands, suggested that these similarities resulted from stylistic and

adaptive convergences that were generically unrelated
(1971). Dumond's suggestion of a widespread Takli Alder
phase has the additional merit of filling the stratum suggested by Chard (1960) to explain widespread ethnographic similarities among the now-distinctive cultures of
the North Pacific region.

Dumond has also suggested, "The common ancestor of
Eskimos and Aleuts will be found on a time level considerably earlier than 4000 B.C. and in circumstances that
allow for the subsequent development of two relatively distinct subsistence patterns—one for exploiting the open
coastal environment, to be developed by descendants who
became Aleuts; a second for exploiting the tundra-covered
territory adjacent to coastlines that freeze, to be developed
by descendants who became Eskimos" (1969:1114).

Helge Larsen published a final report on the 1949–50
Trail Creek excavations in 1968 indicating that men had
visited and eaten there ca. 11,000 B.C. but left no artifacts
—only butchered bone. The next occupants used microblade side blades thought to relate to the Northwest
Microblade tradition (although Anderson cites this as a
member of the American Paleoarctic tradition—see below: 1970c:4). The sequence of occupations then continues to Denbigh, Trail Creek-Choris, Norton-Near
Ipiutak, Western Thule, late prehistoric, and historic Eskimos (Larsen 1968:76)—an ambitious list of tenants from
two caves containing only 243 artifacts with often disturbed stratigraphy.

Additional information on early flake industries in Al-
aska was obtained by Ralph Solecki, Gordon Lowther, and
Edwin Wilmsen, and Karl Schlesier and Lyle James.
Schlesier considered these sites to form the British Moun-
tain tradition (of MacNeish), considering this a valid cul-
tural unit: "Despite the questions concerning the British
Mountain Tradition, its existence can neither be over-
looked nor wished away" (Schlesier 1967:218). Some
Arctic archaeologists would contend that the sites of the
British Mountain tradition are partial artifact inventories

from several cultural complexes (Herbert Alexander, personal communication) or are not artifacts at all. Recent research by Bryan Gordon at Trout Lake on the Yukon Arctic slope yielded a British Mountain complex dating ca. 3500 B.C. (1970; personal communication), giving substance to the hope that the riddle of British Mountain is close to solution.

Recent research by William Irving and C. Richard Harington on Pleistocene mammal deposits in Alaska and the northern Yukon have suggested the presence of man in this region prior to the Wisconsin glacial maximum. At Old Crow Flats, a caribou bone scraper and a toothed scraper have been dated to ca. twenty-nine thousand and twenty-seven thousand years (G 1567 and G 1640—Irving and Harington 1970), but these data are equivocal, as the artifacts and associated bones are secondary riverine deposits and surface finds. The dates document the probable time of death of the animals, but in the absence of *in situ* data and an association with other cultural remains, it is questionable whether the dates document human utilization and the presence of man.

In 1965 Robert Humphrey surveyed the Utukok River finding sites related to southern Plano complexes and to the Campus site. He revisited the site of the fluted point find reported by Thompson in 1948. Humphrey returned in 1966, finding several fluted points and blanks *in situ* at several surface sites on Driftwood Creek. Humphrey saw the southern Clovis finds as descendants of the Driftwood Creek complex, which he saw as a way-station of the developing Paleo-Indian culture en route from Asia, supporting the arguments of C. Vance Haynes and John Witthoft. A radiocarbon date on mammoth tusk associated with the Driftwood Creek complex is greater than 13,-000 B.C.

Frederick Hadleigh-West and Hans-Georg Bandi excavated near Donnelly Dome, Twelve Mile Bluff, and Minto Flats in 1963, 1966, 1967, and 1968. The assemblage resembled those assigned to the Northwest Micro-

blade tradition, but Hadleigh-West denied any strength to
this connection, lumping several sites, including the Donnelly Ridge site, into the Denali complex (guess-dated at
more than ten thousand years).

Robert McKennan and John Cook conducted excavations on and near Healy Lake in the Tanana drainage in
1966, 1967, and 1969. Data from the tightly stratified
Garden and Village sites have clarified the chronology of
central Alaska. The earliest finds, called the Chindadn
complex, were dated at ca. 9000 B.C., and McKennan and
Cook saw vague similarities with the Akmak levels at
Onion Portage, but they saw no other parallels in North
America (1970a:5). Above this complex was a rather
sparse, ill-defined "transitional" phase dated ca. 7000 B.C.
followed by a local manifestation of the "Tuktu phase of
the Athapaskan tradition" (1970a:2)—MacNeish's Northwest Microblade and Denetasiro? This complex should
date ca. 4500 B.C. from the Tuktu date at Anaktuvuk Pass.
It is important to note that the next complex at Healy Lake
is the Denali phase of the Denali complex as isolated by
Hadleigh-West (1967—see above). Because of its stratigraphic position overlying Tuktu and because of comparisons with other dated sites, they suggest that the Denali
phase should date in the first millennium B.C. (compare
this with Hadleigh-West's estimate of 10,000 years—see
above): ". . . it appears that the core and microblade
technology is much more recent than has been heretofore
believed" (Cook and McKennan 1970b:2). Above these
levels were some microblades and then the remains of the
Healy Lake band of Athapaskans. In one series of excavations, they have increased the age of dated interior
Alaskan sites back to 9000 B.C. and pushed the Denali
complex ahead six thousand years. McKennan and Cook
feel that the Tuktu complex represents the founders of the
Athapaskan tradition, thus giving Athapaskan speakers a
sixty-five-hundred-year antiquity in Alaska (1970b).

Recent excavations by Edwin Hall north of the Brooks
Range and by Herbert Alexander at Anaktuvuk Pass have

raised the possibility that several of the complexes separated by Campbell on the basis of typological analysis from sites at Anaktuvuk Pass (see above) should be lumped together. Hall's excavations at Walker Lake (personal communication), Alexander's at Anaktuvuk Pass (1969), and those of Cook and McKennan at Healy Lake (1968) suggest that Campbell's Tuktu and Naiyuk complexes are one. Alexander also suggested that Campbell's Kogruk, Anaktuvuk Ipiutak, and Kayuk complexes should all be lumped into a Kayuk phase related to Ipiutak (1969: 40), leading to a reduction in the complexity of the archaeological record in North Alaska.

Since the summer of 1961, Arctic archaeologists have eagerly awaited any views of the Onion Portage excavations on the Kobuk River. The first extensive excavations in 1961 revealed a sequence of cultures going back to Denbigh, or earlier times, in good stratigraphic order. Several of the cultures were without known coastal or inland parallels. The main results of the early stages of excavation were principally chronological and sequential, although the geographic position of Onion Portage between the Arctic coast and the interior boreal forest provided a unique opportunity ". . . to determine further what possible surges of influence could have taken place between the interior and the coast" (Giddings 1962:19). This site presented the first good evidence for interaction between the interior and the coast, or between Indians and Eskimos. In 1963, Giddings worked in Greenland, and then returned to Onion Portage to dig deeper, but once more they were unable to excavate to sterile deposits. By this time, they had discovered twenty-eight distinct cultural layers going back to cultures related to Palisades II, which he was guess-dating at ca. 7000 B.C. (Giddings 1965:196), although current dating would be several thousand years more recent.

Giddings reiterated Collins' (1953, 1960) belief that microblade cultures represent an extension of the European Mesolithic that later was represented in cultures that evolved into recent Eskimo. "Throughout all this time and earlier, the language spoken in the far inland forests appears to have been Indian. Who knows that it might not have been Athapaskan?" (1965:203). Giddings' party returned to Onion Portage in 1964, while Douglas Anderson surveyed on the Noatak and associated rivers, finding sites related to Tuktu and Palisades II as well as Denbigh sites. Giddings was killed in the fall of 1964, in the middle of an exemplary career. His last scientific paper was published in 1966, corroborating the beach ridge cultural sequence at Cape Krusenstern with the excavated stratigraphy at Onion Portage.

Giddings' work at Onion Portage was continued by Douglas Anderson and Mrs. Giddings under the general supervision of Froelich Rainey. Excavations in 1965, 1966, 1967, and 1968 elaborated the technological inventories of the cultures previously discovered, and extended the record of human occupation to the 6000 B.C. Akmak phase. Anderson interpreted the Akmak phase to represent a widespread cultural tradition (American Paleo-Arctic) that lasted until ca. 6000 B.C. in Alaska and that he felt was historically related to the Denali complex and the Advanced Paleolithic cultures of eastern Asia and Japan (Anderson 1970a). Recent work by Humphrey on the Utukok River and by Dennis Stanford near Point Barrow revealed cultures that may prove to fill temporal and adaptational gaps in the American Paleo-Arctic tradition (personal communications).

Later cultural complexes formed a Northern Archaic tradition whose development possibly led to historic Athabascan cultures (Anderson 1970b:3, 10). The discovery of a developmental sequence of cultures leading to the Denbigh Flint complex was the first evidence on the evolution of Denbigh. These proto-Denbigh levels were dated ca. 2300 B.C. (Anderson 1970c:10) and found their greatest similarity in the Pre-Dorset cultures of the eastern Arctic.

CONCLUSION

Having reviewed the history of Arctic archaeology, several problems of research and publication are outstanding. The literature of Arctic archaeology is composed largely of preliminary reports and analyses. The number of good monographs containing the artifactual data, their analysis, and explanatory hypotheses and conclusions is relatively small. In partial compensation, the quality of the preliminary reports is high.

A good cultural chronology and knowledge of the general interpretations among excavated cultures is requisite for anthropological archaeology. Unfortunately, because of the vastness of the Arctic, the complexity of its cultures and their cultural dynamics over possibly twenty thousand years of occupation, a well-developed chronology has been long in coming. In its absence, archaeologists interested in problems of social organization, acculturation, etc., would have been forced into speculations that were not closely documented by good archaeological data. Anderson observed this emphasis on chronology and the "genetics" of burins or cores in a slightly different manner. To Anderson's ". . . knowledge few Arctic archaeologists have yet to see their material as remains left by social groups. One way of achieving this is by viewing the sites as composites of activity areas in which the structures are but of one kind of, or rather a compound from, an activity sphere" (1968b:397). The number of possible interpretations of archaeological material increases when trying to do anthropology, and this sensitization to the increased alternatives cannot help but improve our hypotheses, our field techniques, and our methods of interpretation, and might even elicit an explanation or two—all things that our social science should value.

One of the important legacies that Giddings and his colleagues have left us is a vast number of sites reported but not excavated, or excavated but not reported, because they did not fit the problems that these men were pursuing. If archaeology in the Arctic is to become anthropology in the Arctic we must turn new insights and new hypotheses on these rich archaeological resources, building on the chronologies and regional sequences that are the achieved goal of an earlier generation of scholars. Only when this is done may we then say that anthropological archaeology has developed in the Arctic.

REFERENCES

ACKERMAN, ROBERT E.
   1962   "Culture Contact in the Bering Sea: Birnik-Punuk Period." *Arctic Inst. Tech. Pap.* 11:27–34.

AIGNER, JEAN S.
   1966   "Bone Tools and Decorative Motifs from Chaluka, Umnak Island." *Arctic Anthro.* 3:57–83.

ALEXANDER, HERBERT L., JR.
   1969   "Prehistory of the Central Brooks Range—An Archaeological Analysis." Ph.D. thesis, University of Oregon.

ANDERSON, DOUGLAS D.
   1968a "A Stone Age Campsite at the Gateway to America." *Sci. Am.* 218:24–33.
   1968b "Review of W. Oswalt and J. Van Stone, *The Ethnoarchaeology of Crow Village*." *Am. Ant.* 33:396–97.
   1970a "Akmak: An Early Archaeological Assemblage from Onion Portage, Northwest Alaska." *Acta Arctica* No. 16.
   1970b "Athapaskans in the Kobuk Arctic Woodlands, Alaska?" *Canadian Arch. Assoc. Bull.* 2:3–12.
   1970c "Microblade Traditions in Northwest Alaska." *Arctic Anthro.* 7:2–16.

ARCHAEOLOGICAL RESEARCH INC. (ARI)
   1970   *Archaeological Report, Amchitka Island, Alaska.* Washington, D.C.: U. S. Atomic Energy Commission.

BANDI, HANS-GEORG
   1969   *Eskimo Prehistory.* College, Alaska: University of Alaska Press.

BANK, THEODORE P., II
   1953   "Cultural Succession in the Aleutians." *Am. Ant.* 19:40–49.

BIRKET-SMITH, KAJ
   1929   "The Caribou Eskimos." Reports of the Fifth Thule Expedition, 1921–24. 5:1:306 and 5:2:420. Copenhagen.

BOAS, FRANZ
1907 "The Eskimo of Baffin Land and Hudson Bay." *Anthro. Pap. Am. Mus. Nat. Hist.* 15:2.

CAMPBELL, JOHN M.
1959 "The Kayuk Complex of Arctic Alaska." *Am. Ant.* 25:94–105.
1961 "The Tuktu Complex of Anaktuvuk Pass." *Anthro. Pap. Univ. Alaska* 19:61–80.
1962a "Prehistoric Cultural Relations between the Arctic and Temperate Zones of North America" (ed.). *Arctic Inst. Tech. Pap.* 11:181.
1962b "Cultural Succession at Anaktuvu Pass." *Arctic Inst. Tech. Pap.* 11:39–54.

CHARD, CHESTER S.
1960 "Northwest Coast-Northeast Asiatic Similarities: A New Hypothesis." *Sel. Papers of the 5th Int. Cong. of Anthro. and Ethno. Sci.*:235–40.

––– and MERBS, B. P.
1964 "The Alaskan Situla Ware: An Asiatic Transplant in the New World." *35th Int. Cong. of Americanists* 1:11–116.

CLARK, DONALD W.
1966 "Two Late Prehistoric Pottery-Bearing Sites on Kodiak Island, Alaska." *Arctic Anthro.* 3:57–84.

COLLINS, HENRY B.
1937 "Archaeology of St. Lawrence Island, Alaska." *Smithsonian Misc. Coll.* 96(1).
1953 "Recent Developments in the Dorset Area." *Soc. Amer. Arch. Mem.* 9:32–39.
1954 "The Position of Ipiutak in Eskimo Culture." *Am. Ant.* 20:79–84.
1958 "Present Status of the Dorset Problem." *32nd Int. Cong. of Americanists.* Copenhagen, 1956:557–60.
1960 "Recent Trends and Developments in Arctic Archaeology." *6th Int. Cong. of Anthro. and Ethno. Sci.* 1:373–77.
1964 "The Arctic and Subarctic," *Prehistoric Man in the New World.* J. D. Jennings and E. Norbeck (eds.), Chicago: University of Chicago Press 85–114.

COOK, JOHN P., and MCKENNAN, ROBERT
1970a "The Village site at Healy Lake, Alaska: An Interim Report." Paper presented at the thirty-second annual meeting of the Society for American Archaeology.
1970b "The Athapaskan Tradition: A View from Healy Lake in the Yukon-Tinana Upland." Paper presented at the tenth annual meeting of the Northeastern Anthropological Association.

DALL, WILLIAM H.
1875 "On Further Examination of the Amaknak Cave, Captain's Bay, Unalaska." *Proceed. California Acad. Sci.* 5:196–200.

1877   *On the Origin of the Inuit.* Contributions to North American Ethnology, 1.

DEBETZ, GEORGE
   1959   "The Skeletal Remains of the Ipiutak Cemetery." *Actas del 33 Cong. Inter. de Americanists:*57–64.

DEKIN, ALBERT A., JR.
   1969   "Paleo-climate and Prehistoric Cultural Interaction in the Eastern Arctic." Paper presented at the thirty-fourth annual meeting of the Society for American Archaeology.
   1970   "Paleo-Climate and Paleo-Ecology of the Eastern North American Arctic During Its Occupancy by Man (2500 B.C. to date)." Paper presented to the third annual meeting of the Canadian Archaeological Association.

DENNISTON, GLENDA B.
   1966   "Cultural Change at Chaluka, Umnak Island: Stone Artifacts and Features." *Arctic Anthro.* 3:84–124.

DUMOND, DON E.
   1964   "A Note on the Prehistory of Southwestern Alaska." *Anthro. Pap. Univ. Alaska* 12(1)33–45.
   1965   "On Eskaleutian Linguistics, Archaeology and Prehistory." *Am. Anthro.* 67:1231–57.
   1969   "Prehistoric Cultural Contacts in Southwestern Alaska." *Science* 166:1108–15.

FITZHUGH, WILLIAM W.
   1970   "Environmental Archaeology and Cultural Systems in Hamilton Inlet, Labrador: A Survey of the Central Labrador Coast from 300 B.C. to the Present." Ph.D. dissertation, Harvard University.

FORD, J. A.
   1959   "Eskimo Prehistory in the Vicinity of Point Barrow, Alaska." *Anthro. Pap. Am. Mus. Nat. Hist.* 47(1).

GIDDINGS, JAMES L., JR.
   1950   "Early Man on the Bering Sea Coast." *Ann. New York Acad. Sci.* 13(1):18–21.
   1951   "The Denbigh Flint Complex." *Am. Ant.* 16:193–203.
   1952   "The Arctic Woodland Culture of the Kobuk River." *Mus. Monog., Univ. Mus.,* Philadelphia: University of Pennsylvania.
   1960   "The Archaeology of Bering Strait." *Current Anthro.* 1:121–35.
   1961   "Cultural Continuities of Eskimos." *Am. Ant.* 27:155–73.
   1962   "Onion Portage and Other Flint Sites of the Kobuk River." *Arctic Anthro.* 1:6–27.
   1965   "A Long Record of Eskimos and Indians at the Forest Edge," *Context and Meaning in Cultural Anthropology,* M. E. Spiro (ed.), 184–215. New York: The Free Press.
   1966   "Cross-Dating the Archaeology of Northwestern Alaska." *Science,* 153:127–35.

GORDON, BRYAN C.
  1970   "Recent Archaeological Investigations on the Arctic Yukon
         Coast," *Early Man and Environments in Northwest North
         America*, R. A. Smith and J. W. Smith (eds.). Paleo-
         Environmental Association, Students' Press, 67–86.

HADLEIGH-WEST, FREDERICK
  1963   *Early Man in the Eastern American Arctic*, a symposium
         (ed.), Univ. Alaska *Anthro. Pap.* 10:2.
  1967   "The Donnelly Ridge Site and the Definition of an Early
         Core and Blade Tradition in Central Alaska." *Am. Ant.*
         32:360–82.

HARP, E., JR.
  1958   "Prehistory in the Dismal Lake Area." *Arctic* 11:219–49.
  1961   "The Archaeology of the Lower and Middle Thelon, N.W.T."
         North Am. Tech. Pap. 8:5–74.
  1964   "The Cultural Affinities of the Newfoundland Dorset Es-
         kimo." *Nat. Mus. Can. Bull.* 200.

HRDLICKA, ALES
  1944   *The Anthropology of Kodiak Island*. Philadelphia: Wistar
         Institute of Anatomy and Biology.

IRVING, WILLIAM
  1953   "Evidence of Early Tundra Cultures in Northern Alaska."
         Anthro. Pap. Univ. Alaska 1(2):55–85.
  1955   "Burins from Central Alaska." *Am. Ant.* 20:380–83.
  1957   "An Archaeological Survey of the Susitna Valley." *Anthro.
         Pap. Univ. Alaska* 6(1):37–52.

——— and HARINGTON, C. RICHARD
  1970   "Pleistocene Radiocarbon Dated Artifacts from Northern
         Yukon Territory." Paper presented at the third annual meet-
         ing of the Canadian Archaeological Association.

JENNESS, DIAMOND
  1925   "A New Eskimo Culture in Hudson Bay." *Geog. Rev.*
         15:428–37.
  1929   "Little Diomede Island, Bering Strait." *Geog. Rev.* 19:78–86.

JOCHELSON, W. VLADMIR
  1925   *Archaeological Investigations in the Aleutian Islands. Car-
         negie Institute of Washington Publication* 367.

KNUTH, EIGIL
  1954   "The Paleo-Eskimo Culture of Northern Greenland Eluci-
         dated by Three New Sites." *Am. Ant.* 19:367–81.
  1958   "Archaeology of the Farthest North." *32nd Int. Cong. of
         Americanists:*561–73.

LAGUNA, FREDERICA DE
  1934   *The Archaeology of Cook Inlet, Alaska*. Philadelphia: Uni-
         versity of Pennsylvania Press.

———; RIDDELL, FRANCIS; McGEEIN, D. F.; LANE, K. S.; and
     FREED, J. A.

1964   "Archaeology of the Yakutat Bay Area, Alaska." *Bur. Amer. Eth. Bull.* 192.

LARSEN, HELGE E.
1950   "Archaeological Investigations in Southwestern Alaska." *Am. Ant.* 15:177–86.
1953   "Archaeological Investigations in Alaska since 1939." *Polar Rec.* 6:593–607.
1961   "Archaeology in the Arctic 1935–60." *Am. Ant.* 27:7–15.
1968   "Trail Creek, Final Report on the Excavation of Two Caves on Seward Peninsula, Alaska." *Acta Arctica* 15:7–79.

——— and RAINEY, FROELICH
1948   "Ipiutak and the Arctic Whale Hunting Culture." *Anthro. Pap. Am. Mus. Nat. Hist.* 42.

LAUGHLIN, W. S.
1951   "Notes on an Aleutian Core and Blade Industry." *Am. Ant.* 17:52–55.
1966   "Introduction" (Aleutian Studies). *Arctic Anthro.* 3:23–27.

——— and MARSH, GORDON H.
1954   "The Lamellar Flake Manufacturing Site on Anangula Island in the Aleutians." *Am. Ant.* 20:27–39.

——— and TAYLOR, W. E.
1960   "A Cape Dorset Culture Site on the West Coast of Ungava Bay." *Nat. Mus. Can. Bull.* 168:1–28.

McCARTNEY, ALLEN P.
1970   " 'Pottery' in the Aleutian Islands." *Am. Ant.* 35:105–7.
1971   "A Proposed Western Aleutian Phase in the Near Islands, Alaska." *Arctic Anthro.* 8(2):92–142.

McGHEE, ROBERT
1970   "Excavations at Bloody Falls, N.W.T., Canada." *Arctic Anthro.* 6(2):53–73.

McKENNAN, ROBERT A., and COOK, JOHN P.
1968   "Prehistory of Healy Lake, Alaska." *8th Int. Cong. Anthro. and Ethno. Sci.* 3:182–84.

MacNEISH, R. S.
1954   "The Pointed Mountain Site Near Fort Liard, N.W.T., Canada." *Am. Ant.* 19:234–53.
1959a   "Men Out of Asia; As Seen from Northwest Yukon." *Anthro. Pap. Univ. Alaska* 7(2):41–70.
1959b   "A Speculative Framework of Northern North America Prehistory as of April 1959." *Anthropologica* 1:1–17.
1962   "Recent Finds in the Yukon Territory of Canada." *Arctic Inst. North Amer. Tech. Pap.* 11:20–26.
1963   "The Early Peopling of the New World as Seen from the Southwestern Yukon." *Anthro. Pap. Univ. Alaska* 10(2):93.

MATHIASSEN, THERKEL
1925   "Preliminary Report of the Fifth Thule Expedition: Archaeology." *21st Int. Cong. Americanists:*202–15.

1927 "Archaeology of the Central Eskimos." *Report of the Fifth Thule Expedition, 1921–24*. 4:1 and 2. Copenhagen.
1931 "The Present State of Eskimo Archaeology." *Acta Arch.* 2(2).
1935 "Eskimo Migrations in Greenland." *Geog. Rev.* 28:408–22.

MAXWELL, MOREAU S.
1960 "The Movement of Cultures in the Canadian High Arctic." *Anthropological* 2:1–13.
1962 "Pre-Dorset and Dorset Sites in the Vicinity of Lake Harbour, Baffin Island, N.W.T." *Nat. Mus. Can. Bull.* 180:20–55.

MELDGAARD, JORGEN
1952 "A Paleo-Eskimo Culture in West Greenland." *Am. Ant.* 17:22–30.
1960 "Origin and Evolution of Eskimo Cultures in the Eastern Arctic." *Can. Geog. Jour.* 60:64–75.

MULLER-BECK, HANSJURGEN
1966 "Paleo-Hunters in America: Origins and Diffusion." *Science* 152:1191–1210.

NELSON, NELS C.
1937 "Notes on Cultural Relations Between Asia and America." *Am. Ant.* 2:267–72.

NOBLE, WILLIAM C.
1971 "Archaeological Surveys and Sequences in Central District of MacKenzie, N.W.T." *Arctic Anthro.* 8(1):102–35.

PINART, ALPHONSE
1875 *La Caverie d'Aknanh, Ile d'Ounga (Archipel Shumagur, Alaska)*. Paris: Leroux.

RITCHIE, WILLIAM A.
1951 "Ground Slates: Eskimo or Indian?" *Penn. Arch.* 21:46–52.

SCHLESIER, KARL
1967 "Sedna Creek: Report on an Archaeological Survey on the Arctic Slope of the Brooks Range." *Am. Ant.* 32:210–22.

SOLBERG, OLE MARTIN
1907 *"Beitrage zur Vorgeschichte der Ost Eskimo." Steinerne Schneidegerate und Eaffenscharfen aus Grönland* 2:1.

SOLECKI, R. S., and HACKMAN, R. J.
1951 "Additional Data on the Denbigh Flint Complex in Northern Alaska." *Jour. Wash. Acad. Sci.* 41:85–88.

SPAULDING, ALBERT C.
1962 "Archaeological Investigations on Agattu, Aleutian Islands." *Anthro. Pap. Mus. Anthro. Univ. Mich.* 18.

STEENSBY, H. P.
1917 "An Anthropogeographical Study of the Origin of Eskimo Culture." *Meddelelser om Grønland* 53:39–288.

TAYLOR, WILLIAM E., JR.
   1959   "Review and Assessment of the Dorset Problem." *Anthropologica* 1:24–46.
   1963   "Hypothesis on the Origin of Canadian Thule Culture." *Am. Ant.* 28:456–64.
   1964   "Interim Account of an Archaeological Survey in the Central Arctic, 1963." *Anthro. Pap. Univ. Alaska* 12(1):46–55
   1967   "Summary of Archaeological Field Work on Banks and Victoria Islands, Arctic Canada, 1965." *Arctic Anthro.* 4:221–43.
   1968   "The Arnapik and Tyara Sites; An Archaeological Study of Dorset Culture Origins." *Soc. Am. Arch. Mem.* 22.

WILMSEN, EDWIN N.
   1964   "Flake Tools in the American Arctic: Some Speculations." *Am. Ant.* 29:338–44.

WISSLER, CLARK
   1918   "Archaeology of the Polar Eskimo." *Anthro. Pap. Am. Mus. Nat. Hist.* 22(3). New York.

WORKMAN, WILLIAM B.
   1966   "Archaeological Reconnaissance on Chirikof Island, Kodiak Group: A Preliminary Report." *Arctic Anthro.* 3:185–92.

3 CANADA

William C. Noble

> "Canadian archaeology is a child of recent years
> that has not yet reached full stature."
>
> (Jenness 1932:71)

Dr. Diamond Jenness's opening remarks, delivered for the
fiftieth anniversary of the Royal Society of Canada, are
most apropos for 1932. In keeping with his life-growth
analogy, however, it is now fair to state that archaeology
in Canada has attained a young adult stature in most of
the Dominion's ten provinces. This paper will first trace
the historical roots of archaeology in Canada, and then
focus on current regional developments and problems. It
will become clear that qualitative as well as quantitative
differences exist in Canadian archaeology, particularly with
regard to existing chronology.

As elsewhere in North America, archaeology in Canada
is historically grounded in anthropology. In many cases,
the very Indians whose ancestry is being traced survive
today. In the past, much of the theory in Canadian archaeology has been embedded in, and drawn extensively from,
ethnographic and ethnological literature, so much so that
its prime purpose was often to provide a prehistoric dimen-
sion to known indigenous cultures. It is important to know
that Canadian archaeology in many cases was, and continues to be, a "handmaiden" to ethnology. Many are the
rich and rewarding relations between the two disciplines,
but new purposes, techniques, and interdisciplinary approaches are changing this relationship. Now it may just
as easily be considered a "handmaiden" to studies of
Pleistocene geology, physical anthropology, paleobotony,

Canada

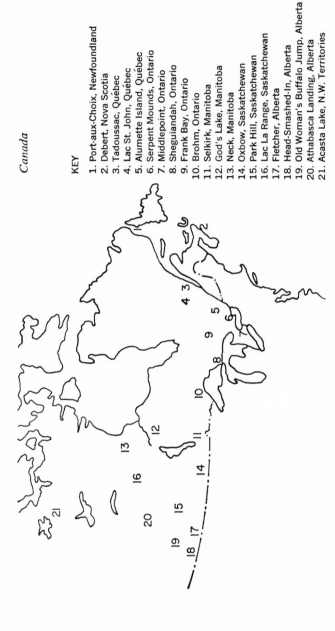

KEY

1. Port-aux-Choix, Newfoundland
2. Debert, Nova Scotia
3. Tadoussac, Québec
4. Lac St. John, Québec
5. Alumette Island, Québec
6. Serpent Mounds, Ontario
7. Middlepoint, Ontario
8. Sheguiandah, Ontario
9. Frank Bay, Ontario
10. Brohm, Ontario
11. Selkirk, Manitoba
12. God's Lake, Manitoba
13. Neck, Manitoba
14. Oxbow, Saskatchewan
15. Park Hill, Saskatchewan
16. Lac La Range, Saskatchewan
17. Fletcher, Alberta
18. Head-Smashed-In, Alberta
19. Old Woman's Buffalo Jump, Alberta
20. Athabasca Landing, Alberta
21. Acasta Lake, N.W. Territories

paleozoology, and paleo-ecology. Yet, when all the data are assembled from the various contributing sources, the archaeologist must get down to his primary concerns: the description, analysis, and interpretation of past peoples and their cultures. Directed toward a people-oriented goal, with interdisciplinary research and a search for causal explanations, Canadian archaeology approaches a greater degree of sophistication and refinement than it has ever enjoyed.

EARLY DEVELOPMENT

In Canada, early prehistoric researches languished during a period of professional and nonprofessional antiquarianism. Frequently, such research stemmed directly from studies of natural history. Interest in the origins of the American aborigines was stimulated by the accumulating evidence of early man in the Old World. Early work began with burial sites in Ontario and adjacent Quebec between 1835 and 1860. The burial mounds of Ontario's sister province, Manitoba, attracted attention in 1868, as did the shell heaps along the eastern coasts of the Atlantic Maritime Provinces. Early archaeological endeavors in the Prairie Provinces of Saskatchewan and Alberta were part of the natural-history observations and collections conducted by the post-1880 scientist-explorers of the Geological Survey of Canada, including Joseph Burr Tyrrell's 1886 journey through Manitoba to northern Alberta, and his later 1893 journey through northern Saskatchewan to the barrenlands. On each occasion, Tyrrell brought archaeological samples back among his collections. James Richardson, another geologist, broke the ground west of the Rocky Mountains in 1871 with his description of archaeological materials in British Columbia.

It is to be noted that while archaeological work began somewhat later in western Canada than in the east, the early western beginnings were made by scientific personnel who took pains to document their findings. This was not done in eastern Canada until the 1850s and 1860s when scholars such as Sir Daniel Wilson and Sir John Dawson lent their educated interests to the developing discipline. Prior to 1850, indiscriminant antiquarian relic-hunting prevailed in Upper and Lower Canada.

Sir Daniel Wilson, Professor of History and English Literature and later President of University College, Toronto, clearly stands as the first professional scholar in the early development of Canadian archaeology. Although not a field man, Wilson's interests in racial osteology and Huron archaeology are classics of his time. Internationally known, Wilson corresponded with Lewis Henry Morgan, Charles Darwin, and many other contemporary eminent European scholars. He commanded a wide-ranging respect and influence, both abroad and at home, and has provided excellent material for biographical studies by Thomas F. McIlwraith (1964) and Bruce G. Trigger (1966).

Similarly, Sir John W. Dawson, eminent geologist and Principal of McGill University, Montreal, stands as an early professional contributor in the early development of Canadian archaeology. Dawson began his interests in prehistory with a collection of Iroquois artifacts from a site at Montreal that he presumed to be that of Jacques Cartier's 1535 Iroquois village of Hochelaga. Published in 1859, 1860, and 1861, these archaeological materials and others from Upper Canada were later incorporated in Dawson's (1880) *magnum opus, Fossil Men and Their Modern Representative*. In this widely read volume, Dawson attempted to compare and place Canadian specimens within the Danish three-age system.

The early organization of Canadian archaeology stemmed primarily from local naturalist, historical, and scientific societies. Centered respectively in the urban cities of Toronto and Montreal, the Royal Canadian Institute and the Canadian Naturalist and Geologist Societies were particularly active. The individual archaeological collections of the two societies later provided, in part, the bases for the collections of the Royal Ontario Museum and McGill University. Outside of Ontario and Quebec, other scholarly societies fostered early interests in prehistoric subjects. Both the Nova Scotian Institute of Natural Science and the Nova Scotia Historical Society in Halifax are examples, as are the Historical Societies of New Brunswick and Manitoba.

Clearly a stimulus to, and a by-product of, early archaeological interest in Canada were museums in which accumulating artifacts could be stored and exhibited. The first museum in Canada was that of Abraham Gesner, opened in 1842 at Saint John, New Brunswick. Housing Indian remains and Micmac ethnographic materials, as well as many other natural-history objects, this early museum later became the New Brunswick Museum. Early too were the university museums opened at Laval (1852), Quebec City, and at McGill (1856) in Montreal, while in Toronto the aboriginal collections of the Canadian Institute founded in 1852 were incorporated into the collections of the Ontario Provincial Museum, subsequently renamed the Royal Ontario Museum, Canada's largest museum today. Another early museum in eastern Canada was that of the Halifax-based Provincial Museum of Nova Scotia, founded in 1868.

Canada's second-largest museum, the National Museum of Canada, also has a long and distinguished history. It began within the Geological Survey of Canada, established in 1842. This oldest scientific branch of the federal service moved from Montreal to Ottawa in 1880, and later occupied the Victoria Memorial Museum, opened in 1910. Formal separation of the Natural History branch did not occur until 1920, but the two continued to occupy the same building until 1952. Many of the early archaeological collections now in the National Museum are attributable to the diligence of the early Geological Survey scientist-explorers.

In western Canada, the earliest museums were founded in British Columbia. The Provincial Museum at Victoria was established in 1887, while the Vancouver City Museum opened its doors shortly afterward. Since the turn of the

century, provincial, university, and local museums have
been established in every province of the Dominion.

Concomitant with the rise of historical, naturalist, and
scientific societies, and the development of museums, were
the Canadian journals offering outlets for articles of an
archaeological nature. Initially appearing in 1852–53, the
Canadian Journal has the distinction of being the first
journal to cover Canadian archaeology. Following close at
hand, archaeological articles soon appeared in the *Canadian Naturalist and Geologist,* which was founded in 1852.
Other early journals include those of the Nova Scotian
Institute of Natural Science (1871), the Nova Scotia Historical Society (1870), the Natural History Society of New
Brunswick (1882), the Royal Society of Canada (1882),
the Historical and Scientific Society of Manitoba (1882),
the *Canadian Record of Science* (1884), the *Annual Archaeological Reports* of Ontario (1887), and the *Canadian Magazine* (1893). Each journal reflects the knowledge of
its era and helped contribute to the early advancement of
archaeology in the Dominion.

In the following pages, an attempt will be made to
document the progress of archaeology in each of Canada's
provinces, excepting British Columbia, proceeding geographically from east to west. The archaeology of British
Columbia is covered in Roderick Sprague's chapter on the
Pacific Northwest in this volume. This synthesis endeavors
to expand and update Diamond Jenness's (1932) interesting yet undocumented paper, as well as a more recent
summary by James F. Pendergast (1963).

NEWFOUNDLAND AND THE LABRADOR

As the most recent Province to enter Confederation
(only in 1949), Newfoundland and its mainland territory,
the Labrador, has a discontinuous history of archaeological
exploration. Major investigations only began in this eastern
province after 1925.

T. G. B. Lloyd can be credited as the province's first archaeologist. Particularly interested in the fate of the now extinct Beothuck Indians, Lloyd endeavored to elucidate their history through ethnographic and archaeological remains. His researches took him from the island to southeastern Labrador, whence possible aboriginal migrations may have stemmed. Much later, J. P. Howley (1915) continued Lloyd's early work on the Beothuck with a classic and scarce volume entitled *The Beothucks or Red Indians.*

It is, however, only after 1925 that trained archaeologists broached Newfoundland and the Labrador. Pursuing his interests in Beothuck, Diamond Jenness (1934) visited the island several times during the late 1920s, followed later by the inexhaustible William J. Wintemberg. Wintemberg continued work on the Beothuck problem as well as researching Dorset culture remains along the northwestern coast of Newfoundland. In northern Labrador, William Duncan Strong (1930) broke first ground, followed by the Hopedale excavations of Junius Bird (1945). Frank G. Speck's (1940) short article on Beothuck bone pendants augmented earlier artwork studies of Howley, Jenness, and Wintemberg.

Interest in the Dorset and Archaic remains of Newfoundland and southern Labrador prompted Elmer Harp (1964) to devote many field seasons in this province. Much of Harp's work has laid the basis for a more thorough understanding and lengthened cultural-chronological sequence of aboriginal occupation in the province. In particular, his Dorset excavations and the 4000 B.C. Forteau Bay Archaic specimens lend significant contributions.

Since 1965, Newfoundland has been the scene of concentrated archaeological research, largely under the auspices of the National Museum. The protracted contract work of Garth Taylor, Helen E. Devereux, and Urve Linnamae promises to expand considerably the known occupations by the Beothucks, Micmac, Dorset, and Archaic peoples. Too, the excavations of rich Archaic burials at Twillingate by Donald G. MacLeod, and the exotic Port-aux-Choix interments found by James Tuck (1970) provide substantial new information on eastern Archaic burial practices. At the same time, continuing osteological analyses (Harp and Hughes 1968; Hughes 1969) help draw the archaeology and physical anthropology of the province closer together.

In central Labrador, the 1968–69 canoe surveys of Donald MacLeod offer new data to augment William Fitzhugh's recent surveys in the Lake Melville and Hamilton Inlet regions, where Shield Archaic is certainly represented. At extreme northern Newfoundland, at L'Anse-aux-Meadows, Anne (1968) and Helge Instad (1968a; 1968b) have finally established Norse habitation in the New World. L'Anse-aux-Meadows currently provides the probable location of Leif Erikson's Vinland. Finally, mention can be made of the National Historic Sites excavations conducted at the masonry forts of Signal Hill and Castle Graves, southeastern Newfoundland (Rick 1970).

NOVA SCOTIA

The archaeology of Nova Scotia, as with Newfoundland, has had a discontinuous history. Nineteenth-century work begins with the antiquarian investigations of William Gossip, followed by Bernard Gilpin's attempts to apply portions of the Danish three-age classification to lithic artifacts he collected from the southern sector of the province. Professor Duns briefly commented on lithic and native copper specimens from the province in 1880, and "Stone Age" terminology continued to be used there until 1900. Exemplifying this are the publications of the Reverend Dr. George Patterson (1890), who donated his collections to Dalhousie University, Halifax, where a modest museum opened in 1912. Native-born Harry Piers (1915) also contributed early works to Nova Scotian archaeology, but it was not until 1913 that trained excavators entered the province.

Harlan I. Smith and William J. Wintemberg (1929), working for the National Museum of Canada, excavated various shell-heaps in 1913–14 at Merigomish Harbour, Northumberland Strait, and at Mahone Bay on Nova Scotia's southeastern coast. The refuse from these mounds was, and still is, considered to be ancestral Micmac Indian.

Until very recently, little professional archaeology had been conducted in Nova Scotia since the time of Smith and Wintemberg. J. Russell Harper's (1957b) description of two historic Micmac burials from Pictou is perhaps an exception to the otherwise local private collections of such men as E. S. Eaton and W. A. Dennis. The work of John S. Erskine (1960) continued shell-heap investigations in the province. With the discovery of the Paleo-Indian site at Debert, central Nova Scotia, professionals once again turned their sights to that province. The reconnaissances of J. S. Erskine, Douglas S. Byers, and Richard S. Mac-Neish paved the way for full-scale excavations by George F. MacDonald (1968). MacDonald's monograph on Debert clearly stands as one of the best-written Paleo-Indian reports for the New World, and he has demonstrated 8000 B.C. occurrences of early man in the central Canadian Maritimes, much earlier than previously thought probable.

Popular articles by Natalie Stoddard and Nova Scotia's provincial archaeologist, John S. Erskine, have endeavored to classify aboriginal tool types and cultures in the province, but much formal analysis remains to be done. Considerable money and energy has been directed toward historic archaeology in Nova Scotia by the federal government since 1961. In that year, excavation and reconstruction commenced at the Fortress of Louisberg on Cape Breton Island, followed by other work at the Halifax Citadel and the early seventeenth-century habitations of Port Royal and Fort Anne in the Annapolis Valley (Rick 1970).

NEW BRUNSWICK

Archaeological researches in New Brunswick began with
the brief 1881 examinations of coastal shell mounds by
Spencer F. Baird. His work was soon followed by that of
Dr. George F. Matthew, who described certain prehistoric
specimens he had uncovered at Bocabec near the extreme
southern boundary of the province. Professor Loring W.
Bailey, another early member of the Natural History Society of New Brunswick, also contributed useful articles
that helped extend the known distribution of various "Stone
Age" lithic artifacts. On the whole, however, early archaeological pursuits in New Brunswick produced meager and
often sporadic results, despite well-meaning enthusiasm.

With Dr. William MacIntosh's 1907 appointment as the
first full-time curator of the New Brunswick Museum, a
concerted and organized study of ethnological and archaeological materials was established. MacIntosh (1913) published on Iroquois pottery found at Grand Lake as well
as on local varieties of lithic implements. After 1915, interest in New Brunswick archaeology prompted Wintemberg to make extensive site surveys through the counties
of Charlotte, Kent, Queens, Northumberland, Sunbury, and
York.

More recently there has been a revival of archaeological
activity in the province. The work at Portland Point by
J. Russell Harper (1956) in his affiliation with the New
Brunswick Museum has revealed historic, late ceramic,
and terminal Archaic materials, as well as a Laurentian
Archaic burial. His work was followed by that of a National Museum contractee, Richard N. Pearson, who surveyed in 1960–62 around St. Andrews and the Tobique
and Miramichi Rivers. In the face of construction of the
impending Mactaquac hydroelectric dam, David Kettel
surveyed a short section of the St. John River with disappointing results in 1964. Later survey on this same river

in 1967 by Dr. David Sanger of the National Museum of Canada revealed numerous components representing the Archaic to late prehistoric periods.

In 1968, Mary J. Sanger's 1967 work at the Eidlitz site, St. Andrews, continued under the auspices of the Province of New Brunswick. At the same time, her husband surveyed in the highlands along the Tobique River and at the headwaters of the Miramichi, where Shield Archaic components (Tobique complex) differ from the Laurentian and terminal Archaic assemblages in the lowlands. In 1968 also, Charles A. Martijn surveyed the north shore of the province for the New Brunswick government.

David Sanger's recent work in 1969–70 around Passamaquoddy Bay promises to contribute additional valuable information, as will Mrs. Judy Keenlyside's 1970 survey of the east coast.

Long a major interest in New Brunswick, historic sites archaeology received a high scholarship example with the untiring and knowledgeable contributions of Dr. William F. Ganong (1899). His influence is clearly detected in the joint investigations of Samuel Kain and Charles Rowe (1902). For a more complete synthesis of historic researches in the province, the reader is directed to the publications of Kenneth E. Kidd (1969) and John Rick (1970).

PRINCE EDWARD ISLAND

The archaeology of this small Maritime island province remains virtually unknown and unpublished. Early work was conducted by J. Walter Fewkes (1896) at a shell mound on Rustico Bay of the island's south shore, where local residents presently recall an examination in this same region by Wintemberg. Few notes have ever been published on this aspect of Wintemberg's untiring career, but presumably his survey was conducted sometime during the late 1920s.

Working for the National Museum of Canada, Richard

N. Pearson (1966) examined eighteen sites along the island's southeastern shore in 1960–62.

QUÉBEC

The development of archaeology in "La Belle Province" is largely the result of post-1920 endeavors, since Sir John Dawson's early interests were not soon continued after his time. It is true that L'Abbé Huart briefly described relics found at the mouth of the Saguenay River at an early date, but it was not until Dr. Frank G. Speck discovered the important Tadoussac site in 1915 that professional activity commenced. Wintemberg investigated and excavated this rich Archaic component in 1927, as well as recorded other sites in the vicinity of the nearby Moulin Baude River. Farther to the north on the headwaters of the Ottawa River, Frederick Johnson picked up pottery on Lac Kakabonga during late 1920 ethnological field work, and this material was later incorporated into Wintemberg's (1942: 135) synthesis of aboriginal pottery in Canada.

Intensive continuous work, however, did not resume in Québec until some twenty years after Wintemberg's Tadoussac excavations. Such work commenced with the 1947–48 canoe surveys of the unrelated team of Edward S. Rogers and Murray H. Rogers (1948, 1950). A third survey in 1950 by Edward Rogers and Roger A. Bradley (1953) expanded the earlier Rogers' collection, thereby providing an important addition to the materials from a little-known sector of central interior Québec. Much of the Rogers' collection from Lakes Mistassini and Albanel contains Shield Archaic, Late Woodland, and historic specimens. Too, the work of Valerie Burger (1953) opened new ground in the Kempt and Manouwane Lakes region of interior southwestern Québec.

Since 1960, considerable work has been undertaken by French Canadians. Indeed, the recent programs directed toward the training of young Québec archaeologists have been singularly successful, and mark an important advance in the archaeological development of the province. The 1962 establishment of the Société d'Archéologie de Québec and wide-ranging educational programs continue to foster additional research and popularization of Québec archaeology.

Michel Gaumond's excavations at Sillery have been followed by the energetic work of René Lévesque (1962, 1968), who effected profitable interdisciplinary analysis of the Early Woodland Batiscan site (Lévesque, *et al.* 1964). Batiscan represents one of the few definite Early Woodland components north of New York State. The contributions of René Ribes (1964, 1965, 1966, 1969) have helped pinpoint various components between Lake Meckinac and Three Rivers, while Gordon Lowther's (1965) reinvestigation of the Tadoussac site helps clarify certain questions raised by Wintemberg's earlier work. More recently, excavations have been conducted at the important Point-aux-Buissons site under the administration of Jacques Bordaz of the Université de Montreal, where many young Québec archaeologists are being trained.

Elsewhere in southeastern Québec, Charles A. Martijn (1969) has conducted substantial research at Temiscouta and Ile-aux-Basques, while Thomas E. Lee has briefly reported on the Gaspé Peninsula as well as Lac St. John and Lake Abitibi in central Québec (Lee 1965). Martijn has also contributed new data from central Québec, as well as providing important syntheses (1969, 1970) written in conjunction with Edward Rogers and Jacques Cinq-Mars. Along the north shore of the St. Lawrence it is hoped that Gerard LaPlante, Claude Bernard, and J.-Henri Fortin will continue to publish on sites they have found between Sept-Iles to the Saguenay River.

The Québec side of the Ottawa River Valley has seen continuous archaeological activity since 1960. In particular, Clyde C. Kennedy's (1967) excavations on Morrison's Island have revealed Laurentian Archaic specimens radiocarbon dated ca. 2700 B.C. Too, the surveys of Roger

Marois (1968), recently appointed Québec archaeologist
at the National Museum in Ottawa, have covered portions
of the lower Ottawa and Gatineau Valleys, and Lake
Abitibi, while James V. Wright briefly examined site lo-
calities in 1969 on the upper Ottawa River. Of the Iroquois
sequence in Québec, James F. Pendergast, Trigger, Martijn,
and Jacques Cinq-Mars continue to offer refinements. Finally, historic sites archaeology has received protracted investigation since 1925 (see Kidd 1969; Rick 1970).

ONTARIO

Archaeologically, Ontario constitutes the richest province in the Dominion, with its proliferation of sites and a
record of archaeological activity extending back to the
1830s. Much of the wealth of data presently available de-
rives principally from the dedicated and untiring work of
such men as Sir Daniel Wilson, Dr. David Boyle, Andrew
F. Hunter, Dr. Robert B. Orr, William J. Wintemberg, and
James V. Wright. Each has contributed substantially to the
development of Ontario archaeology through publications
and guidance to countless individuals. Ontario too has been
fortunate in that the first anthropology department in Canada was established in 1926 at the University of Toronto
by the late Professor Thomas F. McIlwraith. From this
institution a long list of archaeology students have received
their initial training, particularly since 1947 under the direction of Dr. J. Norman Emerson.

Archaeology in Ontario clearly arises from antiquarian
relic hunting. Opened in 1836, the Call Farm ossuary burials near Hamilton were soon followed by excavations at
the Bytown (Ottawa) ossuary in 1843, and another was
opened in 1847 by Captain T. G. Anderson. Such indiscriminant investigations provoked a reasoned editorial comment in the first volume of the *Canadian Journal* in 1852,
suggesting a thirteen-point plan for the accurate and complete recording of Indian remains. Unfortunately, little

heed was paid to this commentary, presumably penned by Sir Daniel Wilson, and wanton destruction of countless ossuaries became common Sunday afternoon sport throughout the middle and late 1800s.

Also from a burial site were the Brockville copper implements and other relics described by Thomas Reynolds in 1856. This find was followed by the activities of E. W. Guest, Thomas C. Wallbridge, and Dr. F. R. Fairbank, but clearly the most extensive work was that conducted by Dr. J. C. Taché of Laval University. Taché salvaged remains from sixteen Huron ossuaries, including the widely publicized Kinghorn pit initially opened in 1856, but he left no published record of his activities. Dr. Edmund W. Bawtree also published on Huron ossuaries, as did Trinity College geology professor Henry Montgomery. C. A. Hirschelder represents another early excavator of historic Huron ossuaries.

With the establishment of the Ontario Provincial Museum in 1886, Dr. David Boyle became its first archaeological curator. Indefatigable, Boyle conducted the first truly systematic archaeology in the province. He also was responsible for the establishment of the Annual Archaeological Reports for Ontario (1887–1926), which he masterfully edited until his death in 1911. Boyle published many articles in this series as well as in other journals.

Around Boyle there developed a group of dedicated men who continued to lay the foundations for Ontario archaeology with active field work and publications in the Annual Archaeological Reports of the Ontario Provincial Museum. Andrew F. Hunter clearly ranks as one of the more outstanding contributors. Affectionately known as Ontario's "horse and buggy" archaeologist, Hunter surveyed and documented over six hundred sites in his native Simcoe County, home of the historic Huron-Petun Iroquois. Similarly, Colonel George E. Laidlaw conducted pioneer archaeological surveys in his home county of Victoria. Other researchers who contributed original work around the turn of the century include Dr. A. F. Chamberlain, Dr. J. H.

Coyne, T. W. E. Sowter, Robert T. Anderson, Frank W. Waugh, Rev. Arthur E. Jones, J. Hugh Hammond, and Dr. Rowland B. Orr, who succeeded David Boyle as provincial archaeologist in 1911.

But Boyle's foremost protégé was William J. Wintemberg, who was encouraged to work at the Ontario Provincial Museum, where he maintained a close connection until 1911, when he began his thirty years' service for the National Museum in Ottawa. Wintemberg's copious articles, and in particular his standardized reports on the Roebuck (1936), Uren (1928), Lawson (1939), Middleport (1948), and Sidey-MacKay (1948) villages, have long provided the bases for studies of the late prehistoric occupations of southern Ontario. Sir Francis H. S. Knowle's (1937) skeletal analysis for the Roebuck village marks the first such osteological study in Ontario since the time of Sir Daniel Wilson.

Since 1936, considerable work has been conducted in southern Ontario by a variety of researchers. Wilfred Jury has examined at least nine different historic and prehistoric components between Lake Erie and Georgian Bay, while Dr. Phileo Nash commenced the University of Toronto's interest in Ontario archaeology with his 1938–39 excavations at the A.D. 1450 Pound site near Aylmer. Emerson F. Greenman in 1938 began work for the University of Michigan near Manitoulin Island with excavations on Old Birch Island and at the Paleo-Indian George Lake site near Killarney. Embarking upon ten years of active field work, Kenneth E. Kidd commenced with the 1939 excavation at Rock Lake in southwestern Algonquin Provincial Park. His subsequent meticulous excavations at the Jesuit Mission of Ste. Marie I (1949), as well as work at Orr Lake, the Ossossanée Huron ossuary, and the Middle Woodland Krieger site, stand as well-known endeavors. Kidd also drew together the first synthesis of fluted points found in the province in 1951 and prepared a pioneering synthesis (Kidd 1952) of historical developments in Ontario archaeology.

During the post-World War II era, Ontario archaeology continued to flourish, both in terms of work accomplished and in the number of trained personnel actively engaged in research. Professor Thomas F. McIlwraith began training students in 1946–47 at the historic Huron village of Cahiagué, and in 1948 at the nearby Sopher Huron site. In 1947 also, Douglas Leechman and Frederica de Laguna initiated an archaeological survey along the St. Lawrence River between Cornwall and Cardinal, with excavation at the prehistoric Parker site. In that same year, J. Norman Emerson (1955) excavated the Middle Woodland Kant site on the Bonnechere River, south of Ottawa, while Dr. William A. Ritchie (1949), also attempting to examine Middle Woodland manifestations, surveyed portions of the lower Trent River system in 1948 between Picton and Rice Lake. Studies of the Ontario Iroquois sequences were considerably strengthened when Dr. Richard S. MacNeish (1952a) completed his 1947–49 survey of Iroquois collections. His synthesis, introducing the direct historic approach and the technique of pottery type seriation, allowed him to formulate an initially disturbing *in situ* hypothesis for northeastern Iroquois origins. MacNeish (1952b) also excavated the Paleo-Indian Brohm site near Thunder Bay, Lake Superior.

Dr. J. Norman Emerson was the first to test ceramic seriation in Ontario with reference to Huron-Petun development. His prodigious excavations in 1947–65 at no less than eleven large Iroquois villages (Emerson 1954, 1956, 1960, 1966) have yielded substantial new data, as well as provided training for many students. In 1956–57, he also conducted excavations at the Middle Woodland Ault Park site on the St. Lawrence River, with subsequent work in 1958–59 on Lake Superior, near Marathon, and the following summer at the Pic River. Since his active support in establishing the Ontario Archaeological Society in 1951, Emerson has also engaged in training Canadian students for archaeological jobs throughout Canada. Two of his early students include Robert E. Popham and the late Douglas Bell.

Major contributions also have been made to Ontario archaeology by Thomas E. Lee, formerly with the National Museum. Lee's surveys through southwestern Ontario in 1949–50 were followed by an examination of a historic fort on the Ottawa River, which is a probable candidate for that of Adam Dollard. His extensive yet unpublished surveys through the Bruce Peninsula and neighboring Manitoulin Island brought to light many sites including the Inverhuron (Lucus) Archaic component and the important Paleo-Indian sites of Giant (Lee 1954) and Sheguiandah (1954, 1955). After 1955, Lee (1958) continued to contribute to archaeology in southern Ontario, but on a diminished scale. Frank Ridley, too, has conducted significant work in the province. Long interested in Huron and Neutral Iroquois (Ridley 1952a, 1952b, 1958, 1961), he has complemented such studies with pioneer investigations in outlying regions of northern Ontario (Ridley 1956, 1962). In particular, his stratified Frank Bay site on Lake Nipissing (Ridley 1954) remains unique in the province, despite small assemblage samples.

The late 1950s saw other activities of a wide-ranging nature. Richard B. Johnston (1968a, 1968b) carried out meticulous excavations at the "Serpent Mound" near Peterborough, while Robert C. Dailey and James V. Wright (1955) salvaged materials from the Malcolm site on the north shore of the St. Lawrence prior to that site going underwater with the seaway. Paul W. Sweetman recorded a unique display of petroglyphs at Stoney Lake, as well as salvaging red ocher burials from the Pennycook site in Haliburton. In Algonquin Provincial Park, Dr. Charles H. D. Clarke broke new ground, as did Dr. James B. Griffin and George I. Quimby during their 1957 launch trip around northern Lake Superior. In 1958, the University of Toronto began work on Lake Superior, soon followed by the extensive surveys and excavations of Dr.

James V. Wright (1963) of the National Museum of Canada.

Wright's (1965) work in northern Ontario in 1960–69 involved road and canoe surveys from the Manitoba to Quebec borders, with detailed work at Lac Seul, Thunder Bay, Lake Nipigon, Rossport, Pays Plat, Schreiber, Little Pic River, Marathon, Heron Bay, Michipicoten, Sand River, Montreal River, and Attawapiskat Lake. The detailed analyses and syntheses of these endeavors provide much of the bases for the known cultural sequences in that region of Ontario. Dr. Walter A. Kenyon (1961) has also devoted considerable time in the Rainy River district, as well as on the lower Albany River, while Kenneth C. Dawson (1969) continues to pursue detailed surveys in other regions of northwestern Ontario.

In southern Ontario, the progress of work over the past decade has been extensive. James V. Wright (1966) brought considerable refinement into Iroquois archaeology with the introduction of horizon and tradition synthesis concepts. He also drew together an important synthesis of certain Archaic traits (Wright 1962), followed by major excavations in 1960 at the Middle Woodland Donaldson site (Wright and Anderson 1962), and in 1962 at the developmental Iroquois village of Bennett (Wright and Anderson 1969). With the completion of his monumental osteological analysis of the Fairity ossuary, Dr. James E. Anderson (1963) was able to postulate further his hypothesis for *in situ* development of the Iroquois physical type—a line of evidence further corroborating MacNeish's initial hypothesis. Drs. Rufus Churcher and Walter Kenyon (1960) also contributed a demographic study of the prehistoric Huron Tabor Hill population.

Because of their rich nature, Ontario Iroquois sites received continued attention during the 1960s. In particular, Colonel James F. Pendergast has analyzed materials from nineteen components in southeastern Ontario, thereby establishing the frameworks for St. Lawrence Iroquois de-

velopment. William S. Donaldson has also contributed to
Huron-Petun archaeology, as has Elsie M. Jury. Other researches include those of Conrad E. Heidenreich; E. Ross
Channen and N. D. Clarke; William C. Noble; Peter Ramsden; Charles Garrad, and Walter A. Kenyon. Such has
been the wealth of accumulated data that William C. Noble
(1968, 1969) has been able to synthesize and present an
interpretation of certain developments in prehistoric Iroquois social organization.

Other studies during the 1960s include George F. Mac-
Donald's survey on the upper Grand River; Barry Mitchell's work on various components in the middle Ottawa
River Valley; Noble's recording of pits, cairns, and petroglyphs at Rock Lake in 1962; James Wright's 1964 salvage
of Middle Woodland and prehistoric Neutral Iroquois materials at Fort Erie; William C. Noble's 1965 excavation
of the late Middle Woodland Surma site, Fort Erie; Dr.
Edward S. Roger's synthesis of dugout canoes in the province; Paul W. Sweetman's excavations on Thorah Island
in Lake Simcoe; and Michael W. Spence's work on Middle
Woodland sites in the Trent River Valley.

Since 1968, the tempo of work in Ontario has continued
at a high pitch. Trent University students have excavated
various components in the rich Trent River Valley, as well
as at Point Pelee on Lake Erie. Numerous University of
Toronto students, including Messrs. Alan Tyyska, Dean
Knight, Peter Ramsden, and William Fox, to name but a
few, have also conducted work on Iroquois and Archaic
sites for Dr. William Hurley. McMaster University, too,
has engaged in excavations of Middle Woodland and historic Neutral sites under C. E. Stortroen and William C.
Noble. During the summer of 1968, Marian E. White
conducted a survey through two Ontario counties in the
Niagara Peninsula, while James V. Wright continued wide-
ranging activities near Orillia and Inverhuron. In short,
the range of archaeological investigation in Ontario continues to be prolific.

MANITOBA

Archaeological investigations in Manitoba began with the 1867 reconnaissance of Donald Gunn, who examined various burial mounds in the southern regions of the province. Twelve years later, during the course of geological exploration, Dr. Robert Bell of the Geological Survey of Canada picked up pottery at the mouth of the Nelson River that has since been identified as Black Duck ware. The conspicuous burial mounds south of Lake Winnipeg drew the most attention throughout the early years of Manitoba archaeology.

Apparently it was Dr. M. P. Schultz who entrenched the idea that the Manitoba mounds were the product of a vanished race of "Mound-Builders." This novel idea, subsequently proved mythical, pervaded Manitoba archaeology well into the 1900s. Rev. George Bryce's work exemplifies this, as does that of Charles N. Bell, T. H. Lewis, and Andrew McCharles. After 1890, however, interest in plains archaeology generally waned. The work of Toronto geologist Henry Montgomery marks an exception, as does that of William B. Nickerson, whose detailed archaeological surveys through southwestern Manitoba in 1912–15 have only recently been published (Capes 1963).

Subsequent work continued to be sporadic and short on publication. Charles N. Bell described a single native copper implement, while Vladimir J. Fewkes reported on villages and mounds near Sourisford. Fewkes also drew attention to the corded pottery from Manitoba possibly being derived from Asia. Curiosity prompted W. H. Rand to open the Rosser and Morden mounds, while amateur Chris Vickers, beginning his investigations in 1943, contributed substantial new data from the southern regions of the province. R. D. Bird and M. S. Stanton also represent mid-1940 researchers.

During the 1950s professionally trained personnel turned

their attention to Manitoba. Douglas Leechman's description of an elephant bone artifact in the National Museum's collections was followed by field work conducted by Dr. Richard MacNeish in 1951–53. MacNeish's surveys in southeastern Manitoba led to his classic 1958 monograph, which with modifications remains definitive for certain Archaic, Middle, and Late Woodland manifestations in the southern regions of the province. Together with Katherine H. Capes, MacNeish (1958) also reported on the United Church site on Rock Lake. Unfortunately, Boyd N. Wettlaufer's survey through Manitoba has never been published, but Walter M. Hlady's work helped prepare the initial outlines for a chronological sequence in the province.

Since 1960, Manitoba archaeology has flourished, largely through the training of students at the University of Manitoba under Dr. William J. Mayer-Oakes. Walter M. Hlady diligently continued to pursue his field studies on Laurel and Selkirk remains, while Nancy S. Cameron made the first osteological analysis of aboriginal Manitoba crania from a series excavated by Henry Montgomery. James V. Wright also began his surveys in the Shield country of northern Manitoba in 1963, while Mayer-Oakes and Timothy Fiske surveyed and salvaged remains from sites under impending destruction with the South Saskatchewan River Floodway Project. In the northern part of the province William N. Irving collected artifacts from the Twin Lakes site, while in 1965 James V. Wright, accompanied by William C. Noble, surveyed Southern Indian Lake. Wright returned to this lake in 1966, and in 1967 surveyed portions of God's Lake and the Nelson River.

From 1965 to the present, many of Mayer-Oakes' students have begun to publish. They include: Matthew Hill; Allan A. Simpson; Leo F. Pettipas; Joyce Dennis; and Eugene M. Gryba. Jack Steinbring continues to pursue studies of Paleo-Indian and Archaic remains in the province, while Mayer-Oakes (1967) has effected interdisciplinary studies associated with research on glacial Lake

Agassiz. Dr. Ronald J. Nash has penetrated into northern Manitoba with surveys on the Seal River and near the towns of Thompson and Churchill. In all, the scope of Manitoba archaeology continues to broaden with systematic and problem-oriented research.

SASKATCHEWAN

The development of archaeology in this western province is essentially very recent. Prior to 1935, only three men published works of note. Joseph B. Tyrrell, of the Geological Survey of Canada, collected small samples of lithic artifacts from the north end of Cree Lake during his northern traverse to the headwaters of the Dubawnt River. But few of his era followed suit in the province. Years later, Henry Montgomery examined archaeological components in the southern sector of the province, but his work too was not soon followed. Traveling through Saskatchewan and Alberta in 1925, William J. Wintemberg made a reconnaissance, collecting data for his posthumous paper of 1942, devoted to the distribution of aboriginal pottery in Canada. Such were the limited early researches in Saskatchewan archaeology, albeit professionally trained individuals clearly laid the groundwork.

After Wintemberg's visit, various amateurs in the province began amassing collections. That this activity was conscientiously intended is reflected in the 1935 establishment of the Saskatchewan Archaeology Society at Saskatoon, with William J. Orchard as its first president. Orchard (1942) later published a curious little text synthesizing various Saskatchewan finds, as well as others from the Canadian prairies. From Reindeer Lake in the north, P. Downes collected late-dating pottery, while Edgar B. Howard focused attention on certain of the Paleo-Indian projectile points from the southern regions of the province. Work during the 1940s generally waned in Saskatchewan, although Oliver C. Furniss did report on newly discov-

ered fur posts, and Walter M. Hlady synthesized known
Plainview Paleo-Indian finds from the prairies as a whole.
Dr. Richard S. MacNeish also made a brief examination
of sites near Fond du Lac on eastern Lake Athabasca in
1949 for the National Museum of Canada.

Boyd N. Wettlaufer clearly contributed the first major
researches in modern Saskatchewan archaeology. His initial surveys in southern Saskatchewan led to major excavations at the stratified Mortlack and Long Creek sites
(Wettlaufer 1956, 1957; Wettlaufer and Mayer-Oakes
1960). During the latter 1950s, Dr. Robert W. Nero and
Bruce A. McCorquodale also reported on new finds, particularly the important Oxbow and Parkhill sites. Eugene
Y. Arima conducted a survey in northeastern Saskatchewan that remains unpublished, as are the results of Robert Nero's survey on Lake Athabasca.

During the latter 1950s, Alice and Thomas Kehoe contributed numerous articles on Saskatchewan archaeology.
In 1959 Alice B. Kehoe presented new data on pottery in
the northern plains. Thomas F. Kehoe's (1958, 1966) interests in tipi rings and Clovis sites in the southern part
of the province were complemented by studies of effigy
monuments (Kehoe and Kehoe 1959) and possible migrations of Athapaskans through the northern plains
(Kehoe and McCorquodale 1961).

Archaeological research in Saskatchewan has steadily
increased during the past decade, particularly since 1965.
Working for E. A. Christiansen, D. M. Lane excavated
the Chamberlain stratified ceramic site in 1969, while Mr.
Don R. King opened up the prehistoric Bracken Cairn.
Surveying through north-central Saskatchewan and north-
ern Alberta in 1964, James V. Wright, accompanied by
William C. Noble, located new components of Archaic
and Selkirk materials at Hudson Bay and north through
Waskesiu National Park.

Roscoe Wilmeth's surveys through southern Saskatchewan have disclosed a fossilized implement from the Gren-
fel site, possibly of Clovis age. Too, a Scottsbluff point has

been reported from Lacadena by Ian G. Dyck, while Zenon Pohorecky continues searching for pre-10,000 B.C. sites. More recently, Dr. James F. V. Millar, University of Saskatchewan, has excavated a series of Oxbow sites near Saskatoon, including an Oxbow cemetery yielding 105 to 300 individuals. Finally, Margaret Hanna's (1970) recent synthesis of Saskatchewan and Prairie archaeology represents an important contribution to the prehistory of the western Canadian provinces.

ALBERTA

As in Saskatchewan, the growth of archaeology in this province is a comparatively recent development. Early Geological Survey officers such as Joseph B. Tyrrell visited and photographed historic sites during the latter 1800s, but few collections were made. Brief and sporadic investigations continued to be the rule until 1949. Never fully published, William J. Wintemberg conducted an archaeological reconnaissance through southern Alberta in 1925. This work was followed by the 1937–38 reconnaissances of Wesley L. Bliss and Junius B. Bird.

Boyd N. Wettlaufer inaugurated the first major archaeological excavations in Alberta during the summer of 1949. At the impressive Head-Smashed-In buffalo jump, just west of Fort MacLeod, he worked through a deeply stratified sequence; the results remain to be published. Thomas F. Kehoe (1958) documented various sites within the Blackfoot Indian Reservation of southern Alberta in 1952–53; while Dr. Douglas Leechman, Margaret Hess, and Roy Fowler reported on pictographic artwork. Hugh A. Dempsey's (1956) ethnohistoric researches clearly provided alternative interpretations for some of the larger stone rings in Alberta, as well as stimulating a closer bond between archaeological and historical approaches.

The year 1955 marks an important date in the development of Alberta archaeology. In that year, the Glenbow

Foundation of Calgary began the first of its many archaeological programs under the directorship of Dr. Douglas
Leechman.

During the summers 1955–56, Dr. H. Marie Wormington conducted archaeological surveys of collections and
sites for the Glenbow Foundation (Wormington and
Forbis 1965:1), and secured the services of Dr. William
Mulloy and Dr. E. Mott Davis. Mulloy's work in the
southern regions of the province, north to Edmonton, was
followed by Davis's excavation in central Alberta and documentation of collections in the Peace River district. Dr.
Wormington was also responsible for introducing Dr.
Richard G. Forbis to Alberta in 1957. In that year, Forbis
undertook excavations at the stratified Ross site near Leth-
bridge. This activity was followed by work at the Old
Women's Buffalo Jump (Forbis 1962) and the Cluny
Earthlodge in 1958–60. For the first time a firm sequence
of aboriginal occupation was established in southern Alberta as a result of these endeavors.

Buried Oxbow culture materials came to light in the
province during Glenbow's 1961 excavations at Castor
Creek, while in that same year Don R. King salvaged remains from a rock cairn on the Red Deer River near
Rumsey (Wormington and Forbis 1965:3). Another
cairn, British Block, was also investigated near Medicine
Hat, and preliminary testing was undertaken in 1962 at
the 1799–1833 fort of Rocky Mountain House. In 1962
also, geologist Dr. Archie M. Stalker encountered near
Tabor an immature skeleton, buried under deposits that
suggest that it is one of the earliest human skeletons yet
recovered in the New World (Wormington and Forbis
1965:117).

In 1963, William C. Noble excavated the historic Rocky
Mountain House fort for Richard G. Forbis, and then
initiated work at the stratified Kenney site near Pincher
Creek. Concisely presented, Forbis (1963) published a
definitive paper outlining the numerous problems involved
in applying the direct historic approach to tribal groups

in the Canadian West. Such was clearly evident in the case of Rocky Mountain House. In 1963, too, Dr. Alan Bryan and Dr. Ruth Gruhn joined the faculty of the University of Alberta, Edmonton, thereby expanding the number of professional archaeologists in the province to three.

In 1964, the Glenbow Foundation continued its investigations in southern Alberta under the direction of Richard G. Forbis. Brian O. K. Reeves completed excavations at the Kenney site and at the Paleo-Indian Fletcher site previously investigated in 1963 by Forbis (1968). Selwyn S. Dewdney completed studies of pictographs in the province, while James V. Wright and William C. Noble completed a road and canoe survey through northern Alberta from Athabasca Landing and Peace River to Hay River in the Northwest Territories. In addition to his mapping of a human effigy near Consort, Lewis A. Bayrock (Wormington and Forbis 1965:98) discovered an early site near Tabor shortly postdating 9000 B.C. (Wormington and Forbis 1965:117).

Of significance in 1964 was the establishment of the first separate Department of Archaeology in North America at the University of Calgary under the chairmanship of Dr. Richard S. MacNeish. From this institution, four archaeology doctorates were first conferred to Canadian students in 1968, and many other students continue to be trained there.

Since 1965, archaeological research in Alberta has blossomed. Many individuals, including Leslie B. Davis, Robson Bonnichsen, William J. Byrne, Ronald Getty, O. A. Christensen, and Jerry Bellamy, to mention a few, continue to work on new data. Too, the potentially very early findings of Dr. C. S. "Rufus" Churcher near Medicine Hat could extend the known sequences of occupation back to forty thousand years in the southern regions of the province. Roscoe Wilmeth undertook a limited survey of the Bow River in 1967, while Dr. David Sanger (1968c) published on a prairie microblade industry near High River. Certainly, the ambitious paleocultural/environmental studies of Brian Reeves in Waterton Lakes National Park marks an important new approach in Alberta archaeology.

CONCLUSION

Summing up, it is apparent that the development of Canadian archaeology has come a long way since Jenness's early evaluation. A good deal of work has been accomplished, such that regional sequences are available for most of the provinces, and many young archaeologists are being trained across the country. It is to be hoped that emphasis will be placed on producing field researchers, although in the not too distant future more syntheses will be necessary.

Three factors have helped to bring unity into Canadian Archaeology to date. One is Charles Borden's (1952) uniform site designation scheme, based upon the latitude-longitude coordinates of a site. This scheme has been nationally applied. Second, the establishment of the Canadian Archaeological Association 1968 has brought together researchers across the country, and it promises to be a growing, viable organization. A third unifying factor is certainly Roscoe Wilmeth's (1969) synthesis of radiocarbon dates from sites within each Province and the Northwest Territories.

Of the archaeology in Canada, the western provinces seem to hold the key for greater understanding of problems associated with earliest man in North America. Both Saskatchewan and Alberta have early claims that should be investigated thoroughly. Studies of changing adaptations to changing ecological conditions are also under way, and will receive expanded attention in the future. A start toward case studies of changing social organization has been made with the northeastern Iroquois (Noble 1969), and the Northwest Coast tribes should also provide excellent material.

As has been shown, Canadian archaeology has progressed from a childhood state to young adulthood stature, and all present trends indicate a continuing and more sophisticated development in the future.

REFERENCES

ANDERSON, JAMES E.
  1963 "The People of Fairity: An Osteological Analysis of an Iroquois Ossuary." *Nat. Mus. Can. Bull.* 193:28–129.

BANCROFT, H. H.
  1875 Native Races of the Pacific States.

BIRD, JUNIUS
  1945 "Archaeology of the Hopedale Area, Labrador." *Anthro. Pap. Am. Mus. Nat. Hist.* 39.

BORDEN, CHARLES E.
  1952 "A Uniform Site Designation Scheme for Canada." *Anthro. in Brit. Col.* 3:44–48.

BURGER, VALERIE
  1953 "Indian Camp-sites on Kempt and Manouwane Lakes in the Province of Quebec." *Penn. Arch.* 23:32–45.

CAPES, KATHERINE H.
  1963 "The W. B. Nickerson Survey and Excavations 1912–15, of the Southern Manitoba Mounds Region." *Anthro. Pap. Nat. Mus. Can.* 4.

CHURCHER, C. S., and KENYON, W. A.
  1960 "The Tabor Hill Ossuaries: A Study in Iroquois Demography." *Human Biology* 32:249–73.

DAILEY, ROBERT C., and WRIGHT, JAMES V.
  1955 "The Malcolm Site." *Tran. Royal Can. Inst.* 31(1):3–23.

DAWSON, SIR JOHN W.
  1880 *Fossil Men and Their Modern Representatives.* Montreal.

DAWSON, KENNETH C.
  1969 "Archaeological Investigations at the Site of the Longlac Historic Trading Post, Thunder Bay District, Ontario." *Ont. Arch.* 12.

DEMPSEY, HUGH A.
  1956 "Stone 'Medicine Wheels': Memorials to Blackfoot War Chiefs." *Journ. Wash. Acad. Sci.* 46:177–82.

EMERSON, J. NORMAN
  1954 "The Archaeology of the Ontario Iroquois." Ph.D. dissertation, University of Chicago.

1955   "The Kant Site: A Point Peninsula Manifestation in Renfrew
        County, Ontario." *Trans. Royal Can. Inst.* 31(1):24–66.
1956   "Understanding Ontario Iroquois Pottery." *Ont. Arch.* 3.
1960   "A Further Note on the MacDonald Site." *Ont. Hist.*
        52(1):60–61.
1966   "The Payne Site: An Iroquoian Manifestation in Prince Ed-
        ward County, Ontario." *Nat. Mus. Can. Bull.* 206:126–257.

ERSKINE, JOHN S.
1960   "Shell Heap Archaeology of Southwestern Nova Scotia."
        Proceed. Nova Scotian Inst. Sci. 24.

FEWKES, J. WALTER
1896   "A Prehistoric Shell Heap on Prince Edward Island." *Am.
        Antiquarian* 1:3–6.

FORBIS, RICHARD G.
1962   "The Old Women's Buffalo Jump, Alberta." *Nat. Mus. Can.
        Bull.* 180:56–123.
1963   "The Direct Historical Approach in the Prairie Provinces."
        Great Plains Jour. 3:1–8.

GANONG, WILLIAM F.
1899   "A Monograph of Historic Sites in the Province of New
        Brunswick." *Proceed. Trans. Royal Soc. Can.* 2:213–357.

HANNA, MARGARET
1970   "The Prehistory and Archaeology of the Canadian Prairies."
        Honours B.A. thesis, University of Manitoba.

HARP, ELMER
1964   "The Cultural Affinities of the Newfoundland Dorset Es-
        kimo." *Nat. Mus. Can. Bull.* 200.

——— and HUGHES, DAVID
1968   "Five Prehistoric Burials from Port-aux-Crois, Newfound-
        land." *Polar Notes.* 8:1–47.

HARPER, J. RUSSELL
1956   "Portland Point, Crossroads of New Brunswick History:
        Preliminary Report of the 1955 Excavation." *New Brunswick
        Mus. Hist. Stud.* 9:1–20.
1957   "Two Seventeenth-Century Micmac 'Copper Kettle' Burials."
        Anthropologica 4:11–36.

HOWLEY, J. P.
1915   *The Beothucks or Red Indians.* Cambridge, England.

HUGHES, DAVID R.
1969   "Human Remains from Near Manuels River, Conception
        Bay, Newfoundland." *Nat. Mus. Can. Bull.* 224:195–207.

INSTAD, ANNE STINE
1968   "The Norsemen's Discovery of America." *37th Inter. Cong.
        Amer.* 4:89–95.

INSTAD, HELGE
1968   "The Norsemen's Discovery of North America: A Theory

and a Discovery at L'Anse aux Meadows, Northern New-foundland." *37th Inter. Cong. Amer.* 4:97–106.

JENNESS, DIAMOND
1932 "Fifty Years of Archaeology in Canada." *Royal Soc. Can. Anniversary Volume 1882–1932:*71–76.
1934 "The Vanished Red Indians of Newfoundland." *Can. Geog. Journ.* 8:27–32.

JOHNSTON, RICHARD B.
1968a "Archaeology of Rice Lake, Ontario." *Anthro. Pap. Nat. Mus. Can.* 19.
1968b "The Archaeology of the Serpent Mounds Site." *Occas. Pap. Royal Ont. Mus.* 10.

KEHOE, ALICE B.
1959 "Ceramic Affiliations in the Northwestern Plains." *Am. Ant.* 25:237–46.

KEHOE, THOMAS F.
1958 "Tipi Rings: The 'Direct Ethnological' Approach Applied to an Archaeological Problem." *Am. Anthro.* 60:861–73.
1966 "The Distribution and Implications of Fluted Points in Saskatchewan." *Am. Ant.* 31:530–39.

——— and KEHOE, ALICE B.
1959 "Builder of Effigy Monuments in the Northern Plains." *Jour. of Am. Folk Lore* 73:115–27.

——— and McCORQUODALE, BRUCE A.
1961 "The Avonlea Point." *Plains Anthro.* 6:179–88.

KENNEDY, CLYDE C.
1967 "Preliminary Report on the Morrison's Island Site." *Nat. Mus. Can. Bull.* 206:100–24.

KENYON, WALTER A.
1961 "The Swan Lake Site." *Occas. Pap. Royal Ont. Mus.* 3.

KIDD, KENNETH E.
1941 "The Excavation of Fort St. Marie." *Can. Hist. Review* 22:403–15.
1952 "Sixty Years of Ontario Archaeology." *Archeology of Eastern United States,* J. B. Griffin (ed.):71–82.
1969 "Historic Site Archaeology in Canada." *Anthro. Pap. Nat. Mus. Can.* 22.

KNOWLES, SIR FRANCIS H. S.
1937 "Physical Anthropology of the Roebuck Iroquois." *Nat. Mus. Can. Bull.* 87.

LEE, THOMAS E.
1954 "The First Shequiandah Expedition, Manitoulin Island, Ontario." *Am. Ant.* 20:101–11.
1955 "The Second Shequiandah Expedition, Manitoulin Island, Ontario." *Am. Ant.* 21:63–71.

80   WILLIAM C. NOBLE

1958   "The Parker Earthwork, Corunna, Ontario." *Penn. Arch* 28:3–30.
1965   "Archaeological Investigations at Lake Abitibi, 1964." *Centre d'Etudes Nordiques Travaux Divers* 10.

LÉVESQUE, RENÉ
1962   *"Les Richesses."* La Société d'archéologie de Sherbrooke, rapport preliminaire.

———, OSBORNE, F. FITZ, and WRIGHT, J. V.
1964   *"Le Gisement de Batiscan."* *Anthro. Pap. Nat. Mus. Can.* 6.

LOWTHER, GORDON
1965   "Archaeology of the Tadoussac Area, Province of Quebec." *Anthropologica* 7:27–37.

MACDONALD, GEORGE F.
1968   "Debert: A Paleo-Indian Site in Central Nova Scotia." *Anthro. Pap. Nat. Mus. Can.* 16.

MCILWRAITH, THOMAS F.
1964   "Sir Daniel Wilson: A Canadian Anthropologist of One Hundred Years Ago." *Trans. Royal Soc. Can.* 3:129–36.

MACINTOSH, WILLIAM
1913   "Aboriginal Pottery of New Brunswick." *Nat. Hist. Soc. New Brunswick Bull.* 9.

MACNEISH, RICHARD S.
1952a "Iroquois Pottery Types: A Technique for the Study of Iroquois Prehistory." *Nat. Mus. Can. Bull.* 124.
1952b "A Possible Early Site in the Thunder Bay District, Ontario." *Nat. Mus. Can. Bull.* 126:23–47.
1958   "An Introduction to the Archaeology of Southeast Manitoba." *Nat. Mus. Can. Bull.* 157.

——— and CAPES, KATHERINE H.
1958   "The United Church Site on Rock Lake, Manitoba." *Anthropologica* 6:119–55.

MAROIS, ROGER
1968   *"L'Archéologie des Provinces d'Ontario et de Québec."* Thèse de maitre, Université de Montréal.

MARTIJN, CHARLES A.
1969   "Ile aux Basques and the Prehistoric Iroquois Occupation of Southern Quebec." *Musée d'Archélogie Préhistorique, Cahier Archéologique:* 53–114.

——— and ROGERS, EDWARD
1969   "Mistassini-Albanel: Contributions to the Prehistory of Quebec." *Centre d'Etudes Nordiques, Travaux Divers,* 25.

——— and CINQ-MARS, JACQUES
1970   *"Aperçu sur la Recherche Préhistorique au Québec."* *La Révue de Géographie de Montréal* 24(2):175–88.

MAYER-OAKES, WILLIAM J.
1967 "Life, Land and Water." *Occas. Pap. Univ. Manitoba, Dept. Anthro.* 1.

NOBLE, WILLIAM C.
1968 "Iroquois Archaeology and the Development of Iroquois Social Organization (1000–1650 A.D.)." Ph.D. dissertation, University of Calgary.
1969 "Some Social Implications of the Iroquois 'In Situ' Theory." *Ont. Arch.* 13:16–28.

ORCHARD, WILLIAM J.
1942 *The Stone Age on the Prairies.* Regina and Toronto: School Aids and Text Book Publishing Company.

PATTERSON, REV. GEORGE
1890 "The Stone Age in Nova Scotia, as Illustrated by a Collection of Relics Presented to Dalhousie College." *Proceed. Trans. Nova Scotian Inst. Nat. Sci.* 3(3):231–52.

PEARSON, RICHARD N.
1966 "Some Recent Archaeological Discoveries from Prince Edward Island." *Anthropologica* 8:101–9.

PENDERGAST, JAMES F.
1963 "Canadian Archaeology and History in 1962." *Can. Geog. Jour.* 66:132–39.

PIERS, HARRY
1915 "Brief Account of the Micmac Indians of Nova Scotia and Their Remains." *Proceed. Trans. Nova Scotian Inst. Nat. Sci.* 8:99–125.

RIBES, RENÉ
1964 *"Les Sites Préhistoriques de Red Mill." Musée d'Archéologie Préhistorique, Cahier Archéologique* 1:1–24.
1965 *"Préhistoire de la Région de Trois-Rivères." Mauricien Médical* 5:37–50.
1966 *"Station du Sylvicole Moyen à La-Pointe-du-Lac." Musée d'Archéologie Préhistorique* 2:1–21.
1969 *"Recherches Archéologiques dans la Région du Lac Brochet et du Grand-lac Meckinac." Musée d'Archéologie Préhistorique, Cahier d'Archéologie Québécoise* 1–52.

RICK, JOHN H.
1970 "Archaeological Investigations of the National Historic Sites Service 1962–1966." *Can. Hist. Sites Occas. Pap. in Arch. and Hist.* 1:9–44.

RIDLEY, FRANK
1952a "The Huron and Lalonde Occupations of Ontario." *Am. Ant.* 17:197–210.
1952b "The Fallis Site, Ontario." *Am. Ant.* 18:7–14.
1954 "The Frank Bay Site, Lake Nipissing." *Am. Ant.* 20:40–50.
1956 "An Archaeological Reconnaissance of Lake Abitibi, Ontario." *Penn. Arch.* 26:32–36.

1958   "The Boys and Barrie Sites." *Ont. Arch.* 4:18–39.
1961   "Archaeology of the Neutral Indians." Etobicoke Historical Society.

RITCHIE, WILLIAM A.
1949   "An Archaeological Survey of the Trent Waterway in Ontario, Canada, and Its Significance for New York State Prehistory." *Rochester Mus. Arts and Sci. Res. Records* 9.

ROGERS, EDWARD S., and ROGERS, MURRAY H.
1948   "Archaeological Reconnaissance of Lakes Mistassini and Albanel, Province of Quebec, 1947." *Am. Ant.* 14:81–90.
1950   "Archaeological Investigations in the Region about Lakes Mistassini and Albanel, Province of Quebec, 1948." *Am. Ant.* 15:322–37.

——— and BRADLEY, ROGER A.
1953   "An Archaeological Reconnaissance in South Central Quebec, 1950." *Am. Ant.* 19:138–44.

SANGER, DAVID
1968   "The High River Microblade Industry." *Plains Anthro.* 13:190–208.

SMITH, HARLAN I., and WINTEMBERG, W. J.
1929   "Some Shell-Heaps in Nova Scotia." *Nat. Mus. Can. Bull.* 47.

SPECK, FRANK G.
1940   "Eskimo Jacket Ornaments of Ivory Suggesting Function of Bone Pendants Found in Beothuck Sites in Newfoundland." *Am. Ant.* 5:225–28.

STRONG, WILLIAM D.
1930   "A Stone Culture from Northern Labrador and Its Relation to the Eskimo-like Cultures of the Northeast." *Am. Anthro.* 32:126–44.

TRIGGER, BRUCE G.
1966   "Sir Daniel Wilson: Canada's First Anthropologist." *Anthropologica* 8:3–38.

TUCK, JAMES
1970   "An Archaic Indian Cemetery in Newfoundland." *Sci. Am.* 222:112–21.

WETTLAUFER, BOYD N.
1956   "The Mortlack Site in the Besant Valley of Central Saskatchewan." *Saskat. Mus. Nat. Hist. Anthro. Series* 1.
1957   "The Long Creek Site." *The Blue Jay* 15:167–69.

——— and MAYER-OAKES, W. J.
1960   "The Long Creek Site." *Saskat. Mus. Nat. Hist. Anthro. Series* 2.

WILMETH, ROSCOE
1969   "Canadian Archaeological Radio-Carbon Dates." *Nat. Mus. Can. Bull.* 232:68–127.

WINTEMBERG, WILLIAM J.
  1928 "Uren Prehistoric Village Site, Greenville County, Ontario."
        Nat. Mus. Can. Bull. 51.
  1936 "Roebuck Prehistoric Village Site, Greenville County, On-
        tario." *Nat. Mus. Can. Bull.* 83.
  1939 "Lawson Prehistoric Village Site, Middlesex County, On-
        tario." *Nat. Mus. Can. Bull.* 94.
  1942 "The Geographical Distribution of Aboriginal Pottery in
        Canada." *Am. Ant.* 8:129–41.
  1948 "The Middleport Prehistoric Village Site." *Nat. Mus. Can.
        Bull.* 109.

WORMINGTON, H. MARIE, and FORBIS, RICHARD G.
  1965 "An Introduction to the Archaeology of Alberta, Canada."
        Denver Mus. Nat. Hist. Bull. 11.

WRIGHT, JAMES V.
  1962 "A Distributional Study of Some Archaic Traits in Southern
        Ontario." *Nat. Mus. Can. Bull.* 180:124–42.
  1963 "An Archaeological Survey Along the North Shore of Lake
        Superior." *Nat. Mus. Can. Anthro. Pap.* 3.
  1965 "A Regional Examination of Ojibwa Culture History." *An-
        thropologica* 7:189–227.
  1967 "The Laurel Tradition and the Middle Woodland Period."
        Nat. Mus. Can. Bull. 217.
  1968 "The Application of the Direct Historic Approach to the
        Iroquois and the Ojibwa." *Ethnohistory* 15:96–111.

——— and ANDERSON, JAMES E.
  1963 "The Donaldson Site." *Nat. Mus. Can. Bull.* 184.
  1969 "The Bennett Site." *Nat. Mus. Can. Bull.* 229.

4 THE NORTHEASTERN UNITED STATES

David S. Brose

THE THEME OF THE MOUND BUILDERS

During the last quarter of the eighteenth century the reports of travelers into the trans-Appalachian wilderness were filled with tales of the impressive earthworks that filled the Mississippi and Ohio River Valleys. It was also known that many of these mounds contained exotic materials of surprising artistry that were at such variance with the depressed status of the current aboriginal inhabitants that the only explanation deemed reasonable was that they were the product of some earlier race displaced by the savage American Indians. Whence had both the Mound Builders and their victorious protagonists, the Indians, come, and when, and how were the Indians able to prevail over an apparently superior civilization?

There was no lack of proponents for ancient transoceanic voyages, nor was there reluctance to explain the significance of the earthworks by analogy with real or mythical events in other continents. The first reported investigations in the United States were those of Thomas Jefferson, who prior to 1782 cut a trench through a Virginia mound. Jefferson (1784) noted stratigraphic levels, recorded the placement of cultural materials and skeletons, and related this mound to neighboring mounds. He concluded that they were the work of American Indians.

The first half of the nineteenth century saw a number of mound explorations. Dr. J. H. McCulloch in Ohio reported on his 1812 excavations of Ohio mounds and stated that the skeletons were no different from those of Indians. By 1836 Albert Gallatin was able to publish a scholarly summary of what was known of the mounds, suggesting that there was no evidence to support the theory of a separate race of Mound Builders. He distinguished the Ohio earthworks, which were "mere tumuli," from the pyramidal mounds such as Cahokia, which ". . . were probably connected with the worship of the nation . . . having a strong family likeness to the Mexican Pyramids." This was not the popular opinion, and in 1833 Josiah Priest's volume describing the vanished race of Mound Builders sold over twenty-two thousand copies in three months.

The Grave Creek Mound in West Virginia had been tested in 1819 by Rev. D. Dodderidge, and in 1838, Charles Abelard Tomlinson sank a central shaft some seventy-seven feet to the stone-covered log tomb within. In 1839 Dr. Samuel G. Morton of Philadelphia collected over nine hundred human skulls and demonstrated that there was no significant difference between those of the Mound Builders and those of the living American Indians.

In 1845 the American Ethnological Society commissioned Ephriam George Squier, a Chillicothe newspaper editor, to report on the Ohio mounds. Along with Dr. Edwin H. Davis, he opened over two hundred mounds in two years, and in 1848 the Smithsonian Institution brought out their report, *Ancient Monuments of the Mississippi Valley*. Squier and Davis began by classifying all earthworks as enclosures or mounds, and there were several subclasses of the latter (e.g., temple mounds, burial mounds, etc.). Squier and Davis concluded that these represented a different race or era. Pyramidal mounds in the lower Ohio Valley were also noted and were relegated to a different culture. The mounds in Ohio had been excavated by sinking central shafts, and Squier and Davis noted stratigraphic levels, which were measured and described. The recovered artifacts were illustrated and described by type of material. Intrusive burials and associated materials were assigned separate provenience. The terrace locations of the mounds were taken to indicate

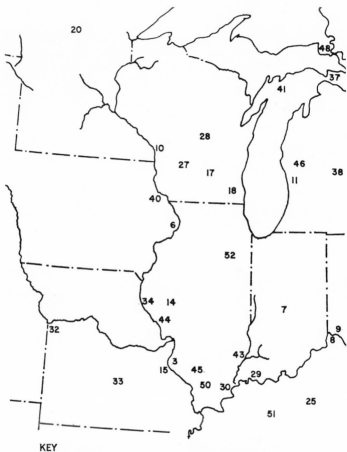

KEY

1. Marietta Mound
2. Jeffersons Mound
3. Cahokia
4. Circleville
5. Grave Creek Mound
6. Elephant Effigy Mound
7. Merom
8. Turner
9. Madisonville Cemetery
10. Trempeleau Mounds
11. Norton
12. Fort Ancient
13. Adena
14. Naples Mound Group
15. St. Louis Mound Group
16. Ripley
17. Kratz Creek
18. Aztalan
19. Abbott Farm—Trenton Gravels
20. Browns Valley Man
21. Reagen Site
22. Bullbrook
23. Williamson
24. Shoop
25. Parrish
26. Lamoka Lake
27. Grand River Mound Group
28. Neale and McClaughy Md Grps

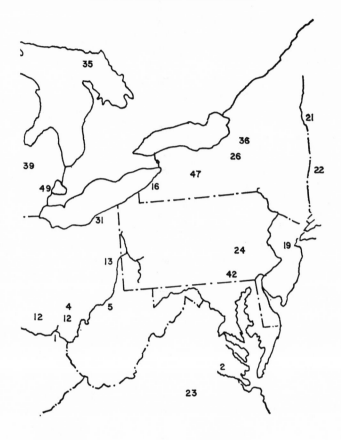

29. Angel Site
30. Kincaid
31. Whittlesey Focus Sites
32. Kansas City Hopewell Sites
33. Grahm Cave
34. Modoc Rock Shelter
35. Georgian Bay Archaic Sites
36. Brewerton
37. Juntanen
38. Saginaw Valley Archaic Sites
39. Schultz Site
40. Mill Creek Sites
41. Summer Island
42. Sheep Rock Shelter
43. Riverton
44. Koster Site
45. Hatchery West
46. Spring Creek
47. Owasco
48. Naomikong Court
49. Holcomb
50. Wassam Ridge
51. Green River Shell Mounds
52. Gentleman Farm
53. "Boyleston Street Fishweir"
   is in Boston Harbor—
   (not on map)

considerable antiquity, and their materials indicated extensive trade over the entire Mississippi Valley. Squier and Davis could discern no significant differences in the southern Ohio mounds, all of which they felt indicated a high civilization somehow related to Mexico. The third Smithsonian *Contributions to Knowledge* (1852) contained Whittlesey's description of the earthworks and villages of northern Ohio, and Volume 7 contained Increase A. Lapham's paper "The Antiquities of Wisconsin" (1855). Volume 8 of the Smithsonian *Contributions to Knowledge* presented a summary and attempted to evaluate the archaeological work done up to that time (Haven 1856).

In 1878, the Smithsonian established the Bureau of American Ethnology (BAE) under the direction of Major John Wesley Powell, who was given the task of ". . . continuing archaeological investigation relating to the Mound Builders and prehistoric mounds." In 1881 Powell set up an archaeological division of the BAE which, under Cyrus Thomas, continued to explore the mounds of the Northeast. Thomas recognized that too much destruction would result if only survey were performed, but there were too few personnel to attempt complete excavations. His solution was to send a number of small crews around to survey mounds and make test excavations in those that seemed most important. In his 1887 report *Burial Mounds of the Northern Sections of the United States,* Thomas classified mounds by types into eight cultural districts: 1. a Wisconsin district with effigy mounds; 2. an Upper Mississippi district with simple conical mounds; 3. an Ohio district where earthen enclosures and embankments were associated with the mounds; 4. a New York district where the earthworks were more or less historic; 5. an Appalachian district with Ohiolike mounds but cultural differences, and 6–8, a number of southern districts. Thomas stressed the complexity of the problems in mound archaeology and stated his belief that these various mounds represented many different cultural groups in many different eras.

THE INSTITUTIONAL PERIOD 1880-1925

By the late nineteenth century the BAE was joined by the Harvard Peabody Museum under Frederick W. Putnam. Putnam had long been interested in the problem of the Mound Builders. As early as 1871–72 he had tested the mounds in central Indiana. Upon becoming curator of Harvard's Peabody Museum in 1875 he expanded his scope of operations. By 1882 he had begun excavations at the Turner Mound in southern Ohio, and within five years had added excavations at Marriott and the Harness Mound group and the Madisonville Cemetery.

He sent John Kimball to excavate mounds on the Mississippi bluffs in Illinois, and in 1885 Putnam visited mound excavations by McAdams in the Illinois River Valley and distinguished these from those of the bluff-dwelling Mound Builders. The Peabody's mound explorations also included the work of Albert Phelps, who excavated shell heaps along the coast of Maine and apparently recorded the exact provenience of every artifact, took stratified random samples, and collected faunal remains with an aim toward reconstructing the prehistoric faunal communities (Putnam 1886:408–9). Putnam also encouraged, and often financially aided, the mound excavations of others such as G. H. Squiers in Wisconsin and Wright L. Coffinberry in Michigan. The Peabody Museum continued to work in southern Ohio until 1911. Much of the actual field work was done by Putnam's students or other assistants, including Roland B. Dixon, Charles Metz, Harlan I. Smith, John R. Swanton, and especially Warren K. Moorehead. Moorehead began field work as a student at Denison University in 1884, and from 1886 to 1890 he excavated around the Fort Ancient works with little institutional support and eventually published on this and neighboring sites (Moorehead 1890). In 1891, Moorehead was sent to obtain exhibit materials for the

1893 Chicago Exposition. Among other sites Moorehead excavated was the Hopewell Mound group. In 1892 Moorehead, along with Gerard Fowke, published *Primitive Man in Ohio,* which listed much of the field work previously done. In 1894 Moorehead became the first curator of the newly founded Ohio State Archaeological and Historical Society. Moorehead's work throughout Ohio was unfortunately characterized by poorly documented provenience data and poor field techniques, as well as a lack of any reasonable interpretive framework.

Moorehead left Ohio in 1897 after spending part of the 1896–97 season at the Harness Mound group, and began excavating a series of Fort Ancient village sites in southern Indiana and northern Kentucky. William C. Mills succeeded to Moorehead's position and began a thirty-year program of excavation. From his earliest publications he demonstrated considerable precision in excavation and recording. Mills excavated the Baum Village site, the Great Mound on Governor Thomas Worthington's estate "Adena," the Gartner Mound and Village site, and the Harness and Seip Mounds.

In 1913 Henry C. Shetrone became Mills' assistant and collaborated with him on his *Archaeological Atlas of Ohio* (Mills and Shetrone 1914), which listed hundreds of mounds, villages, and earthworks by county, although little attempt was made to relate sites by culture, material, or by period. Together Mills and Shetrone excavated at Tremper in 1915, at the Fuert Mound and Village site in 1917, and at the Mound City Group in 1920 and 1921. Shetrone also worked at Campbell Island in 1921, Ginther Mound in 1922, the Wright Mounds, and continued excavations at the Hopewell Group from 1922 to 1925. Shetrone was vitally concerned with the problems of integrating the masses of accumulating data into some reasonable framework. In 1920 he published "The Cultural Problem in Ohio Archaeology" in *American Anthropologist,* in which he offered a number of tentative hypotheses to integrate the Ohio data.

By 1910 considerable work had also been done in Indiana. A number of individuals including Clay Miller, Amos Butler, John Collett, Edward Cox, Moses Elrod, Gerard Fowke, George Homsher, George Levette, David McCaslin, E. R. Quick, and R. S. Robertson had excavated and reported on mounds and village sites throughout the state. Most of this work occurred from 1875–95 and was supported by the Geological Survey of Indiana. By 1915 Clarence Moore had steamed up the Ohio in the *Gopher* and had excavated several small mounds in the southern part of the state, but somehow he missed the nearby major sites.

In Illinois, the BAE, and correspondents of Putnam's, had already excavated and reported several sites. In addition, Henderson had excavated in the mounds near Naples in 1882, Drs. Patrick and Snyder had reported on limited excavations in southern Illinois in 1881, and Fowke and Bushnell had excavated the Montezuma Mounds. From 1877–79 Dr. Patrick excavated at Cahokia, where he was followed by William and Clark McAdams in 1881 and 1907, and by John Snyder in 1900. The American Bottoms were surveyed and tested in 1903–4 for the Harvard Peabody Museum by David Bushnell, who in 1921 directed field work at Cahokia for the Smithsonian. In the autumn of that year W. K. Moorehead, then of the Phillips Academy at Andover, began a series of excavations at Cahokia that was to continue, with support from the University of Illinois, through the end of 1922. Moorehead's reports on these excavations (1922, 1928) were designed to locate village and burial areas, and to prove the artificial nature of the mounds.

Across the Mississippi, Howland had reported on the Big Mound in downtown St. Louis in 1877, and Fowke described the St. Louis area village and mound groups in 1910. In northwestern Illinois W. B. Nickerson was mapping and excavating mounds throughout Jo Daviess County from 1896 through 1901, while Pat Kelley had opened several mounds of the Lowry Group in 1880. In the area around Carbondale, Charles Rau, T. M. Perrine, F. M. Farrell, and G. E. Sellers had excavated and reported on stone graves, rock shelters, fortified villages, and burial mounds between 1856 and 1894. In 1900 W. A. Phillips began investigations of quarry sites and associated villages.

In New York excavation and survey work was accomplished by individuals such as Perkins and Ruttenber, and by the New York State Museum at Albany. It was from this institution that William Beauchamp organized his comprehensive surveys of antiquities that resulted in a series of monographs dealing with discrete facets of material culture. Beauchamp's work culminated in his *Aboriginal Occupation of New York* (1900).

After the turn of the century, students of Putnam began excavations throughout the state: Mark R. Harrington and Alanson Skinner, employed by The American Museum of Natural History and the Museum of the American Indian, Heye Foundation, concentrated on the coastal shell heaps and on aboriginal villages in the estuary areas. Arthur C. Parker, who became the state archaeologist in 1906, worked in the interior and, following Beauchamp, concentrated upon Iroquoian archaeology.

Parker (1907), in his report on the Ripley site, displayed considerable finesse in excavation and recording technique and represented an early attempt to delineate the entire culture of a group from archaeological remains interpreted in the light of ethnography. In 1920–22 Parker published *The Archaeological History of New York*, in which four major periods were recognized: An "Algonkian," which displayed clear Eskimo influence; a Mound Builder occupation; a separate Eskimolike culture, which seemed to exist between the "Algonkian" and Mound Builder occupations; and finally, the Iroquoian culture.

Outside of these centers, individuals and institutions were carrying out surveys and excavations throughout the Northeast. Moorehead, in the employ of the Robert S. Peabody Foundation, undertook archaeological surveys of the state of Maine in 1912, and of the Connecticut and Susquehanna River Valleys even before 1910. Ralph Linton had excavated and reported in 1916 the stratified Crispin Site in New Jersey. Fowke had excavated numerous mounds in southern Pennsylvania and northern Virginia, while in central Pennsylvania Wren was excavating and analyzing aboriginal ceramics, which were compared to those being excavated in the Delaware River Valley by Heye and Pepper, or along the Susquehanna by Skinner. A general dichotomy of "Iroquois" and "Algonkian" served to accommodate these materials.

In Minnesota Jacob Brower published several volumes on village and mound explorations in the southern part of that state, in which he related some of the late burial mounds to the Santee. In 1896 T. H. Lewis excavated Hopewellian mounds in St. Paul, and N. H. Winchell reported in 1898 on excavations in the Little Falls area, where burials without ceramics were found. In 1911 Winchell edited *The Aborigines of Minnesota,* a huge, rambling, illustrated catalog of sites and artifacts throughout the state.

In Michigan, nineteenth-century archaeological work included John Blois' and Henry Gillman's mound excavations in the southeastern part of the state, the work of Leach in Ogemaw County, and Wright L. Coffinberry's explorations of mounds near Grand Rapids. Harlan I. Smith began survey and excavations in the Saginaw Valley while still a student before 1894, and George Fox investigated the Isle Royale copper mines just after the turn of the century. In 1925 Wilbert B. Hinsdale published *Primitive Man in Michigan,* which illustrated what was then known of site and artifact distribution and typology within the state.

In Wisconsin following the work of the Bureau of American Ethnology in the 1880s the State Historical Society began collecting archaeological specimens and the Wisconsin Natural History Society began to acquire private collections. Publication of the *Wisconsin Archaeol-*

ogist began in 1901. The editor of this journal, Charles
E. Brown, attempted to record the distribution and
typology of all sites and artifacts throughout the state. By
1911 the Wisconsin Archaeological Survey was initiated
by the state and run through the society. In 1917 the
Milwaukee Public Museum, directed by Samuel Barrett,
began field work at the Kratz Creek Mound group.
Barrett spent the seasons of 1919, 1920, and 1922 excavating the large fortified mound and village complex at
Aztalan which, he noted, did not relate to anything reported from Ohio.

THE APPROACH OF ANTHROPOLOGY
AND THE HISTORIC APPROACH

By 1925 it had become clear that the mounds had been
built by no vanished race but by prehistoric Indians.
Furthermore, the mounds clearly represented several very
different manifestations that might be geographical or cultural or temporal variations, or worse, some combination
of all three. It was now apparent that there were numerous nonmound-building archaeological manifestations that
might or might not be related, and that could be either
earlier, later, and/or coeval with the mound-building cultures. Some of these cultures could be tentatively tied to
historic Indian groups, but most could not. In order to
define some of these problems, the National Research
Council had formed a Committee on State Archaeological
Surveys in 1920, and during the late twenties, most states
in the northeastern area were covered. Numerous state
and local amateur archaeological societies were formed
during this period.

This period was also marked by a proliferation of
university-related work throughout the area. Not only did
this result in acceleration of data collected, it also introduced theoretical positions that strongly influenced interpretations of the materials. For the first time archaeology

was being performed by students trained as anthropologists. Lest this be considered an unmixed blessing, Haag (1961) has pointed out that most anthropology departments were staffed by Boas students for whom history or historical reconstructions were the basic goal of archaeology. To accomplish this, great quantities of detailed information about any given archaeological manifestation were required. The standard method developed for presenting the results of much of the collection during this period was the interminable, and usually unquantified, trait list. It was this approach that characterized Frank Setzler's work in Indiana, and it is clearly seen in his essay in the Smithsonian Swanton *festschrift* volume (1940). Much of Ritchie's New York work in the 1930s followed this methodology, as did the two archaeological classics of the early 1940s, *The Fort Ancient Aspect* by James Griffin (1943) and *Pre-Iroquoian Occupations of New York State* by William Ritchie (1944).

The historical approach of this period also led to greater efforts to link archaeological manifestations to ethnographically documented groups. This method, which became known as the "direct historic approach," had been advocated as early as 1913 by R. B. Dixon. Some efforts in this direction can be noted in the work of Shetrone and Parker in the early 1920s, but it was in the thirties that this approach flourished, with a culmination in the early 1940s.

THE PROBLEMS OF EARLY MAN

Before the turn of the century it was apparent that the only prehistoric inhabitants of the continent had been Indians. The questions that logically followed were when and whence had they come? While the Southeast and the Far West had offered several candidates for the earliest Americans by the 1840s, serious claims for the Northeast were not made until 1873. In that year C. C. Abbott discovered a camp site in a gravel field near Trenton, New Jersey. Abbott, financed by Putnam, worked this site for nearly twenty years, and by 1889 he was claiming an age of twenty thousand to thirty thousand years for his material. By 1884 F. C. Babbit was claiming to have found vestiges of glacial man in Minnesota, and in 1898 Gerard Fowke spent several months in Siberia looking for evidence of the early migration. The geological analysis of the Trenton gravel by McGhee seemed to establish a "Paleolithic" status for Abbott's finds.

In 1890 W. H. Holmes demonstrated that the Trenton artifacts were similar to numerous Potomac Basin quarry site materials. Holmes claimed that there was no good reason to assume all of the "Paleolithic" materials found in the Northeast were anything other than the work of recent Indians. Fowke's lack of success in Siberia was coupled with the archaeological work of Harlan I. Smith for the Jessup Expedition, which demonstrated no great antiquity for the archaeology of the North Pacific American Coast. After Figgins' 1926 discovery of the indisputable association of early man and extinct fauna at Folsom, New Mexico, interest in early man again became respectable, and during the 1930s a tendency gradually seemed to develop to push "primitive" or unassignable archaeological complexes farther and farther into the past. It was in this atmosphere that Jenks first reported on Browns Valley and Minnesota Man, although later opinion has tended to regard these finds as postglacial.

The large number of archaeological sites with extinct fauna found in the Southwest and Great Plains was not duplicated in the Northeast. To be sure, large numbers of typologically similar artifacts existed in collections throughout the area.

Between 1930 and the early 1950s several unstratified Paleo-Indian sites were reported in this area, including the Reagen site in Vermont (Ritchie 1953), the Bullbrook Site in Massachusetts (Byers 1954), the Shoop Site in Pennsylvania (Witthoft 1952), and the Williamson Site in Virginia (McCary 1951). Artifacts were inserted in seriations derived primarily from the Southwest. This made lithic typology the major method for assigning relative chronology, and numerous papers were devoted to projectile point morphology. The works of John Witthoft and William B. Roosa clearly stand out in this period.

Geochronological methods of dating for this material were first suggested by Greenman in 1940. Wider applications were developed by Greenman, Griffin, and Spaulding in a short paper published in 1956, and later taken up by Quimby, Mason, and Ritchie. These studies attempted to date Paleo-Indian occupations in the northeastern United States by correlation with fluctuations of the pro- and postglacial lake shores. Mason (1962) not only gave a clear summary of this methodology and its history, but went on to suggest that the eastern Paleo-Indian occupations were coeval with the western manifestations, and that clear continuities could be seen (principally in the Southeast) with later materials.

SURVEYS, WPA, AND THE PROBLEMS OF CLASSIFICATION

Although state archaeological surveys had been initiated in the early 1920s, the results were slow in coming. Reports of particular sites or even of entire counties were published. The University of Missouri began a state survey in 1934 and published numerous site reports throughout the thirties and forties but no general summary. In Illinois Fay-Cooper Cole began a state archaeological reconnaissance for the University of Chicago in 1925. Thorne Deuel joined this project in 1930 and excavations continued into the mid-1930s with no published reports other than short seasonal descriptions. In 1928 the Indiana State Survey began a systematic county-by-county investigation. Under the direction of other archaeologists at universities and museums in Minnesota, South Dakota, Michigan,

Nebraska, and Pennsylvania, state archaeological and historical societies in New Jersey, Delaware, New York, Iowa, Ohio, Pennsylvania, Connecticut, Delaware, and Maryland, and numerous private institutions, such as the Peabody Museum at Andover and the Heye Foundation, prodigious numbers of sites continued to be excavated during the thirties. With few exceptions major statements of large regions did not occur. Publications such as Schrabisher's 1930 report of his survey (in Pennsylvania) *Portions of the Delaware River Valley,* Willoughby's *Antiquities of the New England Indians* (1935), and Lilly's *Prehistoric Antiquities of Indiana* (1937) were little better than the atlases and catalogs of thirty years earlier. The *Archaeological Survey of Kentucky* (Webb and Funkhouser 1932) did attempt to describe the physiographic setting of the sites reported, and W. B. Hinsdale's *Distribution of the Aboriginal Population of Michigan* (1932) went well beyond contemporary attempts by explaining site locations in terms of ecological variables.

A major factor contributing to the acceleration of field work in the 1930s was the advent of federal relief projects such as FERA, CWP, or PWA, which employed large numbers of unskilled workmen supervised by a few professional archaeologists (often graduate students). From 1934 to 1942 several WPA projects in the northeastern United States were also carried out, although most work centered in the Tennessee Valley under the supervision of Webb.

Synthetic interpretations of the masses of accumulating data were either ignored in favor of "nonbiased" trait-listing, or were handled by an "Algonkian-Iroquois" dichotomy. Two events occurred during the 1930s that served to vitiate these earlier approaches. In New York, William Ritchie, following earlier inferences by Speck (1926) and Strong (1930), began to excavate numerous nonceramic sites, which he recognized as an early basic northeastern manifestation, possibly ancestral to both the Algonkian and the Eskimo. In 1932 Ritchie reported on

Lamoka Lake, which he classed as an Archaic Algonkian period site. By 1936 Ritchie had abandoned Parker's scheme of sequent Algonkian occupations and was simply referring to all such complexes in the Northeast as Archaic. Although this development was to have major lasting effect, its importance was immediately overshadowed by events originating in the Public Museum in Milwaukee.

William C. McKern had joined that museum in 1925, and by 1928 had focused that institution's archaeological efforts on an analysis of mounds extending across the center of Wisconsin. By 1933 Jeske had excavated the Grand River Mound group and village site; McKern had excavated the Neale, McClaughry, Kletzien, Nitzchke, and Raisbeck Effigy Mound groups; George West had documented the typology, distribution, and technology of aboriginal copper use in northeastern Wisconsin; McKern and Cooper had excavated and reanalyzed several Hopewellian manifestations in southwestern Wisconsin; Barrett and Skinner had excavated both mounds and villages in north-central Wisconsin; and Barrett had published his detailed account of three years' work at Aztalan. In addition to the information from other states, the varieties exhibited by the materials excavated by the Milwaukee Public Museum, and the need to relate one complex to another, lead McKern to formulate his Midwestern Taxonomic Method. The most succinct history of this system of classification is to be found (interspersed with comments on its misuses and shortcomings) as Appendix A to J. B. Griffin's *Fort Ancient Aspect* (1943).

Stratified sites were being excavated in Illinois, New York, and New England, and the temporal sequences in those areas were being established. It had long been recognized that particular archaeological manifestations had restricted geographical distributions. Yet the early formulations of the Midwestern Taxonomic Method reacted to current historical approaches as well as "culture areas" by deliberately eliminating time and space as relevant determinants for cultural classification, relying instead on particular traits of material culture. Avoiding the imprecision of terms such as "culture," the early proposals sought to group sets of several related sites with other sets of sites displaying similar traits, into arbitrary units. These units were then grouped on the basis of similarities of quite different traits into broader and more general classes, and so on. By 1934 (after circulating numerous questionnaires to some members of the profession) McKern, Guthe, and Deuel had revised the system so that the recognition of essential determinant traits lead directly to the recognition of the most general cultural divisions (called basic cultures) within which nonsharing of specific determinant traits could isolate phases. Within phases, new sets of determinant traits could isolate aspects, and within these, foci. A focus was a group of communities sharing most determinant traits. Traits that had not been used for some step of this pigeonholing and that varied between the components of a focus were of no classificatory significance.

In 1935, at the Indianapolis Archaeological Conference, McKern re-emphasized the pure taxonomic nature of the system. He also indicated that the system should begin with the focus and proceed to more general groupings (now termed aspect, phase, and pattern) by mutually exclusive sets of determinant traits. Most discussion at this conference centered on questions of whether the system had valid application outside the Northeast, and whether Hopewell (or Central Basin) should be a phase or aspect of the Woodland Pattern, or a pattern itself.

Following 1935 numerous papers and monographs were published that utilized the McKernian System as a principal means of organizing data. *Rediscovering Illinois* (Cole and Deuel 1937) and *Pre-Iroquoian Occupations of New York State* (Ritchie 1944) demonstrated how the Midwestern Taxonomic Method could render intelligible the information acquired in years of intensive survey in a single state.

The first alterations were the assumptions that taxonomic relationship implied genetic relationship, for in spite of adamant disclaimers, McKern had set it up to resemble a

Linnean system, and it was all too easy to interpret as a picture of cultural diversification through time. Another popular pastime was the use of the system to force ethnic identification from one presumably documented complex to another unknown (but taxonomically closely related) complex. It was in reaction to these "abuses" that Griffin, in 1943, proposed first establishing the foci from *all* of the traits represented in a number of components, and using at least these same "determinate traits" to establish the successively more abstract cultural groupings. Griffin also emphasized the importance of thorough and complete analysis before any attempt was made to classify, and reiterated the dangers of assigning ethnic labels to taxonomic categories. The body of his monograph and McKern's (1945) analyses of the Upper Mississippian materials in Wisconsin are probably the best examples of how the Midwestern Taxonomic Method could be advantageously employed in a single area.

In spite of shortcomings, the Midwestern Taxonomic Method was an overwhelming success. For the first time there existed a method to relate and compare archaeological manifestations from different areas and to express these relationships without recourse to unprovable theories of migrations or improbable ethnic affiliations. It looked as if masses of data could finally be understood in something other than the antiquarian sense. It is hardly surprising that McKern's system was well received.

The first major opposition took the form of "An Interpretation of the Prehistory of the Eastern United States" by James Ford and Gordon Willey (1941). It was noted that proponents of the Midwestern Taxonomic Method tended to let the classificatory techniques lull them into doing little further interpretation. Ford and Willey did not berate the practices of those who employed the method; they instead substituted for McKern's system of arbitrary taxonomic units a series of stages (Archaic, Burial Mound I and II, Temple Mound I and II), which were defined as units of different relative age. The entire prehistoric sequence represented by these stages was felt to have occurred over about twelve hundred years.

This attempt to introduce chronology into classificatory schemes of extensive application had little immediate effect. In 1941 the Woodland Conference was held in Chicago to clear up some of the problems surrounding a Woodland Pattern in the McKernian Method. This conference left its participants feeling that the Woodland Pattern was a concept "with a reasonably solid basis of stratigraphically supported and qualitatively elaborated material, the result of carefully conducted excavations here and there over the area." The Conference on Man in Northeastern North America held at Andover, 1941, found most of the archaeological discussions of McKern, Spaulding, Ritchie, and de Laguna couched in distinctly McKernian terms (Johnson 1946). Although Griffin's paper in that volume specifically stated that no attempt would be made to demonstrate or define cultural groupings, he produced a synthesis by describing McKernian groups in terms of successive cultural stages based on an integration of local relative stratigraphic sequences.

PROBLEM ORIENTATION, CHRONOLOGY, AND MORE THEORY

The years between 1942 and 1955 saw the development of most of today's archaeological strategy. Field work proliferated to the point where even general representation had to be highly selective. Individuals and even institutions began to devote more attention to the solution of problems generated by previous research. In Indiana, Black had excavated the Nowlin Mound in 1936, and in 1939 he began excavations at the Angel Site (which he continued until 1964); at Milwaukee, McKern had focused attention on the Effigy Mound problem in the late 1920s. Again (as in the 1890s), in the period beginning around 1940 most sites were chosen for excavation in order to answer specific questions.

In the Ohio Valley the work of Webb, Snow, Baby, and others concentrated on unraveling the relationships of Adena and Hopewell, while in Illinois the work of Baker, Griffin, Morgan, McGreggor, Bennett, and Maxwell attempted to separate the local Hopewellian from other Woodland manifestations and to understand its local developments. Related to this was Quimby's work in tracing Illinois Hopewell through northern Indiana into western Michigan. In southern Illinois, the University of Chicago excavations at Kincaid were attempting to establish the chronological position of Mississippian intrusions into that area. Greenman was involved in interpreting the late prehistory of the Lake Erie area. In the northern Great Lakes area, Wilford was attempting to segregate Laurel from presumably early Howard Lake materials and the later Black Duck manifestation. In Wisconsin, efforts were concentrated on defining the relationships between Effigy Mounds and Oneota. In Missouri, Iowa, and Kansas, new Hopewellian sites were adding to its geographical extent. Ritchie in New York and Wintemberg in Ontario were excavating numerous Archaic and Woodland sites, and MacNeish (employing the direct historic approach to argue for an *in situ* development) was able to use some of these materials to demonstrate the gradual stylistic changes from Late Woodland to the historically documented Iroquoian ceramics associated with specific tribal groupings.

One significant aspect of problem-oriented research at this time was the extension of the Archaic. The work of Ritzenthaler in Wisconsin, Byers and Johnson at the Boyleston Street Fishweir in Boston and throughout New England, Logan at Grahm Cave in Missouri, Fowler at the Modoc Rock Shelter in Illinois, Ritchie and Carlyle Smith at several New York sites, Greenman in the Georgian Bay region, Webb and Haag in Kentucky shell mounds, Coe in the Carolina Piedmont, Titterington near St. Louis, and numerous others, brought into clear focus the diversity

and importance of the period between Paleo-Indian and
Woodland. Among these, Fowler's work stands out as a
foresighted attempt at combining many of the divergent
theoretical approaches with new methods then being developed for archaeological analyses.

Many of these new techniques had been developed at
other times and in other places. Many had even been employed in this area: Dendrochronology had been tried at
the Chicago laboratory on materials from the Angel and
Kincaid sites. Paul B. Sears had begun to work on pollen
analysis as early as 1932, and by 1937 he had outlined
paleoclimatology in the northeastern United States. Analyses of flora (Jones 1936) and new approaches in the analysis of faunal remains (White 1953) were demonstrating
the importance of understanding the subsistence bases of
prehistoric cultures. In the midst of long (and still very
much alive) discussions over the nature of archaeological
typology, Albert Spaulding brought out a series of articles
beginning with "On the Statistical Discovery of Artifact
Types" (1953), which not only demonstrated the application of statistical techniques to archaeology, but refo-
cused attention on the nature of the cultural variables with
which the archaeologist dealt.

Increasing exposure to European prehistory left many
American archaeologists aware of the fact that American
archaeology had not brought these diverse approaches to
bear on any single problem. As graduate students in anthropology, exposure to the ideas of cultural evolution of
Leslie White and Julian Steward, and to methods of crosscultural ethnographic comparison as propounded by Mur-
dock, left many American archaeologists dissatisfied with
prevailing taxonomic approaches. These vague displeasures
were crystalized with the publication of Walter Taylor's
A Study of Archaeology in 1948.

Inspired by earlier papers of Linton and Kluckhohn,
Taylor devoted the first section of his study to attacking
Webb, Ritchie, and Griffin for the practice of using
bowdlerized trait lists for the external comparison of ar-

chaeological complexes without any real attempt to investigate cultural associations and relationships. Eschewing this comparative taxonomic approach, Taylor advocated the conjunctive approach. The conjunctive approach called for a detailed and quantified analysis of all archaeological materials with an attempt to determine their significance to the culture within which they existed, and how they interrelated with each other and the natural environment in a particular cultural configuration. Taylor also advocated an exact and exhaustive exposition of every artifact and the spatial, artifactual, and social matrix in which it occurred. From this he felt that one could also demonstrate building operations, functional areas of a site, and inferentially, settlement patterns. The conjunctive approach also relied on ethnographic analogy to complete the picture of the prehistoric culture under investigation. Taylor closed with the observations that to implement fully this approach required better conceived intensive excavations, more detailed laboratory analysis of excavated material, and some organization to underwrite the integration of a number of specialists into a full-time analytical complex.

Much of the justification for the Midwestern Taxonomic Method was dissipated with Libby's discovery of radiocarbon dating in 1949. The initial applications to archaeological materials gave northeastern archaeology thousands of additional years in which to operate. Coeval geographical variations were brought to light, often to the detriment of McKernian groupings. More important was the removal of chronological problems from the realm of taxonomy.

The major archaeological syntheses that appeared at midcentury, such as *Indians Before Columbus* (Martin, Quimby, and Collier 1947) or *Archeology of Eastern United States* (Griffin 1952) either predated radiocarbon chronology or were able to make only passing reference to it. In both volumes, the Midwestern Taxonomic Method is influential, although in the former volume *all* groupings were considered distinct "cultures." Griffin felt that the major McKernian groupings were compatible with the emergent radiocarbon data, and he attempted to translate McKernian patterns directly into chronological periods.

The reaction to this began as a series of critical articles by Willey and Phillips in the mid-1950s and culminated with their book *Method and Theory in American Archaeology* (1958). Willey and Phillips condemned Griffin's confusion of ages with stages and attempted to develop a continental culture history phrased in terms of major developmental stages, although this often resulted in temporal and/or spatial disjunctions. A major contribution of this book was its clear delineation of terms such as "tradition" and "horizon."

Taking exception to the Eastern Woodland application of this scheme, which was ". . . specifically appropriate to Mesoamerica and possibly Peru," Joseph Caldwell in his monograph *Trend and Tradition in the Prehistory of the Eastern United States* (1958) attempted to demonstrate not only the uniqueness but also the importance of the Archaic in this area for the understanding of later cultural processes. Caldwell ignored both developmental stages and McKernian groupings in favor of broad economically based patterns crosscut by regional traditions.

In a theoretical sense all three of these approaches to cultural classification are very much alive. Recent syntheses, such as those by Griffin (1967) retain a distinct 1952 flavor. Those by Willey (1966) clearly follow a system of developmental stages, while much of the recent archaeological work in our area has, following Caldwell, ignored both systems and attempted to explain the relationships of economic patterns in specific regions with local traditions.

CULTURE, ECOLOGY, AND STATISTICS

If any single theme can be said to characterize the course of archaeology in the Northeast during the past fifteen years it is its participation in the theoretical and methodological changes taking place throughout American archaeology. The theoretical aspects have been primarily concerned with the logical basis for archaeological analyses, the role of ethnographic analogy in archaeology, and the importance theoretical perspectives will have in archaeological excavation and analyses. The methodological innovations can ultimately be traced back to Taylor's call to analyze culture rather than artifacts. These new attempts employ statistical techniques to extract more anthropological and ecological information from archaeological data, and a basic goal of this "new archaeology" is to produce models of culture change that can then be tested by further excavation.

Among the earliest indicators of current trends were a series of papers by Griffin in 1960 and 1961 in which he argued that the expansion and decline of Hopewell and Mississippian in the Great Lakes could be viewed as the responses to changing climatic patterns. An initial result of these hypotheses was the stimulation of much careful reanalysis of Middle Woodland complexes throughout the Midwest. By the middle 1960s the work of James Brown, Stuart Streuver, Olaf Prufer, James Fitting, and others had demonstrated that "Hopewell" consisted of a number of coeval, stylistically related "cultures," adapted to a number of differing ecosystems.

At the same time Griffin had initiated a project to explore the interrelations of prehistoric cultures and changing ecology within the state of Michigan. Between 1962 and 1968 problem-oriented excavations were carried out at numerous sites ranging from Paleo-Indian through historic. The results of this research can be seen in publications such as Yarnell's (1964) analysis of ethnobotany; Cleland's (1966) discussions of changing ethnozoology; and numerous reports detailing prehistoric cultural ecology and settlement pattern. Much of this field work and the concern with ecological adaptation is summarized in Fitting's (1970) *Archaeology of Michigan.*

Ritchie attempted to introduce ecological parameters to his synthesis of local archaeology in his *Archaeology of*

New York (1965), and this orientation in New York field work is clearly seen in Robert Funk's analysis of Archaic occupations in the Hudson River Valley. In Wisconsin David Baerreis and Reid Bryson published (1965) a detailed revision of Griffin's postulated climatic changes and in 1967 were able to interpret cultural changes in the Mill Creek Culture of Iowa and Wisconsin on the basis of climatic change. In Illinois the problems of cultural ecology and settlement pattern were investigated by Winters' survey of the Wabash River Valley with his subsequent analysis of the Riverton Culture (1966), by the work of Binford and others in the south-central part of the state at Carlyle Reservoir and the Hatchery West site (1970), and by the detailed excavations of Streuver along the Lower Illinois River. In Pennsylvania the massive report on Sheep Rock Shelter (Michels [ed.] 1968) represents a classic integration of cultural and paleoecological data. In Ohio the work of Blank, Prufer, and Shane in the south-central portions of the state and, more recently, Prahl and Brose in the north, represent the application of these parameters to the analysis of prehistoric cultures.

One of the major concerns of the "new archaeology" is its approach to analyses of stylistic variations. The earliest attempts in our area must be those of James B. Stoltman (1962), who applied Spaulding's statistical methods to an analysis of Laurel ceramics in an effort to do rigorous typology. An early and significant analysis of typological variation as a cultural (rather than geographical or temporal) parameter is seen in Binford's (1964) "Red Ochre Cache Blades: A Case of Cultural Drift." The problems of interpreting spatial-temporal variation were elegantly demonstrated in an imaginative series of papers dealing with colonial tombstone motifs in New England, by Dethlefsen and Deetz (1967). Recently there has been attention given to the interpretation of stylistic variation as a function of more limited sociocultural factors; Whallon attempted to analyze changes in late Owasco stylistic ceramic variation in terms of matrilocal residence patterns developing in response to changes in economic emphases. Fitting was able to relate ceramic stylistic variations at the Late Woodland Spring Creek site to functionally differing site areas. Janzen was able to combine Stoltman's earlier analysis of Laurel ceramic typology with Fitting's models from Spring Creek to determine functional areas at Naomikong Point, which probably could be related to variations in social groups. Most recently, David S. Brose (1970) appears to have been able to disclose prehistoric postnuptial residence patterns and some evidence for preferential marriage systems via computerized analyses of ceramic variations and their areal distributions at the Summer Island site. An early paper in this genre was Fitting's analysis of spatial and stylistic variability in the lithic assemblage at the Holcomb site (Fitting, DeVisscher, and Walha, 1966).

Analyses of burial patterns to provide information of social stratification and social organization were first applied by Binford to the Hatchery West site and the Wassam Ridge site in southern Illinois. Good examples of these techniques, often with considerable refinement, can be seen in Winter's (1968) reanalysis of Archaic shell mound burials in northern Kentucky, and Brown's (1969) reanalyses of Fisher Focus burials at the Gentleman Farm site in northern Illinois. Similar attempts are now in progress in the work of Fowler and others at Cahokia, and Halsey at the Middle-Late Woodland period in Michigan and surrounding states.

Concerns with sampling were articulated by Binford in 1964, and he attempted to apply some sophisticated statistical techniques in his work in southern Illinois. These have been followed by the recent work of Streuver and Rackerby in the Illinois Valley, by Fitting and others in Michigan, by Brose's work in northern Ohio, and most recently by Hurley's investigations in Ontario. In general, however, this problem will remain a major stumbling block in northeastern archaeology for some time to come. With the exception of Fowler's and Porter's problem-oriented work at Cahokia, and major interpretative papers such as Fowler's (1970) analysis of the spread of Mississippian cultural ecology and Fitting's (1968) Caldwellian overview of Post-Pleistocene adaptations, most of the archaeology in the Northeast lags behind the type of work detailed above. Yet the demonstrated adaptability of major figures such as Griffin and Ritchie and the newer professional archaeologists who, if not trained in the "processual school" are at least exposed to it, promises that this area will continue to witness and to stimulate the development of North American archaeology.

REFERENCES

ABBOTT, C. C.
  1876   "The Stone Age of New Jersey." *Ann. Report Smith. Instit. 1875:*246–380.

ATWATER, CALEB
  1820   "Description of the Antiquities Discovered in the State of Ohio." *Trans. and Collect. Amer. Antiquarian Soc.* 1:109–251.

BAERREIS, DAVID A., and BRYSON, REID
  1965   "Climatic Episodes and the Dating of Mississippian Cultures." *Wis. Arch.* 46:203–20.

BARRETT, SAMUEL A.
  1933   "Ancient Aztalan." *Bull. Milwaukee Pub. Mus.* 13.

BEAUCHAMP, WILLIAM M.
  1900   "Aboriginal Occupation of New York." *Bull. New York State Mus.* 7(32).

BINFORD, LEWIS R.
  1964   "Considerations of Archaeological Research Design:" *Am. Ant.* 29:423–41.
  1963   "Red Ochre Cache Blades from the Michigan Area: A Possible Case of Cultural Drift." *Southwestern Journ. Anthro.* 19:89–108.

——, BINFORD, SALLY; WHALLON, ROBERT; and HARDIN, MARGARET A.
  1970   "Archaeology at Hatchery West." *Soc. Am. Arch. Mem.* 24.

BROSE, DAVID S.
  1970   "The Summer Island Site." *Case Western Reserve Univ. Stud. in Anthro.* 1.

BROWN, JAMES A.
  1969   "The Gentleman Farm Site." *Ill. State Mus. Rep. Invest.* 13.

BUSHNELL, DAVID I., JR.
  1922a   "Archaeological Reconnaissance of the Cahokia and Related Mound Groups." *Smith. Misc. Coll.* 72(15):92–105.

1922b "Cahokia and Surrounding Mound Groups." *Pap. Peabody Mus. Am. Arch. and Ethno.* 3(1).

1927   "Burials of the Algonquian, Siouan, and Caddoan Tribes West of the Mississippi." *Bureau Am. Eth. Bull.* 83.

BYERS, DOUGLAS S.
1954   "Bull Brook—A Fluted Point Site in Ipswich, Massachusetts." *Am. Ant.* 19:343–51.

——— and JOHNSON, FREDERICK
1942   "Two Sites on Martha's Vineyard." *Pap. Robert S. Peabody Found. for Arch.* 1(1).

CALDWELL, JOSEPH
1958   "Trend and Tradition in the Prehistory of the Eastern United States." *Am. Anthro. Mem.* 88.

CLELAND, CHARLES E.
1966   "Prehistoric Animal Ecology and Ethnozoology of the Upper Great Lakes Region." *Anthro. Pap. Mus. of Anthro. Univ. of Mich.* 29.

COE, JOFFRE L.
1964   "Formative Cultures of the Carolina Piedmont." *Trans. Am. Phil. Soc.* 54(5).

COLE, FAY-COOPER
1951   *Kincaid, A Prehistoric Illinois Metropolis.* Chicago: University of Chicago Press.

——— and DEUEL, THORNE
1937   *Rediscovering Illinois.* Chicago: University of Chicago Press.

DETHLEFSEN, EDWIN, and DEETZ, JAMES
1966   "Death's Heads, Cherubs and Willow Trees: Experimental Archaeology in Colonial Cemeteries." *Am. Ant.* 31:502–10.

FITTING, JAMES E.
1968   "Environmental Potential and the Postglacial Readaptation in Eastern North America." *Am. Ant.* 33:441–45.

1969   "Settlement Analysis in the Great Lakes Region." *Southwestern Journ. Anthro.* 25:360–77.

1970   *The Archaeology of Michigan.* Garden City, New York: The Natural History Press.

———, DEVISSCHER, JERRY; and WAHLA, EDWARD J.
1966   "The Paleo-Indian Occupation of the Holcombe Beach." *Anthro. Pap. Mus. of Anthro. Univ. of Mich.* 27.

FORD, JAMES ALFRED, and WILLEY, GORDON
1941   "An Interpretation of the Prehistory of the Eastern United States." *Am. Anthro.* 3:325–63.

FOWKE, GERARD E.
1902   *An Archaeological History of Ohio.* Columbus: Ohio State Archaeological and Historical Society.

112   DAVID S. BROSE

FOWLER, MELVIN L.
   1959   "Summary Report of Modoc Rock Shelter." *Ill. State Mus.
          Reports of Invest.* 8.
   1959   "Modoc Rock Shelter: An Early Archaic Site in Southern
          Illinois." *Am. Ant.* 24:257–70.
   1969   "Middle Mississippian Agricultural Fields." *Am. Ant.*
          34:365–75.

———, PORTER, JAMES, *et al.*
   1970   "Explorations into Cahokia Archaeology." *Ill. Arch. Sur.
          Bull.* 7.

GREENMAN, E. F.; GRIFFIN, JAMES B.; and SPAULDING, ALBERT C.
   1956   "Dated Beaches and Early Man in Michigan." Pap. of the
          Friends of the Pleistocene, Great Lakes Section, Ann Arbor.

——— and STANLEY, GEORGE M.
   1940   "A Geologically Dated Campsite: Georgian Bay, Ontario."
          Am. Ant. 2:194–99.

GRIFFIN, JAMES B.
   1943   *The Fort Ancient Aspect.* Ann Arbor: University of
          Michigan Press.
   1946   "Cultural Change and Continuity in Eastern United States
          Archaeology." *Pap. Robert S. Peabody Found. for Arch.*
          3:37–95.
   1952   *Archeology of Eastern United States* (ed.). Chicago: Uni-
          versity of Chicago Press.
   1960   "Climatic Change: A Contributory Cause of the Growth
          and Decline of Northern Hopewellian Culture." *Wis. Arch.*
          41:21–33.
   1961   "Some Correlations of Climatic and Cultural Change in
          Eastern North American Prehistory." *Annals New York
          Acad. Sci.* 95:710–17.
   1967   "Eastern North American Archaeology: A Summary." *Sci-
          ence* 156:175–91.

HAAG, WILLIAM
   1961   "Twenty-five Years of Eastern Archaeology." *Am. Ant.*
          27:16–23.

HAVEN, SAMUEL
   1856   "Archaeology of the United States." *Smith. Cont. to Knowl-
          edge* 8.

HINSDALE, W. B.
   1925   *Primitive Man in Michigan.* Ann Arbor: The University of
          Michigan Press.
   1932   "Distribution of Aboriginal Population in Michigan." *Occas.
          Contrib. Mus. Anthro. Univ. Mich.* 2.

JEFFERSON, THOMAS
   1784   *Notes on the State of Virginia.* Richmond: J. W. Randolph.

JOHNSON, FREDERICK (ed.)
   1946   "Man in Northeastern North America." *Pap. Robert S. Pea-
          body Found. for Arch.* 3.

JONES, VOLNEY H.
  1936 "The Vegetal Remains of Newt Kash Hollow." *Univ. of Kentucky Reports in Arch. and Anthro.* 3(4):147–65.

LAPHAM, INCREASE
  1855 "The Antiquities of Wisconsin." *Smith. Cont. to Knowledge* 7.

LILLY, ELI
  1937 *Prehistoric Antiquities of Indiana.* Indiana Historical Society.

MCCARY, BEN C.
  1951 "A Workshop Site of Early Man in Dinwiddie County, Virginia." *Am. Ant.* 17:9–17.

MCKERN, W. C.
  1939 "The Midwestern Taxonomic Method as an Aid to Archaeological Cultural Study." *Am. Ant.* 4:301–13.
  1945 "Preliminary Report on the Upper Mississippi Phase in Wisconsin." *Milwaukee Pub. Mus. Bull.* 16(3).

MARTIN, P. S., and others
  1947 *Indians Before Columbus.* Chicago: University of Chicago Press.

MASON, RONALD J.
  1958 "Late Pleistocene Geochronology and the Paleo Indian Penetration into the Lower Michigan Peninsula." *Anthro. Pap. Mus. Anthro. Univ. of Mich.* 11.
  1962 "The Paleo-Indian Tradition in Eastern North America." *Current Anthro.* 3:227–83.

MICHELS, JOSEPH and SMITH, IRA (eds.)
  1967 *Archaeological Investigations in the Sheep Rock Shelter.* Vols. I and II. University Park, Pennsylvania: Pennsylvania State University Press.

MILLS, WILLIAM C., and SHETRONE, H.
  1914 *Archaeological Atlas of Ohio.* Columbus.

MOOREHEAD, WARREN K.
  1890 *Fort Ancient.* Robert Clarke.
  1892 *Primitive Man in Ohio.* New York: G. P. Putnam's Sons.
  1922 "The Cahokia Mounds." *Univ. of Ill. Bull.* 19(35).
  1928 "Explorations of 1922, 1923, 1924, and 1927 in the Cahokia Mounds." *Univ. of Ill. Bull.* 26(4):7–106.

PARKER, ARTHUR C.
  1907 "Excavations in an Erie Indian Village and Burial Site at Ripley, Chautauqua Co., New York." *New York State Mus. Bull.* 117.
  1922 "The Archaeological History of New York State." *New York State Mus. Bull.* Nos. 235–38.

PUTNAM, FREDERICK W.
  1886 "Report of the Curator." *18th Ann. Report,* Peabody Mus. Amer. Arch. and Ethnol.

QUIMBY, GEORGE I., JR.
    1941   "The Goodall Focus: An Analysis of Ten Hopewellian Components in Michigan and Indiana." *Indiana Hist. Soc. Prehist. Res. Series* 2:63–161.
    1958   "Fluted Points and Geochronology of the Lake Michigan Basin." *Am. Ant.* 24:424–26.

RITCHIE, WILLIAM A.
    1944   "The Pre-Iroquoian Occupations of New York State." *Mus. of Arts and Sci. Mem.* 1.
    1953   "A Probable Paleo-Indian Site in Vermont." *Am. Ant.* 18:249–58.
    1965   *The Archaeology of New York State.* Garden City, New York: The Natural History Press.

——— and MacNEISH, RICHARD S.
    1949   "The Pre-Iroquoian Pottery of New York State." *Am. Ant.* 15:97–124.

SETZLER, FRANK M.
    1940   "Archaeological Perspectives in the Northern Mississippi Valley." *Smith. Misc. Coll.* 100:253–91.

SHETRONE, HENRY C.
    1920   "The Culture Problem in Ohio Archaeology." *Am. Anthro.* 22:144–72.
    1930   *The Mound Builders.* New York: Appleton-Century-Crofts.

SILVERBERG, ROBERT
    1968   *Mound Builders of Ancient America.* New York: Graphic Arts Society.

SMITH, CARLYLE S.
    1950   "The Archaeology of Coastal New York." *Anthro. Pap. Amer. Mus. Nat. Hist.* 43(2).

SPAULDING, A. C.
    1953   "Statistical Techniques for the Discovery of Artifact Types." *Am. Ant.* 18:305–13.

SPECK, FRANK G.
    1926   "Culture Problems in Northeastern North America." *Proc. Amer. Phil. Soc.* 65(4).

SQUIER, EPHRIAM G., and DAVIS, EDWIN H.
    1848   "Ancient Monuments of the Mississippi Valley." *Smith. Contr. to Knowledge* 1.

STEWARD, JULIAN, and SETZLER, FRANK
    1938   "Function and Configuration in Archaeology." *Am. Ant.* 6:366–67.

STOLTMAN, JAMES B.
    1962   "A Proposed Method for Systematizing the Modal Analysis of Pottery and its Application to the Laurel Focus." Master's thesis, University of Minnesota.

STREUVER, STUART
1965 "Middle Woodland Culture History in the Great Lakes Riverine Area." *Am. Ant.* 31:211–23.

STRONG, WILLIAM D.
1930 "A Stone Culture from Northern Labrador and its Relation to the Eskimo-like Cultures of the Northeast." *Am. Anthro.* 32:126–44.

——— (ed.)
1940 "Essays in Historical Anthropology of North America." *Smith Misc. Coll.* 100.

TAYLOR, WALTER
1948 "A Study of Archaeology." *Am. Anthro. Mem.* 69.

THOMAS, CYRUS
1889 "The Problem of The Ohio Mounds." *Bureau Am. Ethn. Bull.* 8.

WEBB, WILLIAM S., and FUNKHAUSER, W. D.
1932 "An Archaeological Survey of Kentucky." *Univ. of Ky. Reports in Anthro. and Arch.* 2.

WHITE, THEODORE
1953 "A Method of Calculating the Dietary percentage of Various Food Animals Utilized by Aboriginal Peoples." *Am. Ant.* 18:396–98.

WHITTLESEY, CHARLES C.
1851 "Descriptions of Ancient Works in Ohio." *Smith. Contr. to Knowledge* 3(7).

WILLEY, GORDON
1966 *Introduction to American Archaeology,* Vol. I. Englewood Cliffs, New Jersey: Prentice-Hall.

——— and PHILLIPS, P.
1958 *Method and Theory in American Archaeology.* Chicago: University of Chicago Press.

WINCHELL, N. H.
1911 *The Aborigines of Minnesota.* St. Paul; Hist. Soc.

WINTERS, HOWARD D.
1963 "An Archaeological Survey of the Wabash Valley in Illinois." *Ill. State Mus. Rept. Invest.* 10.
1968 "Value Systems and Trade Cycles of the Late Archaic in the Midwest," *New Perspectives in Archaeology,* S. R. Binford and L. R. Binford (eds.) 175–222.
1969 "The Riverton Culture." *Ill. State Mus. Rept. Invest.* 17.

WITTHOFT, JOHN
1952 "A Paleo-Indian Site in Eastern Pennsylvania; An Early Hunting Culture." *Pro. Am. Phil. Soc.* 96:464–95.

YARNELL, RICHARD ASA
1964 "Aboriginal Relationships between Culture and Plant Life in The Upper Great Lakes Region." *Anthro. Pap. Mus. of Anthro. Univ. Mich.* 23.

KEY

1. Cahokia
2. New Madrid
3. Etowah
4. Stalling's Island and Hollywood
5. Macon Plateau
6. Kolomoki
7. Hiwasse Island
8. Moundville
9. Irene
10. Crystal River

11. Poverty Point
12. Menard
13. Haley
14. Davis
15. Walls
16. Pecan Point
17. Rose
18. Spiro
19. Marksville and Greenhouse
20. Indian Knoll

The Southeastern United States

5 THE SOUTHEASTERN UNITED STATES

James B. Stoltman

INTRODUCTION

"Archaeological 'facts' take their meaning from their conceptual arrangement and the adequacy or inadequacy of that arrangement, model, or hypothesis accounts for the amount of information made available to the archaeologist." These cogent words from David Clarke's recent book, *Analytical Archaeology,* set the theme for much of the ensuing discussion. A history of the archaeology of any area includes more than a sequential listing of the discoveries of the major data gatherers; it is concerned with growth in information about the past that archaeology has provided. And, as Clarke notes, the amount of information gained from certain data varies with the conceptual framework or model within which those data are viewed. Thus, in this chapter, the development of Southeastern archaeology will be examined in terms of the interrelationships between increasing amounts of data and the waxing and waning of conceptual models of the past that have developed alongside those data. The amount of information available about the past varies with the quality as well as with the quantity of archaeological data. Since data quality depends heavily upon the techniques by which they were gathered, we shall also be concerned in our discussion with growth in techniques in Southeastern archaeology.

Southeastern archaeology, and indeed American archaeology, may be said to have begun with the excavations by Thomas Jefferson (1787) of a prehistoric burial mound in Virginia. As would a modern archaeologist, Jefferson perceived a problem and he set out to solve it via excavation. Moreover, his problem was not to amass antiquities, but to obtain information about the past. By carefully examining a cross section of the mound, he learned that the ancient burial practices were similar to those of some historic Indians, effectively refuting such then-current beliefs as that the mounds were built to cover and support individuals buried in an upright position.

In retrospect Jefferson's observations are remarkably sophisticated, although they fall short of modern standards of reporting. He lived when the prevalent model of human habitation of the New World as a simple dichotomy—the historic "present" and an amorphous, poorly known past —and the contributions he could make to prehistory, no matter how many data were available to him, were severely limited by this point of view. Since the mound dated to a conceptually indivisible past, there existed no framework for making chronological sense of its components.

Thomas Jefferson's contribution is a convenient point of departure. We have seen that he gathered data by excavation in order to obtain information about a specific problem. We have seen that the amount of information he was able to garner from his data was limited both by his particular problem and by his conceptual model of the past. How, and in what ways, Southeastern archaeology has developed since these auspicious beginnings is the subject of the remainder of this chapter.

EIGHTEENTH- AND EARLY NINETEENTH-CENTURY TRAVELERS— INITIAL DESCRIPTION OF PREHISTORIC SITES

During Jefferson's lifetime and continuing through the first half of the nineteenth century, "archaeology" in the Southeast consisted mainly of site descriptions by traveler-naturalists. The most important of these were William Bartram, Henry M. Brackenridge, and Constantine S.

Rafinesque. These men did not ask the kinds of questions that Jefferson had asked about the mounds, nor did they excavate. They were essentially reporters, astute observers of nature, and the man-made monuments were an integal part of the landscape they were describing.

Bartram's *Travels Through North and South Carolina*, published in 1791 (see Van Doren 1928), was especially influential. Within the book are a number of passages referring to mounds. Some of them were overgrown and obviously long abandoned. Others were in use in the sense that they served as substructures for men's council houses, although the Indians who built and used the council houses (Cherokees in this case) specifically denied having erected the mounds. In still other cases Bartram actually witnessed Indians (Choctaws) constructing burial mounds. Although he discriminated between mounds of different age, nowhere did Bartram impute a non-Indian origin to any of them. Nevertheless, accounts of Cherokees disclaiming responsibility for mound construction were often quoted by later authors in support of the view that a mound-builder race distinct from the Indians formerly occupied the Eastern Woodlands.

Both Brackenridge and Rafinesque, by virtue of their correspondence with Thomas Jefferson, can be seen to have been inspired by the latter's interest in archaeology. Brackenridge, in the second decade of the nineteenth century, left reasonably detailed descriptions of mounds in the lower Mississippi Valley. He is credited with being the first to recognize Monk's Mound at Cahokia, the largest of all North American mounds, as a prehistoric site, and he also described such important mound groups as those at New Madrid, Missouri, and Selzertown, Mississippi (later called Emerald Mounds). Rafinesque's principal contribution to Southeastern archaeology was a series of maps and descriptions of Kentucky sites that Squier and Davis included in the monumental report on their Ohio excavations.

EARLY COLLECTORS: 1820–50

While men like Bartram, Brackenridge, and Rafinesque were reporting on Southeastern earthworks, probings into the mounds by nameless pothunters had already begun. Central Tennessee was subjected very early to this scourge. Early Indian abandonment permitted Europeans relatively easy access to the area by the middle of the eighteenth century, and an abundance of easily located stone slab-lined graves (either in mounds or flat cemeteries) yielded a rich reward of grave goods. John Haywood, a prominent jurist whose *Natural and Aboriginal History of Tennessee,* published in 1823, is considered Tennessee's first history, already knew something of the contents of these graves. So far as we know, he did not excavate, although he described at least nineteen major prehistoric sites. Unfortunately, he accepted uncritically, and thus he served to popularize many fanciful tales about the contents of the stone slab graves, including reports of both giants and pygmies.

During the first half of the nineteenth century, there was little controlled excavation in the Southeast and much fanciful speculation. Archaeology did not yet exist as a profession, although a few enterprising individuals were able to earn a living by selling and/or lecturing about the antiquities they found. Two of the more interesting of this ilk were Albert Koch and Montroville W. Dickeson. The former, a German immigrant, was a fossil collector who, in his rambles, stumbled upon two possible mastodon kill sites in central Missouri. Because he was not a trained scientist, his reconstructions of many of the fossils he exhibited were sometimes grotesquely in error. Such practices earned Koch a tainted reputation, so that his claims to have found stone tools, evidence of fire, and other human artifacts in direct association with mastodons in 1838 and again in 1840 have been generally disbelieved, although never really disproved (Montagu and Peterson 1944; Gross 1951).

Dickeson, like Koch, was a traveling showman-lecturer capitalizing on what must have been a considerable public interest in the exotica of the past. Between 1837 and 1846, he excavated numerous mounds in Mississippi and Louisiana, although he published practically nothing (Culin 1900). Rather, he toured the country lecturing on his discoveries while employing a spectacular, crowd-attracting gimmick, a painted panorama (advertized to have covered fifteen thousand feet of canvas) that was unrolled to illustrate dramatically his talks. His most important discovery, first reported in 1846, was a human pelvis found along with the bones of various extinct mammals, including mylodon, megalonx, mastodon, and horse, in a clay layer at the base of an exposure in the loess bluffs near Natchez, Mississippi. Dickeson felt that the fossilization of the pelvis was comparable to that of the megalonx bones thus arguing for their contemporaneity. Subsequently, such prominent scholars as Sir Charles Lyell and Joseph Leidy confirmed Dickeson's observation concerning the comparability of the physical appearance of the bones. Lyell, however, was reluctant to accept this as proof of their contemporaneity because it was his suspicion that the pelvis was not found *in situ* (1849, Vol. II: 151–52). Interestingly, independent confirmation of Dickeson's claims was published before the turn of the century by Thomas Wilson, who had the fluorine content of the pelvis compared with that of an associated mylodon bone. The results of this comparison led him to conclude that "the man and the mylodon, are substantially of the same antiquity" (1895:725). Wilson's contribution went unnoticed, however, until rediscovered in 1951 by Dr. T. Dale Stewart of the Smithsonian Institution.

EARLY EXCAVATORS: 1850–94

Squier and Davis' monumental report of their Ohio excavations appeared in 1848. In this work, the standard reference on the "Mound Builders" for most of the remainder of the nineteenth century, discussion of the Southeast begins with the statement that there is ". . . very little authentic information respecting the monuments of the Southern United States." They had no first-hand knowledge of the Southeast, but relied totally on the reports of others, especially Bartram, Brackenridge, Dickeson, and Rafinesque. In the works of these authorities, and in Squier and Davis, we see a general awareness of the richness of the Southeast's prehistoric past as manifest in numerous, huge earthen monuments. Precisely how these mounds related culturally and temporally to one another and to the spectacular Ohio burial mounds was unknown. That differences existed was obvious, especially in the greater frequencies of flat-topped mounds in the Southeast; nevertheless, the belief was still prevalent that all eastern mounds belonged "to a single grand system" (Squier and Davis 1848:301), that of *the* Mound Builders. Within this unicultural frame of reference, what can be called the Mound Builder model of the past, Mexican analogies obvious in the Southeastern pyramidal mounds automatically applied to all conical burial mounds as well.

As long as the interest in Southeastern mounds went no farther than describing their external appearances or mining for curios, these prehistoric monuments would remain a mystery. However, as the inventory of known sites in the Southeast mounted throughout the nineteenth century, men of scientific bent began to seek answers to the riddles of these sites by excavation.

A major pioneer excavator and cataloger of Southeastern mounds in the late nineteenth century was Charles Colock Jones (1831–93). He was born in Savannah, Georgia and, after being educated at Princeton and finally at Harvard Law School, was elected mayor of his home city in 1860. Jones had an abiding interest in the history of his native state that extended also to prehistory. Both before and after the Civil War, he visited prehistoric sites throughout Georgia (among them Stalling's Island, Etowah, Macon Plateau, Kolomoki, and Nacoochee), described what he saw, and conducted the earliest information-oriented archaeological excavations in the state. He published two books on Georgia prehistory (in 1861 and 1873) and numerous archaeological papers in a variety of popular as well as scientific periodicals.

His *Antiquities,* published in 1873, is his most important archaeological work. This book contains careful illustrations of various artifacts along with discussions of them. By modern standards of artifact description and analysis, the book is inadequate, but viewed in the context of the time, it was a significant contribution. It is a clear manifestation of a growing awareness that artifacts are an invaluable reservoir of information about the past. Another significant contribution by Jones was his observation that not all mounds were of the same age. Thus, after noting, "It is safe to assert that most of the mounds antedate the historic period," he goes on to state, "Compared with each other they differ materially in age" (Jones 1873:131–32).

Jones was also an early dissenter from the widespread belief in the Mound Builders as a lost, non-Indian race. At first he believed in an invasion from Mexico (1861:57), but by 1873 he had come to see the Mound Builders as no more than prehistoric Indians. He reached this conclusion by critically comparing what he knew of Southeastern archaeology with descriptions of Indian life contained in early historic accounts, such as those of De Soto's chroniclers.

Another Jones, Joseph J., also made important contributions to developing Southeastern archaeology in the latter half of the nineteenth century. He was an M.D. who taught chemistry and clinical medicine in New Orleans, and he excavated at least fifteen stone box grave sites in western Tennessee near Nashville in 1868 and 1869 (1876). By careful observation of the burials and their associated artifacts *in situ,* Jones exploded a number of myths about the Tennessee Mound Builders that Haywood and others had popularized. For example, based upon dentition, he demonstrated that burials in small stone graves all were of juveniles, not pygmies. No less than eighty-five drawings of sites and artifacts were included. Most of the grave goods, human effigy pots, bottles, engraved shell gorgets, and monolithic axes, are recognizable today as Mississippian artifacts. His artifact description was the most complete in the Southeastern literature to that date. Another feature of the report was his practice of describing the contents of individual graves rather than treating sites as undifferentiated units. Because of this, it is possible to go to Jones today to re-establish grave lots and thus ascertain some clusters of contemporary artifact types. Jones did not recognize that some of the graves were of different ages from others. In the course of a number of his excavations he recognized vertical stratification, but he failed to use these observations as bases for diachronic studies.

Following Jones, Frederick Ward Putnam (1878) and Gates P. Thruston (1890) also conducted extensive excavations in the Nashville Basin. Because these publications were also replete with drawings of artifacts that had been recovered, these Tennessee sites were the most widely known Southeastern sites in the late nineteenth century. It is little wonder that they attracted early excavators, for the stone graves, which occurred literally by the thousands, were easily discovered with a metal probe and exceedingly rewarding in yields of artifacts; one cemetery alone is said to have produced six hundred to seven hundred whole pottery vessels (Thruston 1890:2).

Interestingly enough, John Wesley Powell, under whose direction the U. S. Bureau of American Ethnology was later to wage a massive campaign against the myth of a lost Mound Builder race, also excavated in one of these Tennessee cemeteries. During the Civil War, while he was on duty for the Union Army near Nashville, he found time to investigate the local antiquities, an interest he had developed in his boyhood home near Chillicothe, Ohio. In a mound containing the characteristic stone graves he found some glass beads and a rusted iron knife. A number of years before, he had made a similar discovery in a mound in Illinois. This time, his ". . . former suspicion became a hypothesis that the mounds from which the glass, copper, and iron articles were taken were constructed subsequent to the advent of the white man on this continent, and that the contents gave evidence of barter between the civilized and savage races" (1894:XL).

After the war, Powell's interests turned away from archaeology. Even after he was appointed director of the newly established Bureau of Ethnology in 1879, he showed no inclination to resume his research in archaeology. However, in 1881, without his knowledge, some of Powell's colleagues enticed Congress to expand the scope of the Bureau's activities to include archaeological exploration into the eastern mounds. With five thousand dollars now earmarked for this activity, Powell appointed Wills de Haas to take charge of mound exploration. Later that same year, de Haas resigned, and the job fell to Cyrus Thomas.

Thomas was an entomologist who served in this capacity on the famous Haydn survey in the Southwest and later taught at Illinois Normal University before coming to Washington. Influenced by Powell's ideas, he led the battle against the Mound Builder myth. Between 1882 and 1886, over two thousand mounds throughout the East were investigated by Thomas and his associates with "The most important question to be settled. . . . Were the mounds built by the Indians?" (1894:21). His final compendium of this research appeared in 1894 as the *Twelfth Annual Report of the Bureau of American Ethnology*. In it excavations in every state in the Southeast are described. Much of their work was understandably focused on the lower Mississippi Valley, where more large temple mound groups are found than anywhere else in the East. In addition, there were conducted what may be the earliest information-oriented excavations in the Caddoan area of south-central Arkansas, along the Valley of East Tennessee, and the important Etowah and Hollywood Mounds in Georgia.

The bulk of the report was devoted to descriptions of the arrangement, form, and structure of the mounds visited. Burials were often described in detail, indicating that methods of excavation and recording must have been meticulous. The report, however, failed to be the final, definitive one Thomas had originally envisioned. The mere description of the sites proved so formidable that a comprehensive artifact analysis was omitted, and this task fell to others at the Bureau, notably Gerard Fowke (1896) and W. H. Holmes (1903), for later publication.

Usually only a few select artifacts (at most) illustrated the cultural assemblage of a site, and most sites were discussed as if they were culturally homogeneous. A notable exception was the Hollywood Mound where Thomas's data documented one of the rare examples to appear in the nineteenth-century literature of cultural superimposition within a Southeastern burial mound.

Thomas devoted the final chapter to a detailed review of the whole Mound Builder problem, citing evidence from ethnohistory and archaeology to document his conclusion, ". . . the remains of the mound section are due to the ancestors of the Indians of that section" (1894:730). His work is generally considered the death blow to the concept of a lost Mound Builder race. The unicultural Mound Builder model of prehistory was also dealt a mortal blow, for, considering the vast distances involved and the profound cultural differences noted within the Mound Builder province, "We are, therefore, forced to the conclusion that the mound-builders belonged to several different tribes or nations" (Thomas 1894:528). Although the term "Mound Builders" continued in use after Thomas's work, never again in the scholarly community did it conjure up the idea of either cultural unity or lost races.

Besides major excavations of burial and temple mounds, the last half of the nineteenth century also saw the discovery of another kind of archaeological site, shell middens. Although these too are artificial eminences, this fact escaped general recognition until the 1860s. For example, Daniel Brinton, the influential linguist-anthropologist who visited Florida in 1856–57, believed that the huge accumulations of fresh-water shells along the St. John's River were natural "hillocks" used by the Indians as convenient places to bury their dead (1859:180, 1867:357). By contrast, even earlier, Sir Charles Lyell (1849, Vol. I: 338–39) had expressed his belief that salt-water shell middens on the Georgia coast were of human origin, the discarded refuse of generations of shellfish gatherers. A similar controversy had raged in Europe in the early nineteenth century and had been resolved in favor of the human origins view in 1851 with the announcement of the results of a major interdisciplinary research program into the Danish "kitchen middens" (Daniel 1950:87–88). News of the Danes' discoveries served as a catalyst to shell midden excavation in this country.

In the Southeast the earliest to excavate shell middens scientifically was Jeffries Wyman, first curator of the Peabody Museum of Harvard University from 1866 until his death in 1874. Wyman, who had an international reputation as an anatomist, apparently became well acquainted with the St. John's shell middens when bad health brought him to Florida in 1852 (Mitra 1933:129). After assuming the curatorship of the Peabody Museum, he dug some shell middens on the coast of Maine and Massachusetts before returning to the St. John's to conduct his first intensive excavations there in 1867. He made subsequent visits in 1869, 1871, and 1874. Preliminary reports of this research appeared between 1868 and 1874, but his final and greatest report was published posthumously in 1875.

Based on his careful excavations in many of the fresh-water shell middens along the St. John's, he demonstrated conclusively, by recording hearths, artifacts, and vertebrate bones throughout the middens, that they were accretions of human refuse. This and other of his observations of these shell middens rate Wyman not only "the first major figure in Florida archaeology" (Goggin 1952:32) but one of the important pioneers in Eastern Woodlands archaeology. In addition, Wyman made the observation that ceramic variation among St. John's shell middens

connoted not simply geographic but also temporal differences. He felt that those mounds lacking pottery were
older than those producing pottery and, further, that
stamped ceramics were younger than both plain and incised types. This was the first ceramic sequence in eastern
North American archaeology and stands to this day. Two
other aspects of Wyman's final publication offer testimony
to his precocity, for they were not duplicated in the archaeological literature of North America until the twentieth century—a quantified table of potsherds from seven
sites based upon temper and decorative differences and a
careful analysis of the fauna recovered from twelve sites.

Following Wyman's work, the 1880s and early 1890s
saw a great deal of excavation in Florida shell middens
by amateurs. Some of this work was excellent, particularly
that of S. T. Walker, whose reports appeared in various
numbers of the Smithsonian Annual Reports. At Cedar
Keys in 1881, a roadcut through a shell midden had exposed the interior stratification, and Walker, an astute
observer, was there to make the most of this unique opportunity. Using the vertical stratigraphy as a chronological framework, he noted that only undecorated pottery
occurred in the lowest levels followed by incised and
stamped wares that were in turn overlain by a finer pottery
with handles, effigies, and some painted or slipped surfaces. In order to learn something about the progression
of prehistoric cultures through time, Walker felt, "The key
to the whole matter is a critical study of ancient pottery"
(1883:680). Walker's message and example, however,
went largely unheeded.

Perhaps the most interesting figure in the history of
Southeastern archaeology was Clarence Bloomfield
Moore (1852–1936). A wealthy Philadelphia socialite,
after a life of worldwide travel and no little adventure
(he once crossed the Andes to the Amazon, which he then
followed to its mouth, and on another occasion he sustained an eye injury while big-game hunting in Africa),
he turned to archaeology. Among his earliest and best

works were his excavations in the shell middens of the St. John's between 1892 and 1894. Traveling by river and with the aid of a crew of up to eight men, Moore was able to revisit all of Wyman's sites, to record forty-three additional sites, and to excavate on a larger scale than anyone before him. His work was surprisingly meticulous (". . . not one spadeful of debris has been thrown out except in his presence . . . dimensions are derived from measurements, and not from estimate") (Moore 1892:917), and he proved to be a careful observer. He amassed further irrefutable evidence in support of Wyman's view that the middens were of human origin while, with *stratigraphic evidence,* he demonstrated that Wyman's opinion about the relative ages of the shell middens was indeed true (1892b:916).

In the sophistication of their observations, particularly in their appreciation of the value of pottery as a valuable tool for understanding something of that prehistory, Wyman, Walker, and Moore were well ahead of their times. It is instructive that these important insights were first gained by excavators of refuse middens rather than of burial or temple mounds. Excavators of such mounds learned quickly that the finest artifacts tended to be concentrated in favorable locations, especially in the center, and thus they were encouraged by the nature of the sites to tunnel directly to the "loot" at the disregard of the stratigraphy. Parenthetically, it may be noted that the tunneling technique, while rewarding in the sense of recovering a maximum number of artifacts with a minimum expenditure of effort, was not without its literal pitfalls. While excavating a southwestern Virginia mound for the Peabody Museum, one of Lucien Carr's helpers was killed by a cave-in while removing a burial at the base of a ten-foot-deep central shaft (Carr 1877:78). By contrast, the shell midden excavators, undistracted by the prospects of rich concentrations of artifacts, tended to excavate extensively and had to make the best of the un-

ceremoniously discarded refuse they were able to find
scattered widely in the deposits.

THE DEVELOPMENT OF COMPARATIVE STUDIES
AND THE GEOGRAPHIC MODEL: 1894–1933

By 1894 the old Mound Builder model of the past had
been discredited, and it was replaced, in the early decades
of the twentieth century, by what can be termed a
geographic model. The new model, which employed a pure
(i.e., temporally undifferentiated) regional framework in
an effort to make order of the ever-growing corpus of data
on Southeastern prehistory, grew up with archaeologists
whose research interests had become pan-Southeastern
and were no longer focused primarily on a single state or
region. Thomas was the first truly pan-Southeastern archaeologist, but because of his focus upon the interrelationships between history and prehistory, his writing is
nearly devoid of attempts to draw comparisons between
prehistoric cultures. Thomas, of course, had recognized
the existence of regional variation within prehistory, but it
was C. B. Moore, and especially W. H. Holmes, with
their extensive, first-hand knowledge of the Southeast,
who first seriously began to look comparatively at the data
of Southeastern prehistory and to recognize patterns
emerging in the geographic distribution of those data.

At the turn of the century and for the next two decades
C. B. Moore was the most active figure in Southeastern
archaeology. Moore was the most prolific excavator and
publisher to have ever worked in the Southeast. Each
summer an advance party would survey a segment of one
of the major Southeastern streams, seeking excavatable
sites and obtaining permission to dig. Beginning typically
in November, Moore embarked in his hundred-foot-long,
low-draught, stern-wheel steamer, the *Gopher*, accompanied by a personal friend, five to ten excavators, the
steamer captain, a local pilot, and a crew of three. Excava-

tions were conducted usually until April. Upon completion of the field season, a survey party prepared for the next year while Moore studied the artifacts and prepared his reports.

Moore's explorations carried him up virtually every large, navigable river in every state in the Southeast except Virginia and North Carolina. The sites he excavated and reported are too numerous to be discussed here, but some of the more important ones include: Irene, Georgia; Crystal River, Florida; Moundville, Alabama; Poverty Point and Gahagan, Louisiana; Haley, Menard, Rose, and Pecan Point, Arkansas; Walls, Mississippi; Indian Knoll, Kentucky; and Hiwassee Island, Tennessee. The descriptions of these sites and many more appeared in over thirty "Parts" of the *Journal of the Academy of Natural Sciences of Philadelphia* between 1894 and 1918.

In examining Moore's publications, two features in particular stand out: the promptness with which they appeared and the high quality of the illustrations. Rarely did a year go by that a report of the preceding fall and winter work did not actually get into print, a record unmatched in the annals of Southeastern archaeology.

To be only slightly facetious, after 1894, Moore's work can be characterized as that of a sophisticated gravedigger. He focused nearly all his attentions upon mounds and flat cemeteries where burials accompanied by rich mortuary offerings were most likely to be found. He must have dug with considerable care, for his publications characteristically record such data as mound stratigraphy and numbers, types, locations, sex, age, and orientation of burials. Perhaps the best aspect of his reports from a modern perspective was his commendable practice of recording grave lots and cross-referencing these with illustrated artifacts. This applied mainly to the more spectacular or unusual artifacts. Since the more spectacular artifacts tended to be archaeologically young, Moore's reports supplied information primarily on the Temple Mound I and II periods. The most notable exceptions are

Poverty Point, Indian Knoll, and various Florida shell heaps, all of the Archaic period.

Another laudable characteristic of Moore's work was his willingness to consult others. Proof of the existence of aboriginal dogs and of the use of native copper was based not on his own claims, but on the testimony of a zoologist and a chemist. The human skeletal remains were turned over to Ales Hrlicka and published as separate appendices in Moore's reports. An archaeologist whose counsel Moore frequently sought was W. H. Holmes.

William Henry Holmes (1846–1933), a towering figure in early American archaeology, began his career as an artist with the U. S. Geological Survey under John Wesley Powell and later (1902–9) succeeded Powell as chief of the U. S. Bureau of American Ethnology (BAE). He was not primarily a field archaeologist. Rather, his influence was most felt, especially in the Southeast, in the realm of data analysis, comparison, and synthesis.

He was a pioneer in the systemic analysis of ceramics. Perhaps his early training as an artist inclined him in this direction, but he soon recognized the value of pottery in tackling chronological and historical problems. After being appointed Curator of Aboriginal Ceramics in the U. S. National Museum in 1882, he began a serious study of the pottery of the Mississippi Valley and of Moore's Florida collections. In 1889 he transferred to the staff of the Bureau of American Ethnology and began studying the ceramics being recovered by Thomas's mound survey. Before he was done, he had incorporated into his study much of Moore's data and that available in a number of other collections. The culmination of these efforts was his classic *Aboriginal Pottery of the Eastern United States* (1903). In this study he defined six ceramic "provinces" within the Southeast: Middle Mississippi, Lower Mississippi, Gulf Coast, Florida Peninsula, South Appalachian, and Middle Atlantic. Here was the first serious effort at constructing an interpretive framework for the study of Southeastern prehistory. This framework, along with Holmes' later

(1914) attempt to define archaeological culture areas, has been referred to above as the geographic model because only geographic distributions entered into its formulation.

One of Holmes' rare field projects was conducted in the quarries and workshops in the vicinity of Washington, D.C. and merits mention. He worked here intermittently from 1889 to 1894. As a result of this research, he became convinced that the crude, "hand-ax"-looking stone artifacts so abundant in the area and widely considered to be "Paleolithic" by analogy with European forms, owed their crudeness not to great age but to the incompleteness of their manufacture (1897:14). He later employed this argument—that crude tools may be quarry "rejects" or "blanks" designed for further shaping—to refute claims of Pleistocene man that were arising from California to New Jersey.

Throughout the period 1894–1933 numerous archaeologists were conducting valuable research in the Southeast, but space permits us to mention some of these only in passing. Most of the research during this period was sponsored by institutions located outside of the Southeast (e.g., Smithsonian Institution, Peabody Museum, Phillips Academy, The American Museum of Natural History, and Heye Foundation) and was carried out by staff members who were non-Southeasterners. Important exceptions were George E. Beyer in Louisiana, William E. Myer in Tennessee, Bennett H. Young in Kentucky, and Calvin S. Brown in Mississippi. The latter two each published an archaeological survey of his home state in 1910 and 1926, respectively. Also during this period, the University of Kentucky physicist-zoologist team of W. S. Webb and W. D. Funkhouser began their research into Kentucky prehistory. Their *Ancient Life in Kentucky* (1928) marks the third major popular survey of a Southeastern state's archaeology published in this period.

A number of prominent scholars whose main research had been outside the Southeast also made forays into the area during this period. In 1896 Frank Hamilton Cushing dug in the mucks of Key Marco in southwestern Florida, where he was rewarded with a spectacularly rich yield of preserved wooden artifacts; Charles Peabody, director of the Department of Archaeology at Andover, dug two Mississippi burial mounds in 1901–2 and Jacob's Cavern in the Missouri Ozarks in 1903; Nels C. Nelson did salvage archaeology in an eastern Florida shell mound in 1917 and sought futilely for Pleistocene man in cave sites in Kentucky and Missouri in 1916 and 1923; F. W. Hodge and George Pepper dug the rich Nacoochee Mound of northern Georgia in 1915; Jesse W. Fewkes excavated a burial mound at the Weeden Island type site in 1923–24; and Warren K. Moorehead descended upon the Etowah site between 1925 and 1927, where he was even more successful than Thomas in extracting embossed copper plates and other Southern Cult burial offerings from Mound C's seemingly endless supply. Moorehead's Southeastern research also took him to the vicinity of Natchez in Mississippi (although this work was never published), to the Caddoan area of southern Arkansas, and into the rock shelters of the Ozarks.

The interval following the active research of Moore and Holmes saw a growing awareness among Southeastern archaeologists that cultural variability existed within as well as between prehistoric sites and that age differences were the explanation of much of this variability. As noted earlier, Thomas had encountered cultural superimposition at the Hollywood Mound, and Charles Peabody had reported a similar phenomenon in a two-stage burial mound in Mississippi.

The earliest serious attempt in the Southeast outside of the Florida shell middens and N. C. Nelson's neglected example at Mammoth Cave (Schwartz 1967:29) to interpret excavation results in terms of a sequence of different prehistoric cultures is found in the work of M. R. Harrington. Following the suggestions of C. B. Moore, then a trustee of the Museum of the American Indian (Heye Foundation), Harrington conducted extensive excavations in southwestern Arkansas (for twenty consecutive months, from 1916 to 1918!), and in the Valley of East Tennessee in 1919. Later, in 1922 and 1923, also for the Heye Foundation, he excavated in the dry caves of the Ozarks in northwestern Arkansas, where preservation of wooden tools, sandals, basketry, bags, nets, etc., created considerable excitement. The most significant aspect of Harrington's work was his explicit realization that within each region he was dealing with cultures of different ages. This is best exemplified in his Tennessee report (1922), wherein he defined a sequence of three "cultures": Round Grave, Second, and Cherokee. We now know that the latter two cultures are mixed bags and that the prehistoric sequence of this region is more complex than Harrington's simple trichotomy. This, however, can not detract from the value of his more basic contribution, a three-dimensional interpretive model.

One other aspect of Harrington's work should be emphasized: He was a leader in the rediscovery of the scientific value of village refuse excavation. The example of Wyman, Walker, Nelson, and Moore had been generally disregarded during the first two decades of the twentieth century as Southeastern archaeologists lavished most of their attention on burial sites, and these efforts had been rewarded with little information about temporal variability. With Harrington's research, we see the temporal ramifications of cultural stratigraphy again being realized and exploited.

Following Harrington's work, a number of other archaeologists in the 1920s consciously excavated village sites. For example, Moorehead dug in the habitation area near the Etowah Mounds in hopes of discovering cultural stratification, and Henry B. Collins was digging in village sites in Mississippi by 1929. Village excavation can also be seen as a further sign of maturation in Southeastern archaeology in that it was symptomatic of a trend away from object-oriented research toward a concern for cultural problems.

Along with an increasing appreciation and documentation of the temporal variability in Southeastern prehistory, there developed a new emphasis upon culture historical problems. A technique that became popular was to select an area or site formerly occupied by a known historic tribe and work by excavation from the known into the unknown. This came to be called the "direct historic approach" to archaeology. Harrington and Collins were pioneers of this approach in the Southeast. Seen in the larger context of early-twentieth-century American anthropology, such an interest in culture history is readily understandable. Thus, it comes as no surprise that the first archaeological conference held in the Southeast—the "Conference on Southern Prehistory" convened in 1932 in Birmingham, Alabama, by the National Research Council—was heavily attended by ethnologists and chaired by Clark Wissler.

THE CWA-WPA ERA: 1933–42

The year 1933 was a revolutionary one for Southeastern archaeology. In that year the Civil Works Administration (CWA), a federal relief program to reduce unemployment, was inaugurated. Through this program, money was allocated in December to be used immediately for hiring over fifteen hundred laborers to do archaeological field work. With short notice, the Smithsonian Institution was given over-all scientific direction of the work, including selecting sites for excavation and providing supervisory personnel. The Southeast benefited more than any other section of the country from this archaeological windfall because the two requisites for an immediate commencement of work were locally available: 1. an abundance of unemployed labor and 2. a mild winter climate.

Six major archaeological projects were begun at once in Florida; one near Macon, Georgia; another at the Shiloh Mound group in southwestern Tennessee; and a ninth at the Peachtree Mound in southwestern North Carolina. A single project in California was the only non-Southeastern project. Meanwhile, large-scale dam construction was being contemplated along the Tennessee River by the Tennessee Valley Authority, and the inauguration of the CWA provided a solution to the dilemma of how to salvage something of the rich archaeological reserves of this valley before they were drowned. In January 1934, CWA labor was approved for work in the Tennessee Valley in the Wheeler and Norris basins, and William S. Webb was appointed supervising archaeologist for all TVA work. Thus, December 1933 to July 1934 was the most intensive period of excavation in the history of Southeastern archaeology (Stirling 1935, Setzler and Strong 1936).

A lull in archaeological activity followed the demobilization of the CWA in 1934, but the creation of the Works Progress Administration (WPA) in the spring of 1936 brought a resurgence of large-scale field work. Between 1936 and the termination of WPA support for archaeology in 1942, many major excavations were conducted throughout the Southeast. Huge crews of laborers, which too few trained supervisors struggled valiantly to hold in check, were turned loose in among other places: two additional Tennessee Valley dam basins (Pickwick and Guntersville); much of north Georgia and along the coast near Savannah; many parts of Kentucky; the North Carolina Piedmont; northeastern Mississippi; eastern Oklahoma; eastern Louisiana; eastern Texas; and eastern Tennessee at the famous Hiwassee Island site.

The volume of data unearthed in these projects was truly staggering. It was excellent data, on the whole, despite the difficulties of directing a hundred or more unskilled workmen with but a few supervisors, but publication lagged for obvious reasons. The first comprehensive publications on this research were Webb's reports of the TVA projects, which began to appear as BAE Bulletins in 1938. The 1940s and 1950s saw more reports trickle out in various publication series, the latest appearing as recently as 1966 (e.g., Caldwell and McCann 1941,

Lewis and Kneberg 1946, Newell and Krieger 1949,
Bell and Baerreis 1951, Fairbanks 1956, Wauchope
1966). The final reports on a number of important sites
remain to appear, notably Macon Plateau, Lamar, Swift
Creek, Marksville, Moundville, and Spiro.

Besides more data than ever before on Southeastern prehistory, the CWA- and WPA-funded projects also provided an invaluable training ground for a whole generation
of archaeologists. Among the young men recruited to serve
as supervisors on these projects were D. A. Baerreis, J. R.
Caldwell, J. L. Coe, D. L. DeJarnette, C. H. Fairbanks,
J. A. Ford, W. G. Haag, J. D. Jennings, T. M. N. Lewis,
G. I. Quimby, W. H. Sears, R. Wauchope, and G. R.
Willey. The two names most associated with over-all
direction of these projects were Mathew Stirling, BAE
chief from 1928 to 1957, and W. S. Webb. Stirling, whose
personal research concentrated on Florida, was able to
publish only a few summary reports on his own field work.

William S. Webb (1882–1964), by contrast, was the
most prolific publisher of this era. He joined the Physics
Department of the University of Kentucky in 1907 after
having served as a federal employee among the Seminoles
in Indian Territory (now Oklahoma). Apparently because
of this experience, he had acquired an intense interest in
Indians, and by the early 1920s he had teamed up with
zoologist W. D. Funkhouser to begin surveying and excavating sites in Kentucky on their own time. In 1926,
although head of the Physics Department, Webb was also
appointed head of the new Department of Anthropology
and Archaeology that had been formed mainly as a
budgetary expedient in order that the gift of a truck for
archaeological research could be legally accepted from
the National Research Council. A new publication series,
University of Kentucky Reports in Archaeology and
Anthropology, was begun three years later. Webb authored or coauthored no less than thirty numbers in the
eight volumes of this series that appeared between 1929
and 1952. All dealt with field work in sites throughout

Kentucky. In addition, after assuming directorship of the TVA projects, he saw four monumental reports through to publication between 1938 and 1951 (Schwartz 1967).

No discussion of this period in Southeastern archaeology would be complete without further mention of the contributions of James Alfred Ford (1911–68). Before his pioneering work in the adjacent portions of Louisiana and Mississippi, the Caddoan area and the lower Mississippi Valley proper were generally regarded as a single cultural province. This was so not because of their archaeological similarity, but because there was an abundance of data from the former and little from the latter. Ford's work more than that of any other individual led to a clarification of the situation.

In 1927, as a youngster just graduated from Clinton (Mississippi) High School, he obtained a job with the Mississippi Department of Archives and History seeking antiquities from local mounds. This work brought him in contact with H. B. Collins, whom he assisted in his village excavations and later accompanied to Alaska as a research assistant. Upon his return from Alaska, he began college, but temporarily gave it up when, in 1933, he was awarded a National Research Council grant to pursue archaeological research in the lower Mississippi Valley. The culmination of this work was his classic *Analysis of Indian Village Site Collections from Louisiana and Mississippi,* published in 1936. He employed the unique technique of collecting broken pottery from the surfaces of village sites and, by integrating these data with the results of strata cuts, defined the first cultural sequence for the region: Marksville, Coles Creek-Deasonville, Historic. His subsequent excavations in the area with WPA labor at the Crooks, Greenhouse, and Tchefuncte sites added embellishments but otherwise left the basic sequence unaltered.

By the late 1930s, work like that of Webb and Ford had led to the establishment of local cultural sequences throughout the Southeast, but there was still no over-all synthetic framework to tie all this disparate information

together. Similar difficulties beset archaeologists all over
the East, which had prompted McKern, as early as 1932,
to propose a hierarchical system of cultural classification
that met rapid acceptance in the Midwest, the so-called
Midwestern Taxonomic Method. Webb was the first to
adopt this taxonomic scheme in the Southeast in his
Wheeler Basin report of 1939, but this precedent was not
widely followed except in the Caddoan area (Krieger
1946). Indeed, in the first comprehensive and substantive
synthesis of Eastern cultural history—Ford's and Willey's
"An Interpretation of the Prehistory of the Eastern United
States" published in the *American Anthropologist* in 1941
—McKern's terminology was not used. Actually there was
much similarity between the major taxonomic units of the
two systems, the "patterns" of McKern and the "stages"
of Ford and Willey. What the former termed "Mississippian" approximated what the latter referred to as
"Temple Mound I and II," while what McKern designated
"Woodland" did not depart too much from what Ford
and Willey classed as "Burial Mound I and II" (except
for ambiguity over Late Woodland); both defined
Archaic as their third major pattern or stage. The major
difference between the two systems was that Ford and
Willey consciously defined their stages as units of different
relative age, whereas McKern originally intended his
patterns to be ageless. Since McKern's patterns almost immediately had connotations of relative age appended to
them, the distinctions between the two systems at this level
of abstraction appear to be largely semantic. Thus, we
here regard these approaches as but variants of a single
archaeological model, the first truly pan-Eastern, three-
dimensional model of prehistory. The new model significantly increased our ability to visualize the broad outlines
of Eastern as well as Southeastern prehistory.

The growing interest in comparison and synthesis in the
1930s was met in another highly effective way: the
regional conference. Because protracted periods of time
were required to process the immense amounts of data be-

ing gathered by CWA and WPA crews (thus delaying publication) and because the earlier literature was woefully lacking in precedents of data analysis within the framework of a three-dimensional model of the past, archaeologists were literally forced to come together to solve their mutual problems. The first such gathering of Southeastern archaeologists (since the Birmingham conference of 1932) was in 1938. The topic of this first Southeastern Archaeological Conference was pottery typology and nomenclature. General principles for describing and naming types were agreed upon, and the first formal pottery type descriptions using these principles were published in 1939 in the initial number of the *Southeastern Archaeological Conference Newsletter*. The Southeastern Archaeological Conference has survived to this day as the major forum for the exchange of ideas about Southeastern prehistory.

In retrospect, the CWA-WPA era saw the establishment of professional, anthropological archaeology in the Southeast. Before this time, most Southeastern archaeologists had received no formal archaeological training. They had learned their trade by trial and error and by consulting the literature. By the 1930s, however, a number of young men interested in Southeastern archaeology were receiving or had completed formal academic training in anthropology at various universities, especially Chicago, Harvard, and Columbia. With the unique opportunity afforded by CWA-WPA funds to conduct field work on an unprecedented scale, these young anthropologists were able to apply their academic training to the obvious advantage of both themselves and the discipline. There thus emerged from this era a group of highly skilled, professional archaeologists who eventually gravitated to universities from which they continued their archaeological research and began the formal training of new generations of archaeologists. A further sign of growing professionalism at this time, not only in the Southeast but throughout the nation, can also be seen in the founding of the national Society for American Archaeology in 1934.

THE MODERN PERIOD: 1942-72

Chronology and taxonomy had developed into important archaeological themes in the prior period, and while they continued as major concerns of the modern period, an era of more sophisticated problem-oriented research had begun. New generations of anthropologically trained archaeologists now directed their field research more toward the history and nature of specific prehistoric cultures. Solutions to these problems were often sought through modern re-excavation of already famous sites, among them Menard, Fatherland, Emerald, Poverty Point, Kolomoki, and Etowah (Ford 1961; Neitzel 1965; Cotter 1951; Ford and Webb 1956; Sears 1956; Kelley and Larson 1957). As before, problems sometimes, in a sense, sought the archaeologist when dam construction threatened inundation of areas of prehistoric habitation (e.g., Caldwell 1953; Sears 1958; Kelley and Neitzel 1961). In other instances the need for new sites to aid in the solution of culture-historical problems fostered systematic regional surveys, such as Willey's Florida Gulf Coast study (1949) and the lower Mississippi Valley survey of Phillips, Ford, and Griffin (1951). These monumental surveys saw the marriage of sophisticated ceramic analysis (an outgrowth of the CWA-WPA period) with controlled village refuse excavation (whose roots go back at least to Harrington), along with an awakening appreciation of the importance of the natural environment to any understanding of prehistory. The resulting sequences of regional ceramic periods provided the frameworks within which the culture-historical analyses were conducted, and they inspired similar regional frameworks to be erected throughout the Southeast. To this day many Southeastern "cul-

tures" or "phases" remain, in reality, little more than
ceramic periods.

In the realm of taxonomy, the modern period has seen
an unparalleled sharpening and refining of conceptual
tools (type, phase, tradition, horizon, region, locality,
period, etc.). None of these was developed uniquely for
Southeastern data. However, Southeastern scholars like
Willey, Phillips, Caldwell, Ford, and Goggin have been
instrumental in their development, so that such concepts
have attained wide acceptance in the Southeast.

A truly revolutionary change in our thinking about the
duration of Southeastern prehistory has come about during the modern period. In 1941 Ford and Willey had con-
densed the prehistoric sequence of the area into less than
twelve hundred years. With the excavation of deeply
stratified early archaic sites (Coe 1964; Miller 1958;
DeJarnette, et al. 1962; Broyles 1966) and the introduction of radiocarbon dating in 1949, human occupation of
the Southeast can now be reliably dated back to the eighth
millennium B.C. An earlier, Paleo-Indian occupation has
become generally recognized since the modern period began (Williams and Stoltman 1965), but the evidence for
Pleistocene man in the Southeast remains inconclusive and
controversial (Williams 1957).

Another surprise accompanying radiocarbon dating was
the unexpected great age demonstrated for the area's
earliest pottery. Fiber-tempered pottery found in pre-
agricultural shell middens of Alabama, Florida, Georgia,
and South Carolina has consistently been dated between
2500 and 1000 B.C. (Bullen 1961; Stoltman 1966), making
it the oldest in North America.

Unlike the past, archaeological research in the Southeast today is being conducted primarily from local institutions, especially state universities where many of the men
who once supervised the CWA-WPA projects still hold
prominent positions. Although the scale of individual field
projects is much smaller than those of the CWA-WPA era,

144   JAMES B. STOLTMAN

the number of projects is greater, the problems more varied, and the quality of work much more controlled and precise.

REFERENCES

BELL, ROBERT E., and BAERREIS, DAVID A.
  1951 "A Survey of Oklahoma Archaeology." *Texas Arch. and Paleont. Soc. Bull.* 22:7–100.

BEYER, GEORGE E.
  1896 "The Mounds of Louisiana." *Pub. Louisiana Hist. Soc.* 1:12–32.

BRACKENRIDGE, HENRY M.
  1814 *Views of Louisiana.* Chicago: Quadrangle Books.
  1818 "On the Population and Tumuli of the Aborigines of North America." *Trans. Am. Phil. Soc.* 1:151–59.

BRINTON, DANIEL G.
  1859 *Notes on the Floridean Peninsula.* Philadelphia: Joseph Sabin.
  1867 "Artificial Shell Deposits of the United States." *Annual Report Smith. Ins.* 1866:356–58.

BROYLES, BETTYE J.
  1966 "Preliminary Report: The St. Albans Site (46 Ka 27), Kanawha County, West Virginia." *The West Virginian Arch.* 19:1–43.

BULLEN, RIPLEY P.
  1961 "Radiocarbon Dates for Southeastern Fiber-Tempered Pottery." *Am. Ant.* 27:104–6.

CALDWELL, JOSEPH R.
  1953 "The Rembert Mounds, Elbert County, Georgia." *Bureau Am. Eth. Bull.* 154:303–20.
  1958 "Trend and Tradition in the Prehistory of the Eastern United States." *Am. Anthro. Ass. Mem.* 88.

——— and McCANN, CATHERINE
  1941 *Irene Mound Site, Chatham County, Georgia.* Athens: University of Georgia Press.

CARR, LUCIEN
  1877 "Report on the Exploration of a Mound in Lee County Virginia." *Reports Peabody Mus. Am. Arch. Eth.* 2(1):75–94.

CLARKE, DAVID L.
  1968 *Analytical Archaeology.* London: Methuen & Co., Ltd.

COE, JOFFRE L.
  1964 "The Formative Cultures of the Carolina Piedmont." *Trans. Am. Phil. Soc.* 54(5).

COLLINS, HENRY B., JR.
1932 "Excavations at a Prehistoric Indian Village Site in Mississippi." *Proc. United States Nat. Mus.* 79(32).

COTTER, JOHN L.
1951 "Stratigraphic and Area Tests at the Emerald and Anna Mound Sites." *Am. Ant.* 17:18–32.

CULIN, STEWART
1900 "The Dickeson Collection of American Antiquities." *Bull. Free Mus. Sci. Art Univ. of Penn.* 2(3):113–68.

CUSHING, F. H.
1897 "Exploration of Ancient Key Dwellers' Remains on the Gulf Coast of Florida." *Proc. Am. Phil. Soc.* 35:329–432.

DANIEL, GLYNNE
1950 *A Hundred Years of Archaeology*. London: Duckworth & Co., Ltd.

DEJARNETTE, D. L.; KURJACK, E. B.; and CAMBRON, J. W.
1962 "Stanfield-Worley Bluff Shelter Excavations." *Jour. Alabama Arch.* 8:1–2.

FAIRBANKS, CHARLES H.
1956 "Archeology of the Funeral Mound, Ocmulgee National Monument." *Nat. Park Service. Arch. Res. Ser.* 3.

FEWKES, JESSE W.
1924 "Preliminary Archeological Explorations at Weeden Island, Florida." *Smith. Misc. Coll.* 76(13).

FORD, JAMES A.
1936 "Analysis of Indian Village Site Collections from Louisiana and Mississippi." *Dept. Cons. Louisiana Geolog. Survey, Anthro. Study* 2.
1951 "Greenhouse: A Troyville-Coles Creek Period Site in Avoyelles Parish, Louisiana." *Anthro. Pap. Am. Mus. Nat. Hist.* 44(1).
1961 "Menard Site: The Quapaw Village of Osotouy on the Arkansas River." *Anthro. Pap. Am. Mus. Nat. Hist.* 48(2).

——— and QUIMBY, G. I.
1945 "The Tchefuncte Culture, An Early Occupation of the Lower Mississippi Valley." *Soc. Am. Arch. Mem.* 2.

——— and WEBB, C. H.
1956 "Poverty Point: A Late Archaic Site in Louisiana." *Anthro. Pap. Am. Mus. Nat. Hist.* 46(1).

——— and WILLEY, G. R.
1940 "Crooks Site: A Marksville Period Burial Mound in La Salle Parish, Louisiana." *Dept. Cons. Louisiana Geolog. Survey, Anthro. Study* 3.
1941 "An Interpretation of the Prehistory of the Eastern United States." *Am. Anthro.* 43:325–63.

FOWKE, GERARD
  1896   "Stone Art." Thirteenth Annual Report of the Bureau of
         Am. Eth.:47–178.

FUNKHOUSER, W. D., and WEBB, W. S.
  1928   "Ancient Life in Kentucky." Kentucky Geolog. Survey 34.

GOGGIN, JOHN M.
  1952   "Space and Time Perspective in Northern St. John's Arche-
         ology, Florida." Yale Univ. Pub. Anthro. 47.

GROSS, HUGO
  1951   "Mastodons, Mammoths, and Man in America." Bull. Texas
         Arch. Paleont. Soc. 22:101–31.

HARRINGTON, M. R.
  1920   "Certain Caddo Sites in Arkansas." Indian Notes and Mono-
         graphs 10.
  1922   "Cherokee and Earlier Remains on Upper Tennessee River."
         Indian Notes and Monographs 24.
  1924   "The Ozark Bluff Dwellers." Am. Anthro. 26:1–21.
  1960   "The Ozark Bluff-Dwellers." Indian Notes and Monographs
         12.

HAYWOOD, JOHN
  1823   The Natural and Aboriginal History of Tennessee. Nashville.

HEYE, GEORGE G.; HODGE, FREDERICK W.; and PEPPER, GEORGE H.
  1918   "The Nacoochee Mound in Georgia." Contrib. from the
         Mus. Am. Indian. Heye Found. 2(1).

HOLMES, WILLIAM H.
  1897   "Stone Implements of the Potomac-Chesapeake Tidewater
         Province." Fifteenth Annual Report of the Bureau of Am.
         Eth.:3–152.
  1903   "Aboriginal Pottery of the Eastern United States." Twentieth
         Annual Report of the Bureau of Am. Eth.:1–201.
  1914   "Areas of American Culture Characterization Tentatively
         Outlined as an Aid in the Study of Antiquities." Am. Anthro.
         16:413–46.

JEFFERSON, THOMAS
  1787   Notes on the State of Virginia. Richmond: J. W. Randolph.

JONES, CHARLES C.
  1861   Monumental Remains of Georgia. Savannah: John M.
         Cooper & Co.
  1873   Antiquities of the Southern Indians, Particularly of the
         Georgia Tribes. New York: D. Appleton & Co.

JONES, JOSEPH
  1876   "Explorations of the Aboriginal Remains of Tennessee."
         Smith. Contr. to Knowledge 22.

KELLEY, A. R.
  1938   "A Preliminary Report on Archaeological Explorations at
         Macon, Georgia." Bureau of Am. Eth. Bull. 119:1–69.

—— and Larson, Lewis H.
1957 "Explorations at Etowah, Georgia 1954–56." *Archaeology* 10:39–48.

—— and Neitzel, R. S.
1961 "The Chauga Site in Oconee County, South Carolina." *Univ. of Georgia Lab. Arch. Report* 3.

Krieger, Alex D.
1946 "Culture Complexes and Chronology in Northern Texas with Extension of Puebloan Dating to the Mississippi Valley." *University of Texas Pub.* 4640.

Lewis, Thomas M. N., and Kneberg, Madeline
1946 *Hiwassee Island.* Knoxville: University of Tennessee Press.

Lyell, Charles
1849 *A Second Visit to the United States of North America,* Vols. I and II. New York: Harper & Bros.

Miller, Carl F.
1958 "Russell Cave: New Light on Stone Age Life." *The Nat. Geog. Mag.* 113:426–37.

Mitra, Panchanan
1933 *A History of American Anthropology.* University of Calcutta, India.

Montagu, M. F. A., and Peterson, C. B.
1944 "The Earliest Account of the Association of Human Artifacts with Fossil Mammals in North America." *Proceed. Am. Phil. Soc.* 87:407–19.

Moore, Clarence Bloomfield
1892 "Certain Shell Heaps of the St. John's River, Florida, Hitherto Unexplored." *Am. Nat.* 26:912–22.
1894 "Certain Shell Heaps of the St. John's River, Florida, Hitherto Unexplored." *Am. Nat.* 28:15–26.
1907 "Moundville Revisited." *Jour. Acad. Nat. Sci. Phil.* 13(3):337–405.
1907 "Crystal River Revisited." *Jour. Acad. Nat. Sci. Phil.* 13(3):406–25.
1910 "Antiquities of the St. Francis, White, and Black Rivers, Arkansas." *Jour. Acad. Nat. Sci. Phil.* 14(2):254–362.
1912 "Some Aboriginal Sites on Red River." *Jour. Acad. Nat. Sci. Phil.* 14(4):481–644.
1913 "Some Aboriginal Sites in Louisiana and in Arkansas." *Jour. Acad. Nat. Sci. Phil.* 16(1):5–102.
1916 "Some Aboriginal Sites on Green River, Kentucky"; "Certain Aboriginal Sites on Lower Ohio River"; "Additional Investigations on Mississippi River." *Jour. Acad. Nat. Sci. Phil.* 16(3):432–511.

Moorehead, Warren King
1931 *Archaeology of the Arkansas River Valley.* New Haven: Yale University Press.

1932   *Etowah Papers.* New Haven: Yale University Press.

MYER, WILLIAM EDWARD
    1928   "Two Prehistoric Villages in Middle Tennessee." *Forty-First Annual Report of the Bureau of Am. Eth.*:485–614.

NEITZEL, ROBERT S.
    1965   "Archeology of the Fatherland Site: The Grand Village of the Natchez." *Anthro. Pap. Am. Mus. Nat. Hist.* 51(1).

NELSON, N. C.
    1917   "Contributions to the Archaeology of Mammoth Cave and Vicinity, Kentucky." *Anthro. Pap. Am. Mus. Nat. Hist.* 22(1).
    1918   "Chronology in Florida." *Anthro. Pap. Am. Mus. Nat. Hist.* 22(2).

NEWELL, H. PERRY, and KRIEGER, ALEX D.
    1949   "The George C. Davis Site, Cherokee County, Texas." *Soc. Am. Arch. Mem.* 5.

PEABODY, CHARLES
    1904   "Exploration of Mounds, Coahoma County, Mississippi." *Pap. Peabody Mus. Am. Arch. and Eth.* 3(2).

——— and MOOREHEAD, W. K.
    1904   "The Exploration of Jacobs Cavern, McDonald County, Missouri." *Phillips Acad. Dept. Arch. Bull.* 1.

PHILLIPS, PHILIP; FORD, JAMES A.; and GRIFFIN, JAMES B.
    1951   "Archaeological Survey in the Lower Mississippi Alluvial Valley, 1940–1947." *Pap. of the Peabody Mus. Am. Arch. and Eth.* 25.

POWELL, J. W.
    1894   "Report of the Director." *Twelfth Annual Report of the Bureau of Am. Eth.* 1890–91:xix–xlviii.

PUTNAM, F. W.
    1878   "Archaeological Explorations in Tennessee." *Reports of the Peabody Mus. Am. Arch. and Eth.* 2(2):305–60.

SCHWARTZ, DOUGLAS W.
    1967   *Conceptions of Kentucky Prehistory.* Lexington: University of Kentucky Press.

SEARS, WILLIAM H.
    1956   "Excavations at Kolomoki" (Final Report). *Univ. Georgia Series in Anthro.* 5.
    1958   "The Wilbanks Site (9CK-5), Georgia." *Bureau of Am. Eth. Bull.* 169:129–94.

SETZLER, F. M., and STRONG, W. D.
    1936   "Archaeology and Relief." *Am. Ant.* 1:301–9.

SQUIER, E. G., and DAVIS, E. H.
    1848   "Ancient Monuments of the Mississippi Valley." *Smith. Contr. to Knowledge.* 1.

STEWART, T. D.
1951 "Antiquity of Man in America Demonstrated by the Fluorine Test." *Science* 113:391–92.

STIRLING, M. W.
1935 "Smithsonian Archeological Projects Conducted Under the Federal Emergency Relief Administration, 1933–34." *Annual Report of the Smith. Inst.* 1934:371–400.

STOLTMAN, JAMES B.
1966 "New Radiocarbon Dates for Southeastern Fiber-tempered Pottery." *Am. Ant.* 31:872–74.

THOMAS, CYRUS
1894 "Report on the Mound Explorations of the Bureau of Ethnology." *Twelfth Annual Report of the Bureau of Am. Eth.*:3–730.

THRUSTON, GATES P.
1890 *The Antiquities of Tennessee.* Cincinnati: Robert Clarke & Co.

VAN DOREN, MARK (ed.)
1928 *Travels of William Bartram.* New York: Dover Publications.

WALKER, S. T.
1883 "The Aborigines of Florida." *Annual Report of the Smith. Inst.* 1881:677–80.

WAUCHOPE, ROBERT
1966 "Archaeological Survey of Northern Georgia." *Soc. Am. Arch. Mem.* 21.

WEBB, WILLIAM S.
1938 "An Archaeological Survey of the Norris Basin in Eastern Tennessee." *Bureau of Am. Eth. Bull.* 118.
1939 "An Archaeological Survey of Wheeler Basin on the Tennessee River in Northern Alabama." *Bureau of Am. Eth. Bull.* 122.
1946 "Indian Knoll, Site Oh 2, Ohio County, Kentucky." *Univ. Kentucky Reports in Anthro. and Arch.* 4(3).

——— and DEJARNETTE, DAVID L.
1942 "An Archeological Survey of Pickwick Basin in the Adjacent Portions of the States of Alabama, Mississippi, and Tennessee." *Bureau of Am. Eth. Bull.* 129.

——— and WILDER, CHARLES G.
1951 *An Archaeological Survey of Guntersville Basin on the Tennessee River in Northern Alabama.* Lexington: University of Kentucky Press.

WILLEY, GORDON R.
1949 "Archaeology of the Florida Gulf Coast." *Smith. Misc. Coll.* 113.

WILLIAMS, STEPHEN
1957 "The Island 35 Mastodon: Its Bearing on the Age of Archaic Cultures in the East." *Am. Ant.* 22:359–72.

——— and STOLTMAN, JAMES B.
1965 "An Outline of Southeastern United States Prehistory with Particular Emphasis on the Paleo-Indian Era." In H. E. Wright, Jr., and David G. Frey (eds.). *The Quaternary of the United States:*669–83. Princeton, New Jersey: Princeton University Press.

WILSON, THOMAS
1895 "On the Presence of Fluorine as a Test for the Fossilization of Animal Bones." *American Naturalist* 29:301–17, 439–56, 719–25.

WYMAN, JEFFRIES
1875 "Fresh-Water Shell Mounds of the St. John's River, Florida." *Memoirs of the Peabody Acad. of Sci.* 1(4).

YOUNG, BENNETT H.
1910 "The Prehistoric Men of Kentucky." *Filson Club Pub.* 25.

6 THE PLAINS

George C. Frison

INTRODUCTION

The Plains constitute a significant portion of North America extending from well inside the Canadian provinces of Alberta, Saskatchewan, and Manitoba to central Texas and from the eastern flanks of the Rocky Mountains to the western borders of the states west of the Mississippi River. The area can be roughly divided into five rather arbitrary divisions. The southern Plains include extreme eastern New Mexico, northern Texas, and all except the southeastern corner of Oklahoma. The central Plains include all of Kansas, Nebraska, the eastern half of Colorado, and the western parts of Missouri and Iowa. The largest division in the area is the northwestern Plains, and these include the southern thirds of Saskatchewan and Alberta and most of Montana and Wyoming. The Middle Missouri is composed of the Missouri River and adjacent areas through North and South Dakota. The northeastern subarea of the Plains occupies southwestern Manitoba, a narrow strip of western Minnesota, and eastern North and South Dakota. Wedel (1961) uses a more restricted area than does Willey (1966), who includes a large share of the Rocky Mountains and northeastern Texas. Objective observers from outside the Plains usually try to be kind but can never conceal their feelings completely, and mention the monotony and dreariness of the environment. Early anthropologists who studied the Plains may have been influenced by this way of thinking. Wissler (1907) considered the peopling of the Plains as the result of introduction of horses along with population

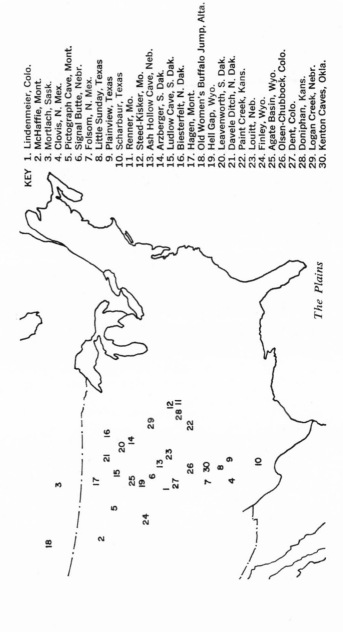

KEY 1. Lindenmeier, Colo.
     2. McHaffie, Mont.
     3. Mortlach, Sask.
     4. Clovis, N. Mex.
     5. Pictograph Cave, Mont.
     6. Signal Butte, Nebr.
     7. Folsom, N. Mex.
     8. Little Sunday, Texas
     9. Plainview, Texas
    10. Scharbaur, Texas
    11. Renner, Mo.
    12. Steed-Kisker, Mo.
    13. Ash Hollow Cave, Neb.
    14. Arzberger, S. Dak.
    15. Ludlow Cave, S. Dak.
    16. Biesterfelt, N. Dak.
    17. Hagen, Mont.
    18. Old Women's Buffalo Jump, Alta.
    19. Hell Gap, Wyo.
    20. Leavenworth, S. Dak.
    21. Davele Ditch, N. Dak.
    22. Paint Creek, Kans.
    23. Louitt, Neb.
    24. Finley, Wyo.
    25. Agate Basin, Wyo.
    26. Olsen-Chubbock, Colo.
    27. Dent, Colo.
    28. Doniphan, Kans.
    29. Logan Creek, Nebr.
    30. Kenton Caves, Okla.

The Plains

displacement of original residents by Europeans, and Kroeber (1939) still held very much to the same way of thinking thirty years later.

A single thing that bound the Plains together in prehistoric times was a continuous sea of grass that supported herds of bison and other herbivores of lesser importance. There is considerable diversity in the Plains north to south and from east to west in rainfall, temperature, altitude, relief, and grass cover. Although every subarea of the Plains was subject to different cultural influences across its borders, there was a homogeneity that made Plains culture distinctive and exhibited the peculiar stamp of adaptation to the Plains environment.

The bison herds constituted a large reservoir of available food, and the Plains inhabitants devised ingenious methods of procurement, but their level of technology never developed to the point of serious exploitation, at least in the postaltithermal period before horses. The tough sod of the Plains was not amenable to working with the bison scapula hoe, and agriculture was thereby limited to flood plains or rivers. As a result, Plains prehistory was never too spectacular, with the possible exception of the earth lodge villages of the Missouri River. The result of this is obvious. Interest in archaeology was centered in areas of more exotic interest, and the only real interest concerning the Plains was in the posthorse Indian culture, which was quite spectacular though short-lived.

PLAINS ARCHAEOLOGY AND THE PALEO-INDIAN

There was, however, one thing that brought one aspect of Plains archaeology to the forefront, and this was the problem of man's entry into the New World. The personalities and events leading up to the final acceptance of a late glacial presence of man associated with extinct fauna in the New World had been well documented by Wilmsen

(1965), and in this area of archaeology the Plains occupied a leading role.

In terms of geology, many parts of the Plains exhibit past and present examples of geomorphological processes in exposed situations. The Plains, in addition, offered a favorable environment for the extinct megafauna of the late Wisconsin period, so it was inevitable that this was where the last doubts of the association of man and extinct fauna would be resolved. Up until the early man problem, mention of the Plains in terms of prehistory was insignificant indeed. Holmes described stone quarries in Oklahoma, Kansas, Texas, and Wyoming in 1919, and at the same time George Will and others were making archaeological investigations along the Missouri River. Mounds in the Dakotas and Manitoba were described around the turn of the century by Montgomery and Comfort. Gilder in Nebraska and Udden in Kansas were also excavating and publishing results at that time. Simms visited and briefly described a "wheel-shaped stone monument" in northern Wyoming in 1903. There were others, but most are little more than casual observations of obvious and interesting features, and none were based on any detailed excavation.

The Colorado Museum of Natural History occupied an important position in the development of Plains archaeology through early man studies. Harold Cook and J. D. Figgins were both paleontologists at that institution who were instrumental in bringing about the acceptance of the association of extinct fauna and man. On the strength of the Long Wolf Creek finds near Colorado, Texas (Cook 1926) and the Folsom site in eastern New Mexico (Figgins 1927), the validity of early man in the New World became established, and within a few years the number of associations of extinct fauna and early man would proliferate with sites such as Lindenmeier (Roberts 1935, 1936), the Clovis sites (Cotter 1937), the Dent site (Figgins 1933), and many others. Complete summaries of the discoveries of this period have been made by

Wormington (1957) and Sellards (1952). Also of importance, as Wilmsen (1965:182) has noted, the Folsom discoveries resulted in the return of geologists to the study of early man, as reflected by the works of Bryan and Ray (1940), Bryan (1941), Antevs (1955), and in more recent years by that of Haynes (1964, 1969) and Leonhardy (1966).

With the establishment of man in the New World at an earlier date, Plains archaeology now became a status activity and was worthy of the attention of anthropologists. Notable among these was Frank H. H. Roberts, whose work at Lindenmeier remains even today as a model of excellence in field techniques and recording. Another was Edgar B. Howard, who attacked the early man problem from a definitely anthropological point of view (1935, 1936) and eventually (1943) did field work at the Finley site, from which the term Eden was derived.

The Plains were to continue much in the forefront of early man, or, as Roberts (1940) called it, Paleo-Indian, a term that has persisted to the present day. As more and more Paleo-Indian material appeared, it was obvious that more than one human group was involved and inevitable that a means of separation would be devised. Typology thus appeared as a fundamental part of Paleo-Indian studies. This topic is presented in detail by Wilmsen (1965:182–83), but several of the protagonists should be mentioned briefly. Renaud (1932) devised an oversimplified typology based on two major categories, fluted and nonfluted. Renaud, however, thought the Folsom type later than Yuma on the basis of surface collections and not field work. Roberts' (1936) reports on Lindenmeier were quite conclusive that the Yuma was a later survival than Folsom, and in 1941 a conference was held in Santa Fe to attempt to bring some order into typology.

Several suggestions were made at the Santa Fe conference and although the problems of typology were not resolved, it was decided the term "Folsom" would now include those showing the characteristics of the Folsom,

New Mexico, material, and "Clovis fluted" and "Ohio fluted" would be applied to other fluted types. The term "Yuma" was kept with the addition of the terms "Eden" and "Oblique" before it. Wormington later suggested that the term "Yuma" be dropped entirely and proposed a new classification. Krieger, at the Sixth Plains Archaeological Conference in 1948, proposed a general sequence for projectile points in North America based on a typology of outline forms. Krieger's studies of typology reached its final expression in 1954 (Suhm, Krieger, Jelks 1954).

Paleo-Indian work on the Plains has continued with a number of important sites and people. Some of these include the Scharbauer site (Wendorf et al. 1955), the Horner site (Jepsen 1953), the Olsen-Chubbock site (Wheat 1967), the Lime Creek sites (Holder and Wike 1949) (Davis 1953), the Simonsen site (Agogino and Frankforter 1960), the MacHaffie site (Forbis and Sperry 1952), and the Hell Gap site in southeastern Wyoming, on which a major report is now in press.

Paleo-Indian studies and the associated personalities have in many ways constituted an area of operation that has often been separate from other areas of interest. There is a feeling of distinction expressed when the investigator is able to say that he is working with Paleo-Indian and a feeling of emotion and reverence in dealing with the older material. Typological studies of Paleo-Indian projectile points are more meaningful than in many other contexts with a better chance of placing temporal and spatial limitations on the limited amount of cultural material recovered. Geology is vital to Paleo-Indian studies, and most geologists are understandably more concerned with rates of deposition and chronology of events rather than with defining cultural systems. Interest has developed also quite understandably in the technological production of the Paleo-Indian material. As a result, there is often the feeling that Paleo-Indian studies exist parallel with other studies. It is, however, encouraging to see that functional typologies of Paleo-Indian assemblages using varied and sophisticated methods of analysis are beginning to provide more anthropologically oriented interpretations.

RIVER BASIN SALVAGE IN ARCHAEOLOGY

With the emphasis on hydroelectric power, water storage, recreation facilities, and flood control, the retention of large bodies of water behind artificial dams began to cover significant land areas. The land covered in this way included probably as much as 80 percent of the archaeological remains, and it was becoming obvious that a large share of history and prehistory would be lost if serious attempts at salvage archaeology were not made before the areas were inundated. As a result, the term "river basin archaeology" became a byword in the profession, and it was probably the greatest single influence in the development of Plains archaeology. The program was funded through agencies of the federal government and was carried out with the cooperation of locally qualified institutions wherever and whenever possible. A summary of development and philosophies of different agencies involved has been presented by Brew (1947). During the period of World War II, a number of large-scale reservoir projects were being planned. The Corps of Engineers and the Bureau of Reclamation called upon the National Park Service, who in turn called upon the Smithsonian Institution to handle the archaeological end of the work. Frank H. H. Roberts was appointed the National Director of River Basin surveys and Waldo Wedel was designated to organize the Missouri River project. The River Basin that affects the Plains is the Missouri, and this survey was the first to be gotten under way in 1946 (Wedel 1946). The Missouri River Basin covers over five hundred thousand square miles, approximately one-sixth of the continental United States, and includes most of the central, northwestern, and northeastern subareas. More than one hundred reservoirs were planned, some quite large. The first problem was to establish priorities, especially in the areas where construction was imminent or already under way. Actual survey work began on August 3, 1946, with three field parties of two men each in thirty-four top-priority sites for a period of about eight weeks. At least 170 sites were reported, but it was immediately obvious that anything approaching a complete survey was impossible during this short a period with so few persons. With the construction of the dam sites progressing at the present rate, Missouri River Basin salvage for archaeology was a race against time.

In the next three years after its inception in 1946, the Missouri River Basin program continued with the usual number of problems—mostly the familiar lack of funds to implement archaeological programs commensurate with the rapidity at which dam construction was progressing. During this period the field headquarters and laboratory were provided by the University of Nebraska through the efforts and recommendation of John L. Champe. Besides the Director, Waldo Wedel, persons on the staff included Paul L. Cooper, Wesley L. Bliss, Marvin F. Kivett, Jack Hughes, and Richard P. Wheeler, all names familiar to Plains archaeologists. In addition to work by these persons, several state agencies also contributed to the effort. These included the University of Kansas, under the direction of Carlyle S. Smith; Montana State University, under the direction of Carling Malouf; the University of Nebraska, under John Champe, Joyce Wike, C. B. Schultz, W. D. Frankforter, and Preston Holder; the Nebraska State Historical Society, under Marvin F. Kivett; and the University of North Dakota, under Gordon Hewes.

Paul Cooper became field director of the Missouri River Project in 1950, and Ralph O. Brown took over that position in 1952. Robert L. Stephenson was promoted to chief in 1954 and remained at this position until 1964, when he replaced Frank H. H. Roberts, who was forced to take sick leave; Warren H. Caldwell in turn replaced Stephenson. The project was always hampered by lack of funds, but still it was able to expand into a large operation in terms of archaeological work. For example, in 1964 there were twenty-four field parties in operation. There were, in addition, a large number of persons of importance to Plains archaeology whose efforts are too numerous to cover but whose work can be found by reference to the *Bibliography of Salvage Archaeology in the United States* (Petsche 1968).

The Smithsonian Missouri River Basin project discontinued its formal operations in 1968. During its existence of twenty-two years, it dominated activities in Plains archaeology. With the large dams along the Missouri River, including Garrison in North Dakota and Oahe and Fort Randall in South Dakota, the Missouri Trench resembles a long, narrow lake; this has been where a large share of the Missouri River Basin money and effort has been expended, and rightly so. The *Bulletin of the Bureau of American Ethnology* has been an outlet for publication of results. Another series appeared in 1966 entitled *River Basin Surveys, Publications in Archaeology,* and both sources have produced an impressive amount of literature on Plains archaeology. The end of the Missouri River Basin project was not the end of salvage archaeology but merely a shifting of operations to different directing agencies.

Salvage archaeology has, therefore, dominated the study of Plains prehistory for over two decades, and this leaves many feelings of ambiguity toward the subject. "Salvage archaeology" is precisely what the term implies. It is impossible to work in the proper operational environment when the water is slowly creeping toward the trenches. It is known at the time that the interpretations will have to be made on the basis of one investigation that is being speeded up, since there will very likely not be a chance to go back later and do further sampling after a chance to analyze and assimilate the first results. Realizing that what will be known depends on what can be salvaged in an inadequate period, the investigator operates in a situation whereby his or her research is not always subject to the necessary follow-up studies. Salvage archaeology is too often not good archaeology, but it is better than no archaeology at all. Unfortunately, the syndrome of salvage archaeology has pervaded the thinking in Plains archaeology and has largely become the methodology applied to all situations. Salvage has therefore been both a good and a bad influence in the development of Plains archaeology. With this as a background, the development of Plains archaeology can perhaps be better understood.

THE CENTRAL PLAINS

The central Plains cover a broad area from western Iowa and Missouri across the entire states of Nebraska and Kansas to the foot of the Rocky Mountains in eastern Colorado and the southeastern corner of Wyoming. William D. Strong (1935), who came to the University of Nebraska in 1929, summarized the early archaeological work in Nebraska, including that of E. H. Barbour, C. Bertrand Schultz, Earl H. Bell, Robert F. Gilder, Charles R. Keyes, and Fred H. Sterns, to mention a few of the more important names. The publication is actually a source book for work done in Plains archaeology to that date. Gilder worked during the first two decades of the present century in the archaeologically rich area of eastern Nebraska, especially near Omaha. Strong and Sterns both worked in the stratified Walker Gilmore site from which the Stern Creek (Plains Woodland) and Nebraska cultures were identified. Strong's own work in extreme western Nebraska on top of Signal Butte was especially significant. This stratified site with three levels of post-altithermal occupation has been used in interpretation of culture sequence for the central and northwestern Plains. Strong devised a projectile point typology based on outline form and proposed also a valid culture sequence for the central Plains. Keyes, through surveys and studies of local collections, perceived the existence of several archae-ological manifestations including the familiar Oneota and Mill Creek. Barbour and Schultz described the fossil bison and associated projectile points from the Scottsbluff Bison Quarry. It was at this period of the early 1930s that Waldo R. Wedel, the present central figure of Plains anthropol-ogy, began his long and distinguished career with field work in Nebraska and Kansas.

The influence of William D. Strong continued and the University of Nebraska in Lincoln remained the major center of development for Plains archaeology. A follow-up to Strong's (1935) work was the volume by Earl H. Bell (1936), with articles on various parts of the state by persons such as Paul Cooper, Marion Dunlevy, John Champe, G. H. Gilmore, and Willem Van Royen. Early work in the rock shelters of western Nebraska was done by Robert Cape and Earl Bell. Prepottery remains were scarce, but significant work in this field was Kivett's (1958:337) work at Logan Creek. Kivett has been a regular contributor to Plains-Woodland studies (Hill and Kivett 1940; Kivett 1952). Other Plains-Woodland and Upper Republican Ceramic sites extended into eastern Colorado and southeastern Wyoming. First mention of pottery in this area was by Renaud (1931, 1932, 1933) in his archaeological surveys of Colorado and Wyoming. Work in the western Nebraska rock shelters by Bell and Cape (Bell 1936) yielded pottery. John Champe, who came to the University of Nebraska in 1940, published his significant investigations at the stratified site of Ash Hollow Cave in western Nebraska (Champe 1946). Later work in sites yielding central Plains ceramics in Colorado was done by Cynthia and Henry Irwin (1957, 1966).

There were later cultural groups to be found in the central Plains. The Dismal River manifestation, accepted as protohistoric Plains Apache, is best known from the work of Hill and Metcalf (1941), Champe (1949), and Gunnerson (1960). Pawnee archaeology has been pre-sented by Wedel (1936), and from his and other studies, the Pawnee are generally conceded to be directly descended from the Lower Loup earth lodge dwellers.

The archaeology of Kansas, until quite recently at least, had almost been the exclusive domain of Waldo Wedel. In his monograph (1959) on Kansas archaeology he noted that no other state was so little known archaeologically or ethnologically when he began field work in 1936. Previous work had been little and much earlier, and none had been by professionals. Wedel gives a summary of this (1959:82–89) and was complimentary of Udden for his work in central Kansas at Paint Creek Village before 1900. Other early investigations in Kansas that should be mentioned are those of Martin on an association of extinct bison and projectile point that was found in 1895, and a later investigation of a Pueblo ruin by Williston and Martin (1900). Wedel (1959:95–96) mentions also early survey work in eastern Kansas by Sterns and Fowke.

Wedel's monograph was based on surveys and field work in 1937, 1939, and 1940. It is more than an introduction to Kansas archaeology and is actually a synthesis of the archaeology of the central Plains, although this was not his first attempt in this direction. Wedel has, in addition, been a pioneer in studies of human ecology for the Plains, and he also documented the western extensions of Hopewell in Missouri. In recent years, work in the central Plains has been greatly intensified through the federal salvage operations and work by various state institutions.

THE MIDDLE MISSOURI

In archaeological terms, the Middle Missouri refers to the Missouri River trench through North and South Dakota. To the west, a number of rivers such as the Knife, Heart, Grand, and White extend back into the high Plains, while east of the Missouri is glaciated country, and the drainage pattern as well as the topography are quite different.

Archaeological interpretations for this area are in debt to the early travelers in the area. Sieur de la Verendrye gave a valuable account of the Mandans in 1738, during their heyday, before their decimation by smallpox. Verendrye came overland and although he was quite disappointed in the Mandans, he left accounts of them valuable for prehistoric cultural interpretations.

The Missouri River offers a natural access route to the Plains, and the next visitors of importance were Lewis and Clarke in 1804. These journals are filled with material used by archaeologists, especially concerning the location of Mandan and Arikara sites at that time. A number of explorers, fur traders, naturalists, missionaries, and others left records of their travels and experiences, all of which have been carefully researched for anything of value to archaeological interpretation. A list of these persons would include Alexander Henry in 1806, George Catlin in 1833, Maximilian in 1833–34, Edward Harris in 1843, and Lewis Henry Morgan in 1859. Ethnographic analogy is especially useful in interpreting late prehistoric period archaeological materials on the Plains, and the investigator constantly refers to this body of historic material. In the Plains, especially, it is difficult to perceive a dividing line between history and prehistory.

The development of systematic archaeology in the Middle Missouri is almost synonymous with the name of George F. Will and others associated with him. Will and Spinden performed archaeological work in a number of earth lodge villages in 1905, and their results remain basic reference today. Much of their interpretation as to identification of villages was based on historical accounts from those mentioned above. Will's interest in the Middle Missouri was to continue with publications appearing as late as 1944 (Will 1933, Will and Hecker 1944, Will and Hyde 1917).

Strong (1940) published a progress report on the northern Plains, which he limited to North and South Dakota. At this time there was surprisingly little to add to Will's work except for unpublished archaeological work by the North Dakota Historical Society, the University of South Dakota Museum, the South Dakota Historical Society, and Columbia University. Several of Strong's graduate students were to become prominent in Plains archaeology, including Carlyle Smith, Preston Holder and Albert C. Spaulding, who later published a monograph on the 1939 field work at the Arzberger site (Spaulding 1956). Other persons active in Middle Missouri archaeology at that time were Alfred W. Bowers, E. E. Meleen, and W. H. Over. Bowers did field work among the Mandan and Hidatsa through the Logan Museum of Beloit College and the University of Chicago from 1929 through 1933. Archaeological work was done, along with ethnographic studies, and a synthesis of the results was later published (Bowers 1950). Both Meleen (1938), and Over did work at Mitchell, South Dakota, and Over (1936) worked in Ludlow Cave in western South Dakota, which is more in the area of the northwestern Plains.

All work after this was very much under the influence of the Missouri River Basin salvage program. Little in the way of Paleo-Indian material in any meaningful context has appeared in the Middle Missouri area, and even later prepottery sites have been largely neglected in the light of richer rewards in the earth lodge villages. Some Late Woodland materials and sites have been found and reported, including the Scalp Creek and Ellis Creek sites (Hurt 1952) along the Missouri River in southern South Dakota. In North Dakota, Woodland materials were recovered at Boundary Mound near Fort Yates (Wood 1960) and near Williston (Wood 1956).

As a result of the Missouri River Basin program, a number of people appeared on the scene who were to become significant in Plains archaeology. Donald J. Lehmer worked in the Oahe Reservoir during the early years of the salvage program. In publications of his results he has been criticized for application of the term "branch" to Middle Missouri archaeology and for other methodological tactics (Lehmer 1954). Nevertheless, he has earned the respect of other investigators and inspired the good students working in that area. Another central figure is W. Raymond Wood, who was in a position to begin on the ground floor of Missouri Trench archaeology and has produced an impressive list of research publications, which include his interpretations into Mandan culture history (1967). For a complete listing of Missouri Trench research publications, reference is once more made to Petsche's (1968) volume on sources for archaeological salvage work.

A new trend in archaeological studies appeared during recent years based on a different methodology, but using data already extant. This study, by James Deetz (1965), utilizing quantitative methods to determine degrees of attribute association, was never intended to be a definitive study but demonstrated that there may be different ways of handling archaeological material and using it to interpret nonmaterial items such as social organization. Studies such as these are adding exciting new dimensions to archaeology.

THE NORTHEASTERN PERIPHERY

To the person accustomed to the more westerly parts of the Plains, the area east of the Missouri River in the Dakotas, Minnesota, and Manitoba seem like a different world entirely. The prehistory of this area shows definite affinities eastward rather than to the Plains proper. A good share of the interest in this area by Plains anthropologists and archaeologists undoubtedly stems from the fact that some of the more important late Plains-dwelling tribes, including the various groups of Sioux, the Cheyenne, and the Assiniboine, came from or across here on their way westward. Before these late historical movements occurred, Middle Missouri inhabitants such as the ancestral Mandan must have crossed the same area, since their cultural affiliations are eastward and not to the west. It has been hedgingly suggested that some of the village sites east of the Missouri in North and South Dakota, Iowa, and Minnesota may actually be the evidence of the early Mandan peoples moving westward (Hurt 1951:24–25). Woodland groups before this also have eastward affiliations, so it remains an area quite different, and as Wedel (1961:110) says, it is marginal to the greater cultural area of the Plains, and it deserves his designation as the northeastern periphery.

The archaeological identification of historic tribes has long been a goal, and the results of the interaction of history and archaeology were well displayed in the Cheyenne site in the Cheyenne River near Lisbon, North Dakota. This site had been described earlier by George Grinnell (1918) and Will (1914). Strong excavated in this village (1940:370–76), and his results confirmed its identity as Cheyenne. This was important to Plains archaeology in demonstrating archaeologically the rapid culture change of a group who in the mid-eighteenth century were village horticulturalists and a half-century later were full-fledged nomadic Plains bison hunters. Along similar lines, the Assiniboine have been associated with the Manitoba mounds by comparison of archaeological mound burials at the Stott site with the historic accounts of Alexander Henry the Elder's (MacNeish 1954:47) description of Assiniboine burial practices. The location of the Stott village site was in Assiniboine territory, according to the accounts from La Verendrye's journals. An excellent synthesis of the early movements and interactions of the different tribes of the area has been compiled by Secoy (1953) in his study of Plains military patterns.

Principal archaeological features of the northeastern subarea include numbers of mounds of varying shapes and sizes, and boulder outlines of figures. These types of archaeological manifestations always intrigue people and lead to wide speculation. A good summary of these, with references to early descriptions and investigations, is given by Wedel (1961:215–34). Evidence that many of the mounds are quite late was presented by James Howard (1953) in demonstrating similarities between some of the art objects recovered in the North Dakota area with material of the Southern Ceremonial Complex and concluding that they were late by a drawing scratched on one that clearly resembles a horse.

The northern limits of Indian agriculture have been an intriguing problem of the northeast subarea. Bowers (1965:482) claims that the Hidatsa had traditions of a former agricultural life in the vicinity of Devils Lake. Will (1946:16) did a tree ring analysis of a stump taken from Stump Lake that was probably killed when lake levels rose, indicating that there had been some profound climatic change occurring. Further work in climatic studies of the area might be of value in resolving some late population migrations to the northwestern Plains.

No Paleo-Indian materials other than surface finds have been found in the area to date. Later archaeological manifestations dating to possibly 3000 B.C. have been described from stratified excavations (MacNeish 1958) and, although these sites are just outside of the northeastern subarea, they are without doubt of value for interpretations pertaining to it.

THE SOUTHERN PLAINS

The line separating the central and southern Plains is arbitrary and generally accepted as the Thirty-seventh Parallel, forming the northern boundaries of New Mexico and Oklahoma. The southern Plains include extreme eastern New Mexico, northern Texas, and most of Oklahoma. Situated with the southwestern area, the northeastern Mexico and Texas area, and the lower Mississippi Valley area nearly surrounding it (all of which are archaeologically rich in comparison to it), it is easy to comprehend why it was neglected during the earlier periods of investigation. The problem also exists as to just exactly where the boundary between Plains and the other archaeological areas should be placed, especially to the south and east, and since the prehistoric cultural evidence changes rapidly as ecological conditions change, it is even more difficult to limit discussion to that of the southern Plains alone. Obviously, a careful evaluation of the development of southern Plains archaeology should be undertaken by someone who is more familiar with the area and the personalities concerned than is the writer.

The importance of this area in the early development of Paleo-Indian studies has already been discussed, and this has also overshadowed the cultures of the later periods on the southern Plains. However, in the light of Plains prehistory as a whole, it is fortunate that Castenada made the records he did of Coronado's journey to the Plains in 1541 (Winship 1904). Scanty as these accounts are, it gives the archaeologist a very limited but vitally important glimpse of the aboriginal Plains culture when it was untouched by the disastrous affects of European disruptions. Castenada's short but concise accounts of the Plains inhabitants' tents, dog traction, hunting, butchering, curing of meat, and their nomadic life following the buffalo are a part of every Plains archaeologist's background of knowledge. Later Spanish travelers such as Onate in 1599 added more increments of this kind of knowledge. Other travels of importance to archaeologists would have to include that of the Frenchman Tixier in 1840.

Although archaeology has proliferated in the southern Plains during recent years (as in all other areas because of increased salvage work and other reasons), the early developments were dominated by only a few personalities, and the problem of even these few is that most of the work was concentrated in areas peripheral to the Plains. Alex D. Krieger, who has already been mentioned in the context of Paleo-Indian studies in the area, was certainly the central figure. His work in classifying and establishing cultural chronologies and integrating these with adjacent areas was a major and significant contribution (Krieger 1946, 1947). This was expanded later into the *Handbook of Texas Archaeology*, which was designed for the use of professional and amateur alike (Suhm, Krieger, and Jelks 1954). Others that should be mentioned are Robert E. Bell and David A. Baerreis (1951) for their *Survey of Oklahoma Archaeology*.

Krieger settled finally on a series of stages, which includes the Paleo-American (he objects to Paleo-Indian), Archaic, Neo-American, and Historic. Archaic are non-pottery materials, which are scarce on the High Plains of the Llano Estacado, with the exception of a few bison kills and camp sites (Hughes 1955, Tunnell and Hughes 1955). More recently what appears to be of importance to Plains archaeology is the Bonfire Shelter just across the Pecos River and between the Edwards and Stockton Plateau (Dibble and Lorain 1967), which has late Archaic and Paleo-Indian levels, and which the authors postulate were the result of buffalo jumping. Farther to the east Krieger includes a number of Archaic materials in the Edwards Plateau Aspect. Preceramic materials are common to northeastern Oklahoma (Baerreis 1951), but this is not in a Plains context.

Krieger's Neo-American stage includes pottery-bearing manifestations, which are found over most of the area. Most important are the Antelope Creek focus to the northern part and the Henrietta focus, located more to the south. As in other parts of the Plains, historic accounts are of value to archaeologists. A summary of the historical tribal movements for the southern Plains can be found in Secoy's monograph (1953) *Changing Military Patterns on the Great Plains*.

Salvage programs have been activated in this area as well as in the rest of the Plains. Although none have affected as large an area as the Missouri River Basin project, they are nonetheless important. Reference to the *Bibliography of Salvage Archaeology in the United States* (Petsche 1968) reveals a surprising amount of work in Oklahoma and Texas by a number of investigators, some of which is pertinent to the southern Plains area.

THE NORTHWESTERN PLAINS

This is the largest subarea of the Plains and includes most of Montana and Wyoming, the southern parts of Alberta and Saskatchewan, and the western edge of the Dakotas. Contained within these boundaries are a wide variety of land forms and vegetation zones. The Plains are broken by a number of smaller mountain ranges, such as the Laramie and Big Horn Mountains close to the Main Rocky Mountain front, and other uplifts, such as the Black Hills and Cypress Hills, farther into the Plains. Grasslands dominate most of the area, although there are arid intermontane basins such as the Big Horn Basin, with annual precipitation as low as six inches. Bison herds were common to the entire area, although the more northerly parts in Montana and Canada supported more because of better grass conditions.

In historic times it was the home of many familiar tribes, including the Sioux, Crow, Blackfeet, Cheyenne, Arapahoe, Shoshoni, Assiniboine, and Cree. Only in the posthorse period was the area a culture center based on buffalo exploitation, and this disappeared almost overnight in the early 1880s when the buffalo were decimated and the tribes forced on reservations.

Aside from brief mention of stone quarries and medicine wheels, systematic archaeology got a late start in the area except for the Paleo-Indian sites already mentioned. It was observed by Strong (1940:356) in his assessment of the northern Plains at that time that the area under consideration here was relatively unknown archaeologically. Until quite recently, few persons have expressed more than a passing interest in the archaeology of the area, mostly because rewards are few measured against efforts expended. The most common archaeological features are literally thousands of stone circles sealed with tough plains sod that yield frustratingly small amounts of material and information. After a short experience in this type of archaeology, the investigator is ready to move on to greener pastures.

The first systematic work of any consequence was done by William T. Mulloy, who established a chronological framework for the northwestern Plains based largely on work in Pictograph Cave, a deep, stratified site near Billings, Montana, and on comparisons with other sites in and adjacent to the Plains. Although much has been done since, Mulloy's framework has proven valid. His cultural sequence is based on an early prehistoric (Paleo-Indian) period followed by a dry altithermal period, with little or no evidence of habitation, beginning about 5000 B.C. and ending about 2500 B.C. Following this is a middle prehistoric period (Plains Archaic), ending about A.D. 500, with an early and late division. This is followed by the late prehistoric period, lasting until historic times. Mulloy has been a prolific worker and sound theorist in Plains archaeology. He has worked on the problem of pottery that appears late in the area (1942, 1953), and he also did salvage work for the National Park Service under the Missouri River Basin project (1954a, 1954b, 1965).

Stone circles have long been a subject of controversy in the light of little interpretive evidence. A number of archaeologists, including Mulloy (1965:48–50), Kehoe (1960), Malouf (1961), and Hoffman (1953), have speculated on their true nature. At almost any place on the northwestern Plains they may be found singly or in groups of a hundred or more. Some are apparently quite old, and others are recent. Some are obviously the base surrounding a temporary lodge structure, while most offer no clue whatsoever as to their function. They will undoubtedly continue to be matters for speculation for years to come.

The subject of buffalo procurement has been of paramount importance to the northwestern Plains. The writer postulated, without fear of contradiction, that a person can stand on the Wyoming-Colorado border and look from one buffalo jump, trap, or pound to another continuously to the forests of Canada. The varied topography allowed the use of many landforms favorable to communal hunting techniques. Only recently have intensive studies of buffalo procurement sites been initiated. Barnum Brown (1932) superficially investigated and reported buffalo jumps along the Yellowstone River in Montana. Forbis (1960) worked in a stratified buffalo jump in Alberta, with evidence of a late Archaic use at the bottom. In 1962 a symposium on buffalo jumps was organized and held by the Montana Archaeological Society, with a panel of archaeologists and ethnologists including Richard Forbis, Carling Malouf, Claude Schaeffer, Dee Taylor, Josephine Medicine Crow, George Arthur, and Stuart Conner (Malouf and Conner 1962). It had positive results in focusing interest on the problem, and in recent years large-scale excavations have started to appear at buffalo procurement sites (Frison 1967, 1970; Kehoe 1967). This remains a prime area for further developments in Plains archaeology.

Archaeology in the Canadian Plains has been at much the same pace as farther south. A survey of much of this work is to be found in William C. Noble's contribution to this volume.

Much of northwestern Plains archaeology concerns the historic tribes. John C. Ewers has contributed much to this area of research through editing and synthesis of journals and other historic materials. His monograph on the Blackfoot (1955), along with many others, is a standard source for archaeologists, along with Secoy (1953) for sources of material pertaining to Plains Indian warfare.

A recent development in the northwestern Plains is confirmation of long-suspected habitation centered along and in the mountains bordering the eastern edge of the area (Wedel, Husted, and Moss 1968; Husted 1969:83). These mountain and mountain-Plains border occupations suggest an orientation toward the environmental niche fringing the Plains and beginning at least as far back as the plano period and continuing through the altithermal period, when evidence for occupation of much of the Plains away from the mountains is scanty. With these and other problems, future developments on the northwestern Plains hold considerable interest.

THE PLAINS ANTHROPOLOGICAL CONFERENCE

The Plains being large and sparsely populated, with universities and other institutions that harbor archaeologists few and far between, it was necessary to have some sort of rallying point, and this was eventually provided by the Plains Anthropological Conference. Its beginnings, as might be expected, were unspectacular, and the circumstances of its origin were reported very briefly in *Nebraska History Magazine* (anonymous 1932). A systematic organization for archaeological work began under the auspices of the Smithsonian Institution in 1930, with Carl E. Guthe as general director for the Mississippi Valley and William D. Strong, who was at the University of Nebraska at that time, as director for the Nebraska and Plains area.

The first official conference of Plains archaeologists was held in September 1931, at Vermillion, South Dakota. No numbers of attendance were given, but it was remarked that, though small, interest was great. The next meeting was held in September of the following year at Lincoln, Nebraska, and was called by a committee appointed the year before and consisting of Earl H. Bell of Lincoln, Charles R. Keyes of Mount Vernon, Iowa, and George Will of North Dakota. The registrants numbered twenty-eight and included a significant number of all Plains anthropologists and archaeologists at that time. It was described as larger than the first meeting, and even greater interest was expressed than for the one held the preceding year. The second day of the meeting was devoted to a number of addresses, including those by William D. Strong, E. H. Barbour, A. T. Hill, Charles R. Keyes, Melvin R. Gilmore, S. C. Dellinger, and others prominent in the early development of Plains archaeology.

The third Plains Conference was held in Mount Vernon, Iowa, in 1936, and the fourth was held in Norman, Oklahoma, in 1940. After this, due initially to World War II, there was a lapse of seven years without a conference. Finally, because of increasing activities and a general feeling among Plains anthropologists of a need and desire to resume, the fifth Plains Conference was held in Lincoln, Nebraska, with eighty-one registrants; the Plains Conference continued to meet there annually until 1960, when it was held once more in Norman, Oklahoma.

At the fifth Plains Conference in 1947, a publication was set up under the title of the *Plains Anthropological Newsletter,* with Jesse D. Jennings as editor. It contained news of the annual conferences and short articles on various aspects of Plains archaeology and ethnology. The proceedings of the Sixth Plains Conference, published as No. 11 of the *University of Utah Anthropological Papers,* has been mentioned before as a provocative meeting, during which problems of typology were discussed (Jennings 1950).

In 1951 Franklin Fenenga became editor of the *Newsletter* and took over in this capacity when the journal, the *Plains Anthropologist,* became a reality in 1954. Attendance at the Plains Conference was sixty-five in 1954 and only forty-nine in 1955, but it has steadily grown until it is at present around the two hundred mark, and it has been necessary to resort to concurrent sessions at the annual meetings.

Publication of the *Plains Anthropologist* faltered with No. 8 in 1957 but was resumed in 1960 with James B. Schaeffer as editor; it has been a viable publication since then. Robert Stephenson was elected editor for a short period in 1963, and the job was then taken over by Warren W. Caldwell, director of the Smithsonian River Basin

Project at Lincoln, Nebraska. In 1968, the home of the journal was moved to the University of Kansas at Lawrence, and Alfred E. Johnson became editor. The journal has been expanded to accommodate a larger number of papers and, to date, a total of six memoirs have also been published. Both the Conference and journal have had an important influence on Plains archaeology in the thirteen states and three Canadian provinces comprising the area. Of equal importance, the Plains Anthropological Conference has constituted a medium where two generations of students in Plains archaeology have faced their baptism of fire for entry into the professional world, and the *Plains Anthropologist* has provided an outlet for publication of their findings.

THE NONPROFESSIONAL IN PLAINS ARCHAEOLOGY

The amateur archaeologists have been important in the development of Plains archaeology, although their efforts have not all been on the positive side. Every professional spends some time contemplating the amateur problem. Amateurs form a broad spectrum, from those on one end whose contributions are very much on the positive side to those on the other end who do real damage. In between, however, is a large group that can be of positive value if properly handled. With greater amounts of leisure time, more and more people will continually become interested in archaeology. The only hope and solution is that their interest can be channeled in the proper direction.

Nearly every professional in the Plains, who operates to any extent in the field, maintains contacts with amateurs who function as informants for locations of archaeological sites and materials. These persons are relied upon more than most professionals care to admit. Since the Plains are relatively short in population and long on land areas, lacking anything resembling adequate surveys, the

professional is forced to rely on amateurs for his information. Alex Krieger has acknowledged the importance of
amateurs to Texas archaeology (Suhm, Krieger, and Jelks
1954:7–10) and stated guidelines for their activities.
Wormington expressed much the same ideas in brief but
certain terms (1959). Much of the negative activity of the
amateurs cannot be condoned under any circumstances,
but still the professional has to keep the communication
lines open and at the same time proselytize the amateurs
to his point of view. Collecting is a state of mind, and the
value of an item has to be established. This has forced
some collectors to go to the professionals for help. In this
way a number of valuable sites have come to light and,
occasionally, a collector has been elevated to a better
position by discovering that a worthwhile contribution carries more personal rewards than acquisition of collector's
items. Once the amateurs realize that there are levels at
which they can participate and receive a measure of recognition for their efforts, they can be valuable additions
to inadequate staffs.

Several Plains states have large, viable, chartered archaeological societies that have been strong factors in
promulgating archaeological programs, not only in surveys
and field work, but also in promoting favorable legislation.
A check of the literature will show that many of the sites
that have been important in development of Plains archaeology were discovered and brought to the attention of
professionals by amateurs. Their role has been one of significance.

CONCLUSIONS

To summarize briefly, Plains archaeology first came into
prominence as the result of the discovery of human artifacts in unquestionable association with extinct fauna, indicating an earlier presence of man in the New World
than had previously been proven to everyone's satisfac-

tion. This was not because the Plains were the only province of early man, but rather because it was here that climatic and geological conditions had been more favorable for the necessary conditions of deposition and erosion that left the evidence in meaningful contexts. The earlier discoveries were understandably dominated by the paleontologists and geologists, and this still remains true to an extent. The result has been that early man or Paleo-Indian studies developed as almost a separate tradition in American and Plains archaeology.

The other area of interest in Plains archaeology was at the other end of the spectrum chronologically and centered around the rather spectacular events concerned with the posthorse Plains Indian tribes. Archaeologists specializing in this area of research were forced to operate more in the context of ethnohistorical studies. This resulted in a sharp contrast between the two specializations.

In the period shortly before and during World War II, there arose the realization of a need for archaeological salvage work ahead of the construction of large hydroelectric and flood-control projects that were to destroy forever a significant share of Plains prehistory. This resulted in a program, beginning in 1946, that in many ways shaped the further development of Plains archaeology. Federal agencies that controlled the sources of funds became involved and salvage became a methodology, the results of which were not always the best, but that were the best under the existing circumstances. It also centered the main focus of Plains archaeology in the larger, more spectacular earth lodge villages along the Missouri River, which were most in danger of destruction. At the same time, the Plains Anthropological Conference and its associated journal, the *Plains Anthropologist,* became a medium for the expression of mutual solidarity and also for the expression of divergent views. Today, however, with the expansion of anthropology departments in colleges and universities in the Plains area, research is being expanded to include problems that have been largely ignored in the urgency of salvage operations.

REFERENCES

AGOGINO, G. A., and FRANKFORTER, W. D.
    1960   "A Paleo-Indian Bison-Kill in Northwestern Iowa." *Am. Ant.* 25:414–15.

ANONYMOUS
    1932   "Prehistoric Man in Nebraska and the Great Plains Region." *Nebraska Hist. Mag.* 13:160–65.

ANTEVS, ERNEST
    1955   "Geologic-Climatic Dating in the West." *Am. Ant.* 20:317–35.

BAERREIS, D. A.
    1951   "The Preceramic Horizons of Oklahoma." *Anthro. Pap. Mus. Anthro. Univ. Mich.* 6.

BELL, EARL H.
    1936   *Chapters in Nebraska Archaeology* Vol. 1. University of Nebraska Press.

BELL, ROBERT E., and BAERREIS, DAVID A.
    1951   "A Survey of Oklahoma Archaeology." *Bull. Texas Arch. and Paleont. Soc.* 22:7–100.

BOWERS, ALFRED W.
    1950   *Mandan Social and Ceremonial Organization.* University of Chicago Press.
    1965   "Hidatsa Social and Ceremonial Organization." *Bureau of Am. Eth. Bull.* 194.

BREW, JOHN OTIS
    1947   "Symposium on River Valley Archaeology." *Am. Ant.* 12(4):209–25.

BROWN, BARNUM
    1932   "The Buffalo Drive." *Nat. Hist.* 32:75–82.

BRYAN, KIRK
    1941   "Correlation of the Deposits of Sandia Cave, New Mexico, with the Glacial Chronology: Evidences of Early Occupation in Sandia Cave, and other Sites in the Sandia-Manzano Region." *Smith. Misc. Coll.* 99(23):45–64.

——— and RAY, LOUIS L.
    1940   "Geologic Antiquity of the Lindenmeier Site in Colorado." *Smith. Misc. Coll.* 99(2):1–76.

CHAMPE, JOHN L.
    1946   "Ash Hollow Cave." *Univ. Nebraska Stud.* New Series 1.
    1949   "White Cat Village." *Am. Ant.* 14:285–92.

COOK, HAROLD J.
1926 "The Antiquity of Man in America." *Sci. Am.* 135:334–36.

COTTER, JOHN L.
1937 "The Occurrence of Flints and Extinct Animals in Pluvial Deposits Near Clovis, New Mexico." *Proceed. Acad. Nat. Sci. Phil.* 139:1-16.

DAVIS, E. MOTT
1953 "Recent Data from Two Paleo-Indian Sites on Medicine Creek, Nebraska." *Am. Ant.* 18:380–86.

DEETZ, JAMES
1965 "The Dynamics of Stylistic Change in Arikara Ceramics." *Ill. Stud. Anthro.* 4.

DIBBLE, DAVID S., and LORRAIN, DESSAME
1968 "Bonfire Shelter: A Stratified Bison Kill Site, Val Verde County, Texas." *Misc. Pap. Texas Mem. Mus.* 1.

EWERS, JOHN C.
1955 "The Horse in Blackfoot Indian Culture." *Bureau of Am. Eth. Bull.* 159.

FIGGINS, JESSE D.
1927 "The Antiquity of Man in America." *Nat. Hist.* 27:229–39.
1933 "A Further Contribution to the Antiquity of Man in America." *Proceed. Colorado Mus. Nat. Hist.* 12(2):4–8.

FORBIS, RICHARD G.
1962 "The Old Women's Buffalo Jump, Alberta." *Nat. Mus. Can. Bull.* 180:56–123.

——— and SPERRY, J. D.
1952 "An Early Man Site in Montana." *Am. Ant.* 18:127–32.

FRISON, GEORGE C.
1967 "The Piney Creek Sites, Wyoming." *Univ. Wyoming Pub.* 33(1):1–93.
1970 "The Kobold Site, 24 BH 406: A Post-Altithermal Record of Buffalo Jumping for the Northwestern Plains." *Plains Anthro.* 15:1–35.

GRINNELL, GEORGE
1918 "Early Cheyenne Villages." *Am. Anthro.* 20:359–80.

GUNNERSON, JAMES H.
1960 "An Introduction to Plains Apache Archaeology—the Dismal River Aspect." *Bureau of Am. Eth. Bull.* 173:131–260.

HAYNES, C. VANCE
1964 "Fluted Projectile Points: Their Age and Dispersion." *Science* 145:1408–13.
1969 "The Earliest Americans." *Science* 166:709–15.

HILL, A. T., and KIVETT, M. F.
1940 "Woodland-like Manifestations in Nebraska." *Nebraska Hist. Mag.* 21:147–243.

180   GEORGE C. FRISON

—— and METCALF, GEORGE
    1941   "A Site of the Dismal River Aspect in Chase County, Nebraska." *Nebraska Hist. Mag.* 22:158–226.

HOFFMAN, J. JACOB
    1953   "Comments on the Use and Distribution of Tipi Rings in Montana, North Dakota, South Dakota, and Wyoming." *Montana State Univ. Anthro. and Soc. Pap.* 14:1–14.

HOLDER, PRESTON, and WIKE, JOYCE
    1949   "The Frontier Culture Complex, A Preliminary Report on a Prehistoric Hunter's Camp in Southwestern Nebraska." *Am. Ant.* 14:260–66.

HOWARD, EDGAR B.
    1935   "Evidence of Early Man in North America." *Mus. Journ.* 24:61–175.
    1936   "Early Man in America." *Proc. Am. Phil. Soc.* 76:327–33.
    1943   "The Finley Site." *Am. Ant.* 8:224–41.

HOWARD, JAMES
    1953   "The Southern Cult in the Northern Plains." *Am. Ant.* 19:130–38.

HUGHES, JACK T.
    1955   "Little Sunday, An Archaic Site in the Texas Panhandle." *Bull. Texas Arch. Soc.* 26:55–74.

HURT, WESLEY R., JR.
    1951   "Report of the Investigation of the Swanson Site, 39 BR 16, Brule County, South Dakota." *South Dakota Arch. Comm. Arch. Stud.* 3.
    1952   "Report on the Investigation of the Scalp Creek Site, 39 GR 1, and the Ellis Creek Site, 39 GR 2, Gregory County, South Dakota." *South Dakota Arch. Comm. Arch. Stud.* 4.

HUSTED, WILFRED M.
    1969   "Bighorn Canyon Archaeology." *River Basin Surveys Pub. in Salvage Arch.* 12.

IRWIN, CYNTHIA, and IRWIN, HENRY
    1957   "The Archaeology of the Agate Bluff Area, Colorado." *Plains Anthro.* 8:15–33.

IRWIN-WILLIAMS, CYNTHIA, and IRWIN, HENRY
    1966   "Excavations at Magic Mountain." *Denver Mus. Nat. Hist. Proc.* 12.

JENNINGS, JESSE D. (ed.)
    1950   "Proceedings of the Sixth Plains Archaeological Conference." *Univ. Utah Anthro. Pap.* 11:1–161.

JEPSEN, G. L.
    1953   "Ancient Buffalo Hunters." *Princeton Alumni Weekly* 53:10–12.

KEHOE, THOMAS F.
    1960   "Stone Tipi Rings in North Central Montana and the Adja-

cent Portion of Alberta, Canada: Their Historical, Ethnological and Archaeological Aspects." *Bureau of Am. Eth.
Bull.* 173:417–73.

1967   "The Boarding School Bison Drive Site." *Plains Anthro.
Mem.* 4.

KIVETT, MARVIN F.
1952   "Woodland Sites in Nebraska." *Nebraska State Hist. Soc.
Pub. in Anthro.* 1.
1958   "Notes and News." *Am. Ant.* 23:337.

KRIEGER, ALEX D.
1946   "Culture Complexes and Chronology in Northern Texas, with
Extension of Puebloan Datings to the Mississippi Valley."
Univ. Texas Pub. 4640.
1947   "The Eastward Extension of Puebloan Datings Toward Cultures of the Mississippi Valley." *Am. Ant.* 12:141–48.

KROEBER, ALFRED L.
1939   "Cultural and Natural Areas of Native North America."
Univ. Cal. Publ. Am. Arch. and Eth. 38.

LEHMER, DONALD J.
1954   "Archaeological Investigations in the Oahe Dam Area, South
Dakota, 1950–51." *Bur. Am. Eth. Bull.* 158.

LEONHARDY, FRANK C.
1966   "Domebo: A Paleo-Indian Mammoth Kill in the Prairie-
Plains." *Contrib. Mus. Great Plains* 1.

MACNEISH, RICHARD S.
1954   "The Stott Mound and Village, Near Brandon, Manitoba."
Nat. Mus. Can. Bull. 132.
1958   "An Introduction to the Archaeology of Southeast Manitoba." *Nat. Mus. Can. Bull.* 157.

MALOUF, CARLING
1961   "The Tipi Rings of the High Plains." *Am. Ant.* 26:381–89.

——— and CONNER, STUART
1962   "Symposium on Buffalo Jumps." *Montana Arch. Soc.
Mem.* 1.

MELEEN, E. E.
1938   "A Preliminary Report on the Mitchell Indian Village Site
and Burial Mounds, on Firesteel Creek, Mitchell, Davison
County, South Dakota." *South Dakota Arch. Comm. Arch.
Stud.* 2.

MULLOY, WILLIAM T.
1942   "The Hagen Site." *Univ. Montana Pub. in the Soc. Sci.* 1.
1953   "The Ash Coulee Site." *Am. Ant.* 19:73–75.
1954a "Archaeological Investigations in the Shoshone Basin of
Wyoming." *Univ. Wyoming Pub. in Sci.* 22(1):1–71.
1954b "The McKean Site in Northeastern Wyoming." *Southwestern
Journ. Anthro.* 10:432–60.

182   GEORGE C. FRISON

    1965   "Archaeological Investigations Along the North Platte River
            in Eastern Wyoming." *Univ. Wyoming Pub. Sci.* 31(2):23–51.

OVER, W. H.
    1936   "The Archaeology of Ludlow Cave and Its Significance."
            Am. Ant. 2:126–29.

PETSCHE, JEROME E.
    1968   "Bibliography of Salvage Archaeology in the United States."
            River Basin Surveys Pub. in Salvage Arch. 10.

RENAUD, ETIENNE B.
    1931   "Archaeological Survey of Eastern Colorado." Depart. of
            Anthro., Univ. of Denver.
    1932   "Yuma and Folsom Artifacts." *Proc. Col. Mus. Nat. Hist.*
            11(2):5–18.
    1933   "Archaeological Survey of Eastern Colorado, Third Report."
            Depart. of Anthro., Univ. of Denver.

ROBERTS, FRANK H. H., JR.
    1935   "A Folsom Complex: Preliminary Report on Investigations
            at the Lindenmeir Site in Northern Colorado." *Smith. Misc.
            Coll.* 94(4).
    1936   "Additional Information on the Folsom Complex." *Smith.
            Misc. Coll.* 95(10).
    1940   "Developments in the Problem of the North American
            Paleo-Indian." *Smith. Misc. Coll.* 100:51–116.

SECOY, FRANK R.
    1953   "Changing Military Patterns on the Great Plains." *Mono.
            of the Am. Eth. Soc.* 21. University of Washington Press.

SELLARDS, E. H.
    1952   *Early Man in America.* Austin: University of Texas Press.

SPAULDING, ALBERT C.
    1956   "The Arzberger Site, Hughes County, South Dakota." *Occas.
            Contr. Mus. Anthro. Univ. Mich.* 16.

STRONG, WILLIAM D.
    1935   "An Introduction to Nebraska Archaeology." *Smith. Misc.
            Coll.* 93(10).
    1940   "From History to Prehistory in the Northern Great Plains."
            Smith. Misc. Coll. 100:353–94.

SUHM, DEE ANN; KRIEGER, A. D.; and JELKS, E. B.
    1954   "An Introductory Handbook to Texas Archaeology." *Bull.
            Texas Arch. and Paleont. Soc.* 25.

TUNNELL, C. D., and HUGHES, J. T.
    1955   "An Archaic Bison Kill in the Texas Panhandle." *Panhandle-
            Plains Hist. Rev.* 28:63–70.

WEDEL, WALDO R.
    1936   "An Introduction to Pawnee Archaeology." *Bureau of Am.
            Eth. Bull.* 112.

1947 "Prehistory and the Missouri Valley Development Program: Summary Report on the Missouri River Basin Archaeological Survey in 1946." *Smith. Misc. Coll.* 107(6).

1959 "An Introduction to Kansas Archaeology." *Bur. of Am. Eth. Bull.* 174.

1961 *Prehistoric Man on the Great Plains.* Univ. of Oklahoma Press. Norman.

———; HUSTED, W. M.; and Moss, J. H.
1968 "Mummy Cave: Prehistoric Record from Rocky Mountains of Wyoming." *Science* 160:184–86.

WENDORF, FRED; KRIEGER, A. D.; ALBRITTON, CLAUDE C.; and STEWART, T. D.
1955 *The Midland Discovery.* Univ. of Texas Press. Austin.

WHEAT, JOE BEN
1967 "A Paleo-Indian Bison Kill." *Scient. Am.* 216:44–52.

WILL, GEORGE F.
1914 "The Cheyenne Indians in North Dakota." *Proceed. Mississippi Valley Hist. Assoc.* 7:67–78.

1933 "A Résumé of North Dakota Archaeology." *North Dakota Hist. Quart.* 7:150–61.

1946 "Tree Ring Studies in North Dakota." *Ag. Exp. Stat. North Dakota Ag. Col. Bull.* 338.

——— and HECKER, THAD C.
1944 "The Upper Missouri River Valley Aboriginal Culture in North Dakota." *North Dakota Hist. Quart.* 11:5–126.

——— and HYDE, G. E.
1917 *Corn Among the Indians of the Upper Missouri.* St. Louis: W. H. Miner Co., Inc.

WILLEY, GORDON R.
1966 *An Introduction to American Archaeology,* Vol. 1. Englewood Cliffs, New Jersey: Prentice-Hall.

WILLISTON, S. W., and MARTIN, H. T.
1900 "Some Pueblo Ruins in Scott County, Kansas." *Kansas Hist. Coll.* 6:124–30.

WILMSEN, EDWIN N.
1965 "An Outline of Early Man Studies in the United States." *Am. Ant.* 31:172–92.

WINSHIP, G. P.
1904 *Journey of Coronado.* New York: A. S. Barnes & Co.

WISSLER, CLARK
1907 "Diffusion of Culture in the Plains of North America." *Proc. Fifteenth Int. Cong. Americanists:*39–52.

WOOD, W. RAYMOND
1956 "A Woodland Site Near Williston, North Dakota." *Plains Anthro.* 6:21–24.

1960 "The Boundary Mound Group (32SII): An Eastern Woodland Complex in North Dakota." *Plains Anthro.* 10:71–78.

1967 "An Interpretation of Mandan Culture History." *Bureau Am. Eth. Bull.* 198.

WORMINGTON, H. M.

1957 "Ancient Man in North America." *Col. Mus. Nat. Hist. Pop. Ser.* 4.

1959 "The Amateur Archaeologist." *Southwestern Lore* 25:1–3.

7 THE SOUTHWEST AND INTERMONTANE WEST

Arthur H. Rohn

Evidences of past human occupations in the American Southwest have been apparent to the earliest travelers and settlers of European origin. Arid conditions contributed to remarkable preservation of both structures and usually perishable materials. Thus, when interest in studies of the precolumbian cultures of the New World began to develop, early attention was devoted to the Southwestern ruins.

The Intermontane West lacked comparably spectacular remains, despite its aridity. Prehistoric peoples there did not build similar large villages of durable construction, nor did they manufacture large quantities of painted pottery. Because of this, intermontane archaeology has for the most part lagged behind work in the Southwest to the extent that, until recently, numerous Southwesternists have viewed the Intermontane West as a "northern periphery." However, we now recognize distinctive culture histories in this area, each with its own peculiar set of interrelationships.

A detailed account of the development of archaeological studies in the Southwest and Intermontane West would be both long and dull. Consequently, I will focus attention on those events and developments that have exerted some lasting influence on our knowledge of culture history in these areas or on the practice of archaeology in general. My selection of events will be arranged around topical interests, rather than in a strict chronological order.

In tune with the training of most professional archaeologists, the beginning chapters of many major mono-

KEY

1. Lindenmeier
2. Folsom
3. Pecos
4. Navajo Reservoir
5. Mesa Verde
6. Chaco Canyon
7. Bat Cave
8. Canyon de Chelly
9. Awatovi
10. Tsegi Canyon
11. Glen Canyon
12. Fremont sites
13. Danger Cave
14. Tule Springs
15. California desert sites
16. Point of Pines
17. Snaketown
18. Ventana Cave
19. Casas Grandes

The Southwest and Intermontane West

graphs describing the results of field work in the South-west contain sketches of the previous archaeological work in that area. In several instances the "area" included all possibly related districts or similar materials. Frank H. H. Roberts (e.g. 1929, 1932, 1935) and Harold Gladwin (e.g. 1945) regularly surveyed the past and present of ar-chaeological research in their respective areas with each successive major report of field activities. Perhaps the most thorough such history was done by J. O. Brew (1946) for the Colorado Plateau country. In light of such practice, little need existed for separate histories until the post-World War II data boom forced scholars to constrict the borders covered by their introductory historical sketches. As it turned out, many of these scholars were relatively young and newly trained. They lacked first-hand knowl-edge of many of the events that shaped their own training patterns. And, when the elder statesmen of Southwestern archaeology began to pass away, little formal attention was given to historical development of the discipline.

Following the discovery and early explorations of pre-historic Southwestern sites, a relative flood of reseachers began collecting information to answer questions posed by the initial observations. During this process, considerable attention was paid to developing sound field techniques and devising new ways to increase the kinds of data ob-tainable. Many students and workers from other areas were brought to the Southwest for training. However, be-cause there were already many qualified scholars working there and answering questions, and because many other parts of the world appeared to be "virgin territory" in which a young archaeologist could make his fame, almost none of the younger persons continued his career in the Southwest. The area was considered a "squeezed orange" by both students and their advisers, thereby discouraging nearly a full generation of archaeologists from undertak-ing Southwestern archaeology.

As this became apparent, several of the surviving "grand old men" began setting down some of their reminiscences

—Kidder (1958), Gladwin, Judd (1968), Colton. Close attention was also focused on preserving the notes and papers of some who had recently died. Several publications have resulted from material salvaged from Earl Morris's files (e.g. Carlson 1963, 1965) and a biography of his life has been written (Lister and Lister 1968).

EARLY EXPLORATION

Much of the Southwest belonged to Spain and then Mexico until the middle of the nineteenth century. Although the Spaniards were remarkable explorers and colonizers, their chronicles deal mostly with descriptions of the lands and the peoples inhabiting them. Even when they exhibited a humanistic interest in alien customs, any historical curiosity probed only oral traditions. The Mexicans were too busy with domestic affairs and the administration of their outlying provinces to devote scientific energies to historical questions other than their own. Only on occasion did Spanish travelers, such as Kino, report the presence of old ruins, and then often as temporary shelter for themselves.

With the Gadsden Purchase by the United States, the discovery of gold in California, and the Mormon migration to Utah, early American explorers focused attention on geographic features, which to them included the remains of past occupants of these lands. The earliest explorers who recorded their observations were mostly military men. While on a military campaign against the Navajos in 1849, Lieutenant James Simpson wrote descriptions of ruins in Chaco Canyon and Canyon de Chelly (Simpson 1850).

When gold and silver were discovered in the Rockies and copper in Arizona, new lands had to be administered, colonized, and in many instances pacified. Most surveying and exploration parties included both military personnel and some scientifically educated men who either began recording observations as they traveled or interested others in doing so. The United States Geological and Geographical Survey of the Territories under F. V. Hayden included extensive descriptions of both ruins and artifacts from Colorado and New Mexico by William H. Jackson and W. H. Holmes (Jackson 1876, 1878; Holmes 1878, 1886). Collections made from Southern California and the New Mexico Pueblos by United States Geographical Surveys west of the one-hundredth Meridian under Lieutenant George M. Wheeler were described and analyzed by Frederick Ward Putnam of Harvard's Peabody Museum.

Major John Wesley Powell provided a remarkable impetus to the scientific explorations of the West with his trip down the Green and Colorado rivers in 1869. He became the first chief of the United States Bureau of American Ethnology in 1879. In this position he encouraged and supervised such early archaeological works as Victor Mindeleff's *Study of Pueblo Architecture* (V. Mindeleff 1891) and Cosmos Mindeleff's two works on *Casa Grande Ruin* (C. Mindeleff 1896b) and the Verde Valley (C. Mindeleff 1896a), in addition to the invaluable record of American Indian cultures and languages.

Private financing supported several early explorations among the Southwest's spectacular antiquities. Considerable impetus was provided by the scientifically untrained but remarkably astute Wetherill brothers of Mancos, Colorado (McNitt 1957). Under sponsorship of the Hyde Exploring Expedition, the Wetherills conducted extensive surveys and excavations from 1893 through 1903 in Grand Gulch, Utah; Tsegi Canyon, Arizona; and Chaco Canyon, New Mexico where major work was done in Pueblo Bonito (Pepper 1920). The Hemenway Southwestern Archaeological Expedition opened up central Arizona from the Verde Valley to Casa Grande (Bandelier 1890; Fewkes 1898). Gustav Nordenskïold came from Sweden to finance his own work on the Mesa Verde in 1891 that resulted in one of the finest monographs ever produced (Nordenskïold 1893). T. Mitchell Prudden from New York began his work with a broad survey of sites in the San Juan drainage (Prudden 1903), followed by many years of small-scale excavations in small Pueblo sites in the northern San Juan region.

INTENSIVE DATA COLLECTING

Once knowledge of the extensive remains of past occupants in the Southwest had spread, attention was turned to systematically learning about them and their ways of life. Many institutions throughout the country sponsored field work, and several in the Southwest were established primarily to conduct field investigations.

Agencies of the United States government continued to support active archaeology through the Smithsonian Institution and the Bureau of American Ethnology. With the establishment of Mesa Verde National Park in 1906, Jesse Walter Fewkes was assigned the task of opening many of the ruins for public visitation. He excavated many of the major cliff dwellings—Cliff Palace, Spruce Tree House, Square Tower House, Oak Tree House, Fire Temple, and the like—and began intensive work in sites on the mesa top, such as Far View House, Pipe Shrine House, Sun Temple, and the first Basket Maker III pithouse (actually excavated by his assistant, Ralph Linton). At the same time, Fewkes set several precedents in the business of exhibiting prehistoric sites to the interested public.

From 1915 through 1923, the United States National Museum sent Neil Judd to survey and excavate sites throughout Utah, from the Great Salt Lake to the Grand Canyon, and to repair the large cliff dwelling, Betatakin, in Navajo National Monument, for public visitation. Aside from the spotty attention to archaeological remains given by early explorers, such as the Hayden Survey, Judd conducted the first systematic work in the Intermontane West.

In the Chaco Canyon, with the assistance of the National Geographic Society, Judd directed an intensive campaign of survey and excavations from 1920 through 1927. Pueblo Bonito, the largest known pueblo ruin, received the most attention (Judd 1954, 1964), but important ancillary studies attempted to date the sites through tree-rings (Douglass 1935) and examined the environment and geology affecting the site and its former inhabitants (Bryan 1954).

The Peabody Museum of Harvard and the Peabody Foundation of Phillips Academy, Andover, Massachusetts, supported the remarkable work of Alfred Vincent Kidder in the Four Corners and at Pecos. With Samuel Guernsey, he surveyed and excavated in the general vicinity of Kayenta from 1914 through 1917 (Kidder and Guernsey 1919; Guernsey and Kidder 1921). With each season, Kidder gained additional information and insight into the broad cultural history of the Four Corners that was to culminate in the Pecos Classification. While Guernsey continued to investigate the Kayenta region through 1923 (Guernsey 1931), Kidder had begun to focus his attention on Pecos Pueblo in 1915, where he completed a total of ten seasons through 1929.

Kidder's impact on prehistoric studies extended far beyond the Southwest. He adopted the stratigraphic method introduced by Nels Nelson in the Galisteo Basin, and while refining the technique at Pecos, he trained numerous archaeologists, who later worked in other parts of North America. Throughout the Pecos Ruin, he excavated according to natural accumulation layers and the order of construction. In the twenty-six-foot-deep refuse deposit, where no natural layers were visible, Kidder employed arbitrary excavation levels, from which he developed a very usable seriation of changing ceramic styles (Kidder and Amsden 1931; Kidder 1936). Similar but less complex seriations were also outlined for stone and bone artifacts (Kidder 1932).

Although much of the financial support still emanated from eastern and midwestern sources, several local centers of archaeological work sprang up within the Southwest. The Museum of New Mexico was founded in Santa Fe in 1909 under the direction of Edgar L. Hewett. Byron Cummings moved to the University of Arizona from Utah in 1915 and developed a Department of Anthropology. A similar unit grew at the University of New Mexico. In 1928, three nonarchaeologically trained people instigated the founding of important centers of research activity in Arizona: Harold S. Colton, a zoologist, settled in Flagstaff, where he organized the Museum of Northern Arizona; and Harold S. Gladwin, a onetime stock broker, and his wife began restoration of Gila Pueblo near Globe, Arizona, as a museum and research center.

From this nucleus, the balance of archaeological sponsorship shifted rapidly to institutions located within the Southwest, even though several locally raised and trained workers, such as Earl H. Morris, continued under sponsorship of eastern institutions.

The many individuals who worked or received experience in Southwestern archaeology during this stage include such names as Alfred L. Kroeber, Leslie Spier, Ralph Linton, Sylvanus G. Morley, Earnest A. Hooton, George C. Vaillant, Ralph Beals, George Brainerd, and Julian Steward.

This same period saw the commencement of intensive archaeological work in the Intermontane West. Its prehistoric remains were far less attractive than those of the Southwest until the recognition of much earlier occupations. During the late 1920s and the 1930s, M. R. Harrington of the Southwest Museum in Los Angeles identified sites and complexes affiliated with Pleistocene events (e.g., Gypsum Cave—Harrington 1933). Judd's pioneer investigations of the later cultures, such as Promontory and Fremont, were continued by John Gillin, Julian Steward (1937), and Noel Morss (1931).

World War II interrupted, but did not halt, the process of assembling primary survey and excavation data and refining both local and regional sequences, especially represented by ceramics and architecture. The hub of activity definitely shifted to the locally based institutions, which became active in field school training activities and salvage archaeology in addition to basic research. The intensive collection of primary data still constitutes a major portion of Southwestern and Intermontane archaeology, even though contemporary field workers emphasize additional goals.

SYSTEMS FOR ORGANIZING DATA

When data and knowledge accumulate at such a rate that scholars can no longer keep up with current developments readily, some system of abstraction of the data becomes desirable. The first informal conference held at Pecos in 1927 was stimulated by such a need. A. V. Kidder invited the archaeologists then working in the Southwest to gather at the site of Pecos Pueblo, New Mexico, at the end of the field season. The conferees agreed on some common terminology and on a system of categorization for Puebloan culture history that has been designated the Pecos Classification (Kidder 1927).

The Pecos Classification consists of a series of eight numbered stages covering approximately two thousand years of cultural development. With slight modifications and greatly expanded descriptions of cultural content, many Southwesternists still use this system as a framework within which to discuss Pueblo culture history. Neither the basic concepts, nor the terminology, nor the cultural descriptions were entirely new, but the Pecos conferees achieved a consensus view that remained flexible enough to absorb much new information from subsequent work.

Still, the Pecos Classification has two major shortcomings. It cannot be readily applied to the several non-Puebloan cultures—e.g., Hohokam, Mogollon, Sinagua, Patayan—known from the central and southern regions of the Southwest, where the cultural manifestations are often quite different from Puebloan materials. Nor is it precise enough for detailed studies in districts of the Puebloan subarea itself. Each stage rarely exists in all regions at exactly the same time period due to cultural lag, and occasionally transitional occupations occur.

Partly in response to these problems, Harold S. Gladwin proposed a biological model for ordering different levels of congruence in archaeological data (Gladwin and Gladwin 1934). Gladwin's scheme took the general form of a tree with roots composed of several stems, which in turn were composed of several branches in which were found sequences of phases. Architectural patterns and ceramic styles identified the phases. Branches possessed a strong geographic identity. Stems have always been somewhat amorphous. Roots expressed the separate cultural traditions that Gladwin had effectively contrasted only a short time earlier—the Hohokam and Anasazi (Pueblo). The obvious difficulties inherent in the application of a biological model to problems of human culture have resulted in the virtual cessation of any use of the concepts of root and stem. The geographic strictures built into the branch concept have made it hard to use, although some workers continue to do so. The identification of cultural phases, and their arrangement into sequences, have become major research activities during the past three decades.

In northern Arizona, Harold S. Colton (1939) attempted to improve on the Gladwins' system by incorporating some ideas from the Midwestern Taxonomic Method. He adopted the concept of *focus* in place of phase in order to encompass all known aspects of culture in the unit description, and he recognized the *component* as the manifestation of a given focus at one site. Colton recognized four cultural roots: Anasazi, Hohokam, Mogollon, and Patayan.

On a different level, the great masses of pottery fragments from Southwestern sites required a systematic approach to ceramic studies. Although several approaches were tried, the type classification system has remained the most viable. It has been best described by Lyndon L. Hargrave and Harold Colton (Colton and Hargrave 1937; Colton 1953), although considerable variation has always occurred among individual archaeologists. One group viewed a pottery type as an "ideal" in the potter's mind that she strove to achieve, while others considered a type to consist of a group of specimens that clustered within a relatively narrow range of variation among numerous characteristics of pottery vessels. Still others defined type as a stage along the continuum of a stylistic seriation of ceramic change (e.g., Haury in Gladwin, et al. 1937). From all approaches, an extensive body of named pottery types and type descriptions has emerged.

Seriation as a technique has also enjoyed a long history. Kroeber (1916) and Spier (1917) both constructed simple seriations of surface pottery collections to arrange sites near Zuni, New Mexico, in chronological order. With the rapid growth of type descriptions and well-dated type distributions, surface collections of pottery fragments can often provide surprisingly accurate temporal placement.

Closely related to the work of ceramic classification has been a variety of technological studies related to pottery manufacture. In conjunction with his work at Pecos Pueblo, Kidder asked Anna O. Shepard to analyze the physical properties of the paste, slips, and paints of the Pecos pottery (Shepard 1936). She soon was examining petrographic thin sections of ceramic specimens submitted by archaeologists working in many parts of the Southwest (e.g., Shepard 1939) and other areas of the world, especially Mesoamerica. This work culminated in a standard reference book for all students of prehistoric ceramics, *Ceramics for the Archaeologist* (Shepard 1956).

Of the many concepts that grew out of archaeological work in the Southwest and Intermontane West, only one other deserves separate treatment here. Jesse D. Jennings described the "Desert Culture" as a generalized adaptation to desert environments by foraging peoples through non-

selective utilization of all exploitable natural food resources (Jennings and Norbeck 1955; Jennings 1957).
Although first offered as an explanatory concept to encompass the long unchanging cultural sequence found in western Utah caves, Desert Culture is now frequently used to
describe the pre-agricultural, preceramic cultural stage
found throughout western North America, even though
numerous manifestations along rivers and the coast hardly
occupied desert areas.

ANTIQUITY OF MAN IN THE NEW WORLD

Certainly the most important single event relevant to
the age of human occupation in the entire New World was
the discovery in 1926 of human-made tools in unquestionable association with extinct Pleistocene fauna near
Folsom, New Mexico. Since the Folsom projectile points
exhibited a very distinctive fluting on one or both faces,
additional sites became relatively easy to recognize. Fluted
projectile points, of the Folsom type and related forms,
became the most reliable marker artifacts for Paleo-Indian
occupations in North America.

As additional early man complexes were described from
sites in the eastern Southwest and the western Great
Plains, clear stratigraphy at Blackwater Draw near Clovis,
New Mexico, and in Sandia Cave, also in New Mexico,
established the chronological sequence of a tradition of big
game hunters. The oldest Llano Complex was marked by
Clovis Fluted points and Sandia points, the subsequent
Lindenmeier Complex by Folsom Fluted points, and the
youngest Plano Complex by numerous large unfluted
points.

However, many sites in the western Southwest and the
Great Basin produced materials that did not easily fit into
the Llano-Lindenmeier-Plano sequence of the High Plains
and the eastern Southwest. Yet geological associations and
scattered radiocarbon dates indicated roughly equivalent

antiquity, and even led to numerous claims of much greater age. Over the past forty years some workers have almost seemed to be in competition to find and/or recognize the earliest human remains in North America.

Amid a rash of reports and claims, some field work had lasting importance. Elizabeth and William Campbell, Charles Avery Amsden, and M. R. Harrington delineated such ancient lithic complexes as Lake Mohave (Campbell and Campbell 1937, Amsden 1937), Pinto Basin (Campbell and Campbell 1935), and Borax Lake (Harrington 1948), associated with topographically old features in the California desert. Although some of these complexes have subsequently been reassigned to more recent periods, their definition has remained useful. Harrington also investigated cave sites, among them Gypsum Cave (Harrington 1933), where distinctive projectile points and wooden dart shafts were associated with extinct ground sloth dung, all of which has subsequently been radiocarbon dated about 8500 B.C.

In 1941 and 1942, E. W. Haury directed excavations in the deep, stratified deposits of Ventana Cave located in the desert of southern Arizona (Haury, et al. 1950). Not only were ancient human artifacts clearly associated with Pleistocene fauna in the deepest deposits, but these were covered by a refuse accumulation representing essentially continuous occupation from an early post-Pleistocene Desert Culture to protohistoric Desert Hohokam. More recently, Haury documented two important mammoth kill locations in southern Arizona at Naco (Haury 1953) and Lehner (Haury 1956) belonging to the Llano Complex.

The important site at Tule Springs near Las Vegas, Nevada, was originally investigated by Harrington and his associates at Los Angeles Southwest Museum (Harrington 1934, 1954, 1955). Simple camp remains, crude flake tools, an absence of distinctive projectile points, and an unexpectedly early radiocarbon determination inspired broad disagreements on the antiquity of man in North America. The great extent of the site prompted Richard

Shutler to assemble a multidisciplinary excavation team, including heavy road machinery, to cut deep mile-long trenches for geological and archaeological evaluations, which clarified the stratigraphic relationships and recognized the presence of lignitized wood (dead carbon) that could be confused with charcoal.

The associations of human remains with Pleistocene geologic deposits and features drew quick attention from two noted Pleistocene geologists, who firmly established geochronological methods of dating in North American archaeology. Kirk Bryan of Harvard and Ernst Antevs of Globe, Arizona, produced assessments of the geological associations and ages of most early man finds in the Southwest and western Plains prior to the mid-1950s (e.g., Bryan 1937, 1941; Bryan and Ray 1940; Bryan and Toulouse 1943; Antevs 1935, 1952, 1953). Antevs ultimately described the geologic-climatic method of dating (Antevs 1955).

Among the significant follow-ups to Bryan and Antevs was the establishment of the Geochronology Laboratory at the University of Arizona by Terah L. Smiley in 1957. Smiley has attempted to correlate many of the specialized techniques available for chronological studies of both human and recent geological events in an effort to circumvent obstacles formed by traditional discipline boundaries (Smiley 1955).

PALEOECOLOGY

Despite frequent references to the newness of ecological studies in prehistory, especially with the development of new techniques for the recovery of ecological information, many of the pioneer archaeologists had displayed remarkable ecological insights. For example, Gustav Nordenskïold analyzed thin sections of stone and pottery in 1892 (Nordenskïold 1893), Cosmos Mindeleff described the relation of prehistoric irrigation ditches and horticulture in the Verde Valley (C. Mindeleff 1896a), and T. Mitchell Prudden plotted site distributions relative to stream valleys in the San Juan drainage (Prudden 1903).

Although many subsequent archaeologists appeared oblivious to ecological relationships, a few recognized regular processes in the natural environment as potential keys to dating. Primary stimulus came from an astronomer striving to answer questions unrelated to archaeology. Andrew Ellicott Douglass was seeking to relate cyclic climatic episodes on Earth to periods of sunspot activity. Since long weather station records were unavailable he sought to discover suitable climatic records in nature—in the annual growth rings of certain trees. As he first correlated ring width and moisture in the arid Southwest, and then sought progressively older specimens—first in historic sites, then in prehistoric sites—the capability for dating prehistory through dendrochronology developed.

Douglass began his work at the Lowell Observatory in Flagstaff, Arizona, and moved to the University of Arizona in 1906. Following his dramatic success in dating prehistoric ruins, he founded the Laboratory of Tree-Ring Research in 1938. While continuing to provide tree-ring dates for archaeologists, the laboratory also conducts multidisciplinary studies focused on past climates as recorded by annual growth rings.

At Flagstaff both Colton and John C. McGregor began organizing their published reports of field work along basic ecological lines, devoting attention to foodstuffs and sources of raw material. Lyndon L. Hargrave, with training as an ornithologist, launched himself on a full-blown program analyzing bird bone and feather remains from archaeological sites.

One of the earliest multidisciplinary team approaches was Harvard's Peabody Museum Expedition to Awatovi in 1935–39 under the directorship of J. O. Brew. Specialists included architect Ross Montgomery, zoologist Barbara Lawrence, ethnobotanist Volney Jones, and geologist John Hack. Hack's report, "The Changing Physical Environment of the Hopi" (Hack 1942) ranks among the best environmental works.

As we have already seen, paleoecology also prospered within studies of early man in the New World. By the 1950s, the mold was cast for growing numbers of increasingly complex ecological approaches. Perhaps the most elaborate of all to date has been the joint National Park Service-National Geographic Society Wetherill Mesa Archeological Project in Mesa Verde National Park, Colorado, from 1959 through 1965 (Osborne 1964).

RECENT APPROACHES

Intensive collection of data has continued to the present and is still actively pursued, although along somewhat altered lines. The conditions favoring optimal preservation combined with an extensive array of published field work reports provide an unusual background for research aimed at answering specific problems about demography, ecological adaptations, prehistoric social organization, culture change, and the like. Many new programs rely heavily on comparability with other work. Regional chronologies are available in considerable detail for most regions and are easily correlated with one another through intrusive pottery fragments. Even with the most sophisticated techniques available, it would take many years of intensive work in a new area to achieve a similar store of knowledge.

Perhaps the most promising results will emerge from the relatively long-term programs within relatively small districts. The University of Arizona has combined student field training with such a program at Point of Pines in east-central Arizona from 1946 through 1962, and at Grasshopper, to the northwest, from 1963 to the present. The Point of Pines work produced important chronological refinement for the early Mogollon (Wheat 1955), new awareness of economic activities (Woodbury 1961), and striking documentation of social processes (Haury 1958).

At Grasshopper, quantitative techniques are being used to reconstruct aspects of social organization.

The Field Museum of Natural History in Chicago has been concentrating its field research activities in the upper Little Colorado River drainage of east-central Arizona since 1956. Problems such as population dynamics, environmental influences on subsistence, and cultural change have recently dominated their work (e.g. Martin, Longacre, and Hill 1967), which also contains a heavy quantitative orientation. There are several other similar programs in other regions, on more modest scales, employing different methods and ideas. Yet most workers are now focusing on similar or related problems.

Following World War II, the Southwest also benefited from the rapid growth in awareness of the need for salvage archaeology. As did many other states, Arizona and New Mexico appointed state archaeologists to handle emergency work created by new federal highway construction. With the expansion of oil prospecting, Dr. Jesse L. Nusbaum assumed leadership in encouraging the oil companies to provide funds for salvaging sites in pipeline right-of-ways.

Again, as in other areas, construction of reservoirs prompted archaeological salvage activities. The largest of these were operated in the area to be flooded by Lake Powell behind the Glen Canyon Dam on the Colorado River. The University of Utah and the Museum of Northern Arizona have cooperated in producing one of the most complete publication records in the United States. The Museum of New Mexico salvage project in the Navajo Reservoir on the San Juan River set a fine example in orienting the salvage work toward answering significant questions about the prehistoric human ecology of that district (Dittert, Hester, and Eddy 1961).

Other salvage work has been sponsored for land areas in northern Arizona slated to be damaged by mining activities and by the location of utility lines. Urban renewal in Tucson allowed salvage teams to rescue information on

the old historic settlement there before new building construction covered the site.

Because such a large proportion of all western lands is
owned by the United States government, several federal
agencies have had to manage archaeological resources
along with their other operations. The National Park Service has fostered archaeological field work in its primarily
archaeological areas since its inception in 1906. Prior to
the mid-1950s, the great bulk of this work was done by
non-Park Service employees. However, since then, the
Service has mounted many of its own research and development programs with its own professional staff. Most
of this work and staff has now been concentrated into a
Southwest Archeological Center that has also provided an
invaluable and unique service to Southwestern archaeologists by identifying animal and bird remains from prehistoric sites.

In recent years, both the Bureau of Land Management
and the U. S. Forest Service have begun to inventory
archaeological resources on their lands and to plan development of some of these resources for public visitation. Perhaps the greatest benefit of these activities will be
protection of many sites from destruction through construction activities and illegal excavations.

SUMMARY

The remarkable preservation of usually perishable ancient remains in arid conditions has repeatedly spurred
both interest in and awareness of the pre-European occupants of the New World. The desire to protect and yet investigate the more spectacular of these remains led to the
enactment of a federal Antiquities Act in 1906 and to in-
clusion in the National Parks and Monuments System of
areas with primarily archaeological significance. Consequently, many exhibits in place have been developed

within these and similar state-operated areas for public enjoyment and education.

From the early years of the twentieth century, the Southwest has served as a major training ground for American archaeologists and anthropologists. Although many field workers, from Fewkes on, employed students and trainees as field assistants, two major programs especially had a strong impact on professionals and amateurs in addition to students: A. V. Kidder's work at Pecos and the University of New Mexico's field school and research program in Chaco Canyon. Today, more formal field schools are operated by more than a dozen institutions; trainee positions exist at several of the museums; and many classroom instructors from outside the area take classes on regular tours of the preserved sites.

Preservation in the Southwest has not been limited to material relics of the past. Even the layman can readily recognize the living Pueblo Indians—Tanoans, Keres, Zuni, and Hopi—as the cultural descendants of the prehistoric Anasazi of the Colorado Plateau by the houses they live in and their general way of life. This clear-cut continuity has provided the culture historian with a rare opportunity to combine the results of archaeology, ethnohistory, and ethnography into a story of cultural change and development covering some two thousand years. At the same time he can employ ethnographic data to help decipher some of the more inscrutable puzzles of prehistory.

Significant individual discoveries, other than the first visits of explorers to the sites, are relatively few. Unquestionably the clear association of human-made tools with extinct bison in geologic deposits near Folsom, New Mexico, revolutionized both thinking and subsequent approaches on studies of early man in the New World. A. E. Douglass's discovery of an ancient beam in a later prehistoric ruin near Showlow, Arizona, in 1929 linked an extensive floating tree-ring chronology to the present, thus furnishing an accurate means for dating many Southwestern sites. The recovery of an early pod corn from deep preceramic levels in Bat Cave, New Mexico, by Herbert Dick provided morphological clues to the question of the origin and domestication of *Zea mays*.

As we might expect, most significant contributions have resulted from painstaking work in extensive projects. Kidder's work at Pecos had a major impact in many directions: the refinement of stratigraphic methods, the development of ceramic stylistic seriation, the training of many workers, the link between prehistory and history, the employment of ceramic technological studies, the use of ethnographic analogy in interpretation, the inspiration for regular conferences of field workers, and on and on. Virtually all of Kidder's publications are models of clarity and interpretation.

Harold Gladwin's recognition of the Hohokam culture, marked by red-on-buff-colored pottery, in the desert regions of southern Arizona led to systematic surveys to delineate the geographic range of the distinctive pottery. Extensive excavations at the important site of Snaketown outlined Hohokam chronology and fostered the definitive work on Hohokam prehistory (Gladwin, Haury, Sayles, and Gladwin 1937).

In like manner, Harold Colton chose to concentrate his efforts on northern Arizona, especially around Flagstaff. Through the Museum of Northern Arizona, he correlated studies of prehistory, geology, botany, and zoology within this area. The museum's files contain some of the most complete records for any such region in the world.

Research on the Mogollon culture by Paul S. Martin of the Field Museum of Natural History concentrated in the Pine Lawn and Reserve regions of west-central New Mexico from 1939 to 1956. A long series of reports, published almost annually, documented in considerable detail Mogollon culture history.

The single most significant work in the Intermontane West was the excavation of Danger Cave in northwestern Utah by Jesse D. Jennings. From this study (Jennings

1957) emanated the concept of a Desert Culture and evidence of a long record of human occupation in the Great Basin from the end of the Pleistocene to the arrival of Europeans with almost no change.

Several specific techniques were produced or improved through Southwestern studies. Dendrochronology was invented by A. E. Douglass in Arizona. Geochronology developed out of the efforts of Bryan, Antevs, and Smiley. Stratigraphic methods were refined and taught by Nelson and Kidder after importation from the Old World. Ceramic analysis benefited from the carefully systematic approaches to classification by Colton and to technology by Shepard. Prehistoric human ecology has seen the cooperation of specialists in nonarchaeological disciplines.

Surprisingly few attempts have been made to discuss Southwestern prehistory in a single book. John McGregor's *Southwestern Archaeology* (1941) concentrates mostly on Arizona. H. M. Wormington's *Prehistoric Indians of the Southwest* (1947) offers general descriptive outlines of the culture sequences in Colton's four major subareas. Of these two, only McGregor's book has been updated (1965), although not modified greatly in format. Harold Gladwin synthesized his ideas in very readable style in *A History of the Ancient Southwest* (1957). By far the finest book was the first to appear: Kidder's *An Introduction to the Study of Southwestern Archaeology* (1924), which was reissued as a paperback (1962).

As background for expounding new theoretical ideas, several shorter reviews of prehistory in both the Southwest and Intermontane West have been written. Paul Kirchoff (1954) defined the Greater Southwest to include most of North America's desert lands from southern Oregon through northwestern Mexico, focusing especially on various economic adaptations in this zone. A special seminar convened by the Society for American Archaeology discussed the Southwest in terms of its relationships with surrounding areas (Jennings 1956). As a prelude to his study of pithouse architecture, William R. Bullard (1962) reviewed most Southwestern regional sequences, presenting several alternative interpretations to the Hohokam and Mogollon chronologies.

Future trends for archaeology in the Southwest and Intermontane West may be speculated from the emphases of present work. Ecological studies will undoubtedly continue and be elaborated. Increasing efforts will be aimed at answering demographic questions. More investigators will seek to reconstruct aspects of social organization from archaeological remains, some using quantitative techniques. More attention will be devoted to Mexico's northern states. Hopefully, all these activities can be undertaken before too many of the remaining archaeological sites have been destroyed by vandalism or the rapid growth of modern civilization.

REFERENCES

AMSDEN, CHARLES AVERY
   1937   "The Lake Mohave Artifacts." *Southwest Mus. Pap.* 11:51–97.

ANTEVS, ERNST
   1935   "The Occurrence of Flints and Extinct Animals in Pluvial Deposits near Clovis, New Mexico, Pt II, Age of Clovis Lake Beds." *Proc. Phil. Acad. Nat. Sci.* 87:304–11.
   1952   "Climatic History and the Antiquity of Man in California." *Univ. Cal. Arch. Survey Report* 16:23–29.
   1953   "Artifacts with Mammoth Remains, Naco, Arizona, II: Age of the Clovis Fluted Points with the Naco Mammoth." *Am. Ant.* 19:15–18.
   1955   "Geologic-climatic Dating in the West." *Am. Ant.* 20:317–35

BANDELIER, ADOLF F.
   1890   "Contributions to the History of the Southwestern Portion of the United States." *Pap. Arch. Inst. Am., Am. Series* 5.

BREW, JOHN O.
   1946   "Archaeology of Alkali Ridge, Southeastern Utah." *Pap. Peabody Mus. Am. Arch. Eth.* 21.

BRYAN, KIRK
   1937   "Geology of the Folsom Deposits in New Mexico and Colorado," *Early Man:*139–52. Philadelphia.
   1941   "Correlation of the Deposits of Sandia Cave, New Mexico,

with the Glacial Chronology: Evidences of Early Occupation in Sandia Cave and other Sites in the Sandia-Manzano Region." *Smith. Misc. Coll.* 99(23).

1954 "The Geology of Chaco Canyon, New Mexico, in Relation to the Life and Remains of the Prehistoric Peoples of Pueblo Bonito." *Smith. Misc. Coll.* 122(7).

—— and RAY, LOUIS L.
1940 "Geologic Antiquity of the Lindenmeier Site in Colorado." *Smith. Misc. Coll.* 99(2).

—— and TOULOUSE, JOSEPH H., JR.
1943 "The San Jose Non-Ceramic Culture and its Relation to Puebloan Culture in New Mexico." *Am. Ant.* 8:269–80.

BULLARD, WILLIAM R.
1962 "The Cerro Colorado Site and Pithouse Architecture in the Southwestern United States Prior to A.D. 900." *Pap. Peabody Mus. Am. Arch. Eth.* 44(2).

CAMPBELL, ELIZABETH W., and CAMPBELL, WILLIAM H.
1937 "The Lake Mohave Site in the Archaeology of Pleistocene Lake Mohave: A Symposium." *Southwest Mus. Pap.* 11:9–43.
1935 "The Pinto Basin Site." *Southwest Mus. Pap.* 9.

CARLSON, ROY L.
1963 "Basket Maker III Sites Near Durango, Colorado." *Univ. Col. Stud. Series in Anthro.* 8.
1965 "Eighteenth Century Navajo Fortresses of the Gobernador District." *Univ. Col. Stud. Series in Anthro.* 10.

COLTON, HAROLD S.
1939 "Prehistoric Culture Units and Their Relationships in Northern Arizona." *Mus. Northern Arizona Bull.* 17.
1953 "Potsherds." *Mus. Northern Arizona Bull.* 25.

—— and HARGRAVE, LYNDON L.
1937 "Handbook of Northern Arizona Pottery Wares." *Mus. Northern Arizona Bull.* 11.

DITTERT, ALFRED E., JR.; HESTER, JAMES J.; and EDDY, FRANK W.
1961 "An Archaeological Survey of the Navajo Reservoir District, Northwestern New Mexico." *Monog. School of Am. Res.* 23.

DOUGLASS, ANDREW ELLICOTT
1935 "Dating Pueblo Bonito and Other Ruins of the Southwest." *Nat. Geog. Soc. Contrib. Tech. Pap.* 1.

FEWKES, JESSE WALTER
1898 "Archaeological Expedition to Arizona in 1895." *Bur. of Am. Ethn. Seventeenth Annual Report, Part II.*

GLADWIN, HAROLD S.
1945 "The Chaco Branch; Excavations at White Mound and in the Red Mesa Valley." *Medallion Pap.* 33.
1957 *A History of the Ancient Southwest.* Portland.

———; HAURY, EMIL W.; SAYLES, E. B.; and GLADWIN, NORA
    1937   "Excavations at Snaketown, Material Culture." *Medallion Pap.* 25.

GLADWIN, WINIFRED, and GLADWIN, HAROLD S.
    1934   "A Method for the Designation of Cultures and Their Variations." *Medallion Pap.* 15.

GUERNSEY, SAMUEL J.
    1931   "Explorations in Northeastern Arizona. Report on the Archaeological Fieldwork of 1920–23." *Pap. Peabody Mus. Am. Arch. Eth.* 12(1).

——— and KIDDER, ALFRED V.
    1921   "Basket-maker Caves of Northeastern Arizona." *Pap. Peabody Mus. Am. Arch. Eth.* 8(2).

HACK, JOHN T.
    1942   "The Changing Physical Environment of the Hopi Indians of Arizona." *Pap. Peabody Mus. Am. Arch. Eth.* 35(1).

HARRINGTON, MARK R.
    1933   "Gypsum Cave, Nevada." *Southwest Mus. Pap.* 8.
    1934   "A Camel Hunter's Camp in Nevada." *The Masterkey* 8:22–24.
    1948   "An Ancient Site at Borax Lake, California." *Southwest Mus. Pap.* 16.
    1954   "The Oldest Camp-fires." *The Masterkey* 28:233–34.
    1955   "A New Tule Springs Expedition." *The Masterkey* 29:112–13.

HAURY, EMIL W.
    1936   "The Mogollon Culture of Southwestern New Mexico." *Medallion Pap.* 20.
    1953   "Artifacts with Mammoth Remains, Naco, Arizona, I: Discovery of the Naco Mammoth and the Associated Projectile Points." *Am. Ant.* 19:1–14.
    1956   "The Lehner Mammoth Site." *The Kiva* 21:23–24.
    1958   "Evidence at Point of Pines for a Prehistoric Migration from Northern Arizona," *Migrations in New World Culture History,* Raymond H. Thompson (ed.) 1–6.

——— and collaborators
    1950   *The Stratigraphy and Archaeology of Ventana Cave, Arizona.* Albuquerque: University of New Mexico Press.

HOLMES, WILLIAM H.
    1878   "Report on the Ancient Ruins of Southwestern Colorado, Examined during the Summers of 1875 and 1876." *United States Geolog. and Geog. Survey of the Territories for 1876:*383–408.
    1886   "Pottery of the ancient Pueblos." *Bur. Am. Eth., Fourth Annual Report:*257–360.

HOOTON, EARNEST A.
    1930   "The Indians of Pecos Pueblo." *Pap. Phillips Acad. Southwestern Exped.* 4.

JACKSON, WILLIAM H.
1876 "Ancient Ruins in Southwestern Colorado." *United States Geolog. and Geog. Survey of the Territories for 1874*:367–81.
1878 "Report on the Ancient Ruins Examined in 1875 and 1877." *United States Geolog. and Geog. Survey of the Territories for 1876*:411–50.

JENNINGS, JESSE D. (ed.)
1956 "The American Southwest: A Problem in Cultural Isolation." *Soc. Am. Arch. Mem.* 11.
1957 "Danger Cave." *Soc. Am. Arch. Mem.* 14.

—— and NORBECK, EDWARD
1955 "Great Basin Prehistory: A Review." *Am. Ant.* 21:1–11.

JUDD, NEIL M.
1954 "The Material Culture of Pueblo Bonito." *Smith. Misc. Coll.* 124.
1964 "The Architecture of Pueblo Bonito." *Smith. Misc. Coll.* 147(1).
1968 *Men Met Along the Trail.* Norman: Univ. of Okla. Press.

KIDDER, ALFRED V.
1924 "An Introduction to the Study of Southwestern Archaeology." *Pap. Phillips Acad. Southwestern Exped.* 1.
1927 "Southwestern Archaeological Conference." *El Palacio* 23:554–61.
1932 "The Artifacts of Pecos." *Pap. Phillips Acad. Southwestern Exped.* 6.
1936 "The Pottery of Pecos, Vol. II." *Pap. Phillips Acad. Southwestern Exped.* 7.
1958 "Pecos, New Mexico: Archaeological Notes." *Pap. Robert S. Peabody Found. for Arch.* 5.

—— and AMSDEN, CHARLES AVERY
1931 "The Pottery of Pecos, Vol. I." *Pap. Phillips Acad. Southwestern Exped.* 5.

—— and GUERNSEY, SAMUEL J.
1919 "Archaeological explorations in Northeastern Arizona." *Bureau of Am. Eth. Bull.* 65.

KIRCHOFF, PAUL
1954 "Gatherers and Farmers in the Greater Southwest: A Problem in Classification." *Am. Anthro.* 56:529–60.

KROEBER, ALFRED L.
1916 "Zuni Potsherds." *Anthro. Pap. Am. Mus. Nat. Hist.* 18(1).

LISTER, FLORENCE C., and LISTER, ROBERT H.
1968 *Earl Morris and Southwestern Archaeology.* Albuquerque: Univ. of New Mex. Press.

MARTIN, PAUL S.; LONGACRE, WILLIAM A.; and HILL, JAMES N.
1967 "Chapters in the Prehistory of Eastern Arizona, III." *Fieldiana: Anthro.* 57.

McGregor, John C.
1941   *Southwestern Archaeology*. New York: John Wiley & Son.
1965   *Southwestern Archaeology*. Second Edition. Urbana: Univ.
       of Ill. Press.

McNitt, Frank
1957   *Richard Wetherill: Anasazi*. Albuquerque. Univ. of New
       Mex. Press.

Mindeleff, Cosmos
1896a "Aboriginal Remains in the Verde Valley." *Bureau of Am.
       Eth. Thirteenth Annual Report*.
1896b "Casa Grande Ruin." *Bureau of Am. Eth. Thirteenth An-
       nual Report*.

Mindeleff, Victor
1891   "A Study of Pueblo Architecture: Tusayan and Cibola."
       *Bureau of Am. Eth. Eighth Annual Report:*3–228.

Morris, Earl H.
1928   "Notes on Excavations in the Aztec Ruin." *Anthro. Pap.
       Am. Mus. Nat. Hist.* 26(5).
1939   "Archaeological Studies in the La Plata District, South-
       western Colorado and Northwestern New Mexico"; with
       an appendix, "Technology of La Plata Pottery," by A. O.
       Shepard. *Carnegie Inst. Wash. Pub.* 519.

——— and Burgh, Robert F.
1941   "Anasazi Basketry, Basket Maker II Through Pueblo III. A
       Study Based on Specimens from the San Juan River Coun-
       try." *Carnegie Inst. Wash. Pub.* 533.
1954   "Basket Maker II Sites Near Durango, Colorado." *Carnegie
       Inst. Wash. Pub.* 604.

Morss, Noel
1931   "The Ancient Culture of the Fremont River in Utah." *Pap.
       Peabody Museum Am. Arch. Eth.* 12(3).

Nordenskiöld, Gustav
1893   *The Cliffdwellers of the Mesa Verde, Southwestern Colorado,
       their Pottery and Implements*. (D. Lloyd Morgan, trans.).
       Stockholm: P. A. Norstedt & Soner.

Osborne, Douglas
1964   "A Prologue to the Project." *National Park Service Ar-
       cheological Research Series* 7-A.

Pepper, George H.
1920   "Pueblo Bonito." *Anthro. Pap. Am. Mus. Nat. Hist.* 27.

Prudden, T. Mitchell
1903   "The Prehistoric Ruins of the San Juan Watershed in
       Utah, Arizona, Colorado, and New Mexico." *Am. Anthro.*
       5:224–88.

Roberts, Frank H. H., Jr.
1929   "Shabik'eschee Village: A Late Basket Maker Site in the

Chaco Canyon, New Mexico." *Bureau of Am. Eth. Bull.* 92.
1932 "The Village of the Great Kivas on the Zuni Reservation, New Mexico." *Bureau of Am. Eth. Bull.* 111.
1935 "A Survey of Southwestern Archaeology." *Am. Anthro.* 37:1–35.

SAYLES, EDWARD B., and ANTEVS, ERNST
1941 "The Cochise Culture." *Medallion Pap.* 29.

SHEPARD, ANNA O.
1956 "Ceramics for the Archaeologist." *Carnegie Inst. Wash. Pub.* 609.

SIMPSON, LIEUTENANT J. H.
1850 "Journal of a Military Reconnaissance from Santa Fe, New Mexico, to the Navajo Country." Reports of the Secretary of War, Senate Executive Document No. 64.

SMILEY, TERAH L. (ed.)
1955 "Geochronology." *Univ. Arizona Physical Sci. Bull.* 2.
1957 ."Climate and Man in the Southwest." *Univ. Arizona Bull.* 28(4).

SMITH, WATSON
1971 "Painted Ceramics of the Western Mound at Awatovi." *Pap. Peabody Mus. Am. Arch. and Eth.* 38.

SPIER, LESLIE
1917 "An Outline for a Chronology of Zuni Ruins." *Anthro. Pap. Am. Mus. Nat. Hist.* 18(3).

STEWARD, JULIAN H.
1937 "Ancient Caves of the Great Salt Lake Region." *Bureau of Am. Eth. Bull.* 116.

WHEAT, JOE BEN
1955 "Mogollon Culture Prior to A.D. 1000." *Soc. Am. Arch. Mem.* 10.

WOODBURY, RICHARD B.
1961 "Prehistoric Agriculture at Point of Pines, Arizona." *Soc. Am. Arch. Mem.* 17.

WORMINGTON, H. MARIE
1947 *Prehistoric Indians of the Southwest.* Denver Mus. Nat. Hist.
1955 "A Reappraisal of the Fremont Culture." *Denver Mus. Nat. Hist. Proc.* 1.

KEY

1. Auriferous gravels
2. Lower Sacramento River
3. Sacramento Delta
4. San Francisco Bay Shell Mounds
5. Sites in the Lodi region—Northern San Joaquin Valley
6. Santa Barbara Channel
7. San Diego Coast
8. Lake Mohave

California

8 CALIFORNIA

Claude N. Warren

Consistent and sustained interest in California prehistory commenced in the 1870s, a decade characterized by great collecting expeditions such as those led by Paul Schumacher and Count Leon de Cessac, when a series of papers was published describing the harvest of relics (Putnam 1879; Yates 1900; Meredith 1900). However, this characterization does not do justice to some areas of major influence. Although the archaeology of the day lacked any formal methodology, it was at least beginning to ask questions that would lead to its development.

This kind of relationship is most clearly illustrated by J. D. Whitney's attempt at dealing with the origin of man in California. *The Auriferous Gravels of the Sierra Nevada of California* (1879) represents the culmination of more than ten years' investigation of the geology of the gold deposits of central California. Whitney brought together evidence that man was contemporaneous with extinct fauna of the auriferous gravel, which dated back to the Tertiary Period. In this volume, for the first time, a substantial body of data was presented in a convincing manner under one cover. Consequently the publication was of considerable importance and certainly influenced the thinking of other workers in the area.

Even before Whitney's *magnum opus* was published, we find Putnam (1879:12) writing:

> As the archaeologist has no right to be governed by any preconceived theories, but must take the facts as he finds them, it is impossible for him to do otherwise than accept the deductions of so careful and eminent a geologist as Professor

Whitney, and draw his conclusions accordingly, not with-
standing the fact that this pliocene man was, to judge by his
works in stone and shell, as far advanced as his descendants
were at the time of the discovery of California by the
Spaniards.

Whitney's evidence consisted of a series of stone artifacts, identical in many instances to those used by historic
Indians of the region, found in the mines at varying depths
in tertiary gravels beneath a basalt cap; and a human skull
(the infamous Calaveras skull), reportedly from a mine
shaft at a depth of about 130 feet.

There was nothing seemingly impossible about the claim
of a fully developed human type dating from the
Pliocene, since there were no geologically dated human
fossils discovered at that time. Whitney's interpretation
of these finds reveals his anti-evolutionary stance. These
remains of man and his works were not essentially different from "what had been found in other parts of the
world wherever the lowest stratum of humanity has been
reached, or essentially different from what is now existing
in California itself." Therefore, the "advocates of progres-
sive development must look farther back than the Pliocene
. . . for traces of the primordial stock" (1879:257).
Whitney also noted that there were no Paleolithic, Neolithic, Bronze, or Iron Ages in the New World—"no un-
folding of the intellectual faculties of the human race."
In fact, he maintained that "over most of the continent
man cannot . . . be considered as having made any essential progress toward civilization." In short, Whitney recognized little or no cultural or biological change from the
Pliocene to the historic period in California.

Whitney did raise a question about the origin of man
and the nature of cultural development in California.
Even though much of his work was to be discredited because of the lack of methodology, his questions remained
critical to the study of the prehistory of California.

Though Putnam was obviously influenced by Whitney, he also was considering other interpretations of the peopling of California and tried to utilize linguistic, ethnological, and racial evidence, as well as archaeological data, in reconstructing California prehistory. Putnam's reconstruction was done with broad strokes and few details. He concluded, ". . . The Californians have probably developed by contact of tribe with tribe through an immense period of time, and that the primitive race of America which was as likely autochthonous, and of Pliocene Age, as of Asiatic origin, has retained its impress on the People of California" (1879:18). He thus raised questions not only of origin, but of cultural process and culture history.

While Putnam was drawing some broad generalizations that were suffering methodological shortcomings in that they could not even be considered as testable hypotheses, others were collecting and describing artifacts and to varying degrees their associations. The result of much if not most of this activity was the accumulation of large museum collections. Certain studies, however, were tightly controlled interpretations and must be considered prototypes of later developments.

For example, Schumacher's (1877) work on the Santa Barbara Channel had a rather straightforward statement of purpose:

> The principal aim of the expedition to this region was the collection of implements left by the former inhabitants, the observation of particulars in connection with such finds, the description of the mode of burial practiced by these people, and the delineation of topographical characteristics, together with the preparation of sketches of such former settlements (1877:37).

These goals were indeed achieved with varying success, and we find two sides to Schumacher's work. He was a combination of the treasure hunter ("My attention was especially given to the finding and exhuming of the old cemeteries, which, as my experience taught me, promises the richest rewards") (1877:38) and the archaeologist:

> Among the articles discovered, my attention was again arrested by a deposit of shell flakes, . . . some of which were partially worked into fishhooks, others finished. Other kinds of implements were found, such as double-pointed borers, of coarse, gritty sandstone, flint points, and a whetstone shaped something like a doubled edged knife, all of these kinds of articles had been found before, but never such a full assortment in one place. I had before suspected that these objects were used in the manufacture of fishhooks. I now was convinced of it. . . . (1877:42).

Schumacher (1875) described in some detail the method of manufacturing shell fishhooks as he reconstructed it from the archaeological data. This reconstruction still stands and is considered essentially correct by most archaeologists.

The Putnam and Schumacher studies represent the kinds of contribution to the field of archaeology made in the late 1800s that were to form the basis of later archaeological inquiry. Whitney's publication ignited a controversy that lasted for about two decades and stimulated development of more rigorous methodology. Possibly the reaction against Whitney's interpretation did more to further California archaeology than did any other single study or event, for with criticism of Whitney, the modern era of California archaeology begins.

Holmes' critical review (1901) spotlighted the inadequacies of Whitney's approach and brought to an end the practice of using as scientific evidence, affidavits of "expert" witnesses.

Holmes' careful analysis of the evidence for dating of the Calaveras skull was a superb example of scientific inquiry, which must have set a standard for future field work. However, though Holmes and also Hrdlicka removed both the Calaveras skull and the artifacts reportedly found in the auriferous gravels from the list of early man finds, Whitney's questions regarding the antiquity of man were still unanswered.

As the twentieth century began, archaeological investigations were initiated by the University of California, Berkeley. Professors Putnam and J. C. Merriam supervised field work in certain caves in Shasta County, the auriferous gravel regions, and among the shell mounds of San Francisco Bay. By 1910 a series of articles had appeared; the search for early man was being carried on in the caves of Shasta County (John C. Merriam 1906, F. W. Putnam 1906, W. J. Sinclair 1904), while the last major review of Neocene man in the auriferous gravels was made by W. J. Sinclair (1908).

Several investigations of shell mounds were begun. J. C. Merriam and Max Uhle excavated the Emeryville shell mound (Uhle 1907), and N. C. Nelson completed a survey of the shell mounds of the San Francisco Bay region and excavated Ellis Landing shell mound (Nelson 1909, 1910). Even earlier, in 1900, Phillip Mills Jones began a survey and excavation of mounds near Stockton, California (Jones 1923) as well as undertaking field work on the Channel Islands.

A. L. Kroeber was becoming influential in California anthropology, and in 1909 he discussed California archaeology and outlined the nature of the problems of that period. He considered the primary concerns of California archaeology to be: 1. to determine the first presence of man in California and to fix an absolute date for man's arrival, and 2. to determine the various forms taken by civilization and their historical succession, thus becoming concerned with time in a relative sense. In Kroeber's view the first problem required geological methods for a satisfactory attack, while the second was inseparable from ethnology.

Kroeber noted (1909:2–3) that the

> quarternary and tertiary gravels of California, especially those that are gold-bearing have been searched for indu-

bitable or possible human remains, and examined in their geological aspects. Caves . . . have been explored with a similar object, particularly those that bore abundant animal remains. Finally surface deposits have been examined for their geological relations.

He noted that the investigations of gravels had negative results, and that the caves had produced only possible man-made objects, not "generally admitted by those whose opinion is most authoritative." However, investigation of surface shell deposits had led to "the rather unexpected and gratifying determination that their beginnings are of greater antiquity than might theoretically be presupposed or than had been assumed."

Kroeber's own interests and bias as well as his great intellect were to influence the nature of California archaeology. The embryo of much of what was to come was found in Kroeber's discussion of "cultural archaeology" (1909:3–4):

That phase of archaeology which aims to unfold culture and is therefore essentially historical, shows in California one fundamental feature which is usual in the archaeology of North America. The civilization revealed by it is in essentials the same as that found in the same region by the more recent explorer and settler. The material dealt with by archaeology and ethnology is therefore the same, and the two branches of investigation move closely linked toward the same goal, differing only in their methods. The archaeologist's record being always imperfect, particularly in the case of unlettered peoples, his findings will be incomplete if not supplemented by ethnology. The ethnologist can obtain a more complete picture, but it is only momentary, a cross section as it were; and if he wishes to give to his results historical reality, introduce the element of time, and consider the factors of development, he is in turn dependent upon the archaeologist.

Uhle, as early as 1902, recognized changes in culture of the Emeryville shell mound, and outlined differences between occurrences of artifacts and a change in burial pattern from the lower to the upper layers of the mound. He also noted differences in predominant shellfish species between lower and upper layers. His observations on the base of the mound and the internal structure demonstrated that a considerable period of time was involved in its formation and thus in the human occupation. Uhle (1907:40–41) in fact would distinguish three different cultural expressions, but he does not provide the reader with any considered analysis of the content of any of the three. This simply reflects the stage of the development of classification in archaeology at that time. Archaeologists were concerned with the much broader concepts of cultural stages, as Paleolithic versus Neolithic culture.

This attitude is even more pronounced in Kroeber's paper (1909). He noted that the excavations at Emeryville shell mound upheld the view of a distinct progression and development during the growth of the mound. However, Kroeber felt that the material upon which the interpretation was based tended to negate it. He admitted (1909: 15–16) to some change in certain specialized types

> but on the other hand, mortars, pestles, sinkers, and bone implements, differing in no wise from those of more recent period, are found in the very lowest layers. . . . It does appear that there was some gradual elaboration and refinement of technical processes, but it was a change of degree only, and one in no way to be compared even for a moment with a transition as fundamental as that from paleolithic to neolithic.

It also appears that Kroeber was thinking as much in terms of major cultural stages as less pronounced stylistic changes when he wrote (1909:16) that in view of the antiquity of man in America, it may be doubted whether radical change could be expected in the time represented in the shell mounds:

> . . . particularly where the recent civilization is still so simple as in central California, it is difficult to believe that

a few thousand years would comprise a notable development; not because of any assumption that conservatism increases with degree of primitiveness, but because any radically simpler culture than the recent one in central California must have been so extremely rude as to make its existence a short time ago seem more than questionable to anyone impressed with the evident historical antiquity of a fairly well developed civilization elsewhere in America. *A priori* ideas as to the rapidity of cultural development seem to have been partly responsible for the view that the San Francisco mounds show noticeable development of culture, whereas it is precisely on *a priori* grounds that such change seems most doubtful.

Kroeber also noted at this time that the California shell middens of San Francisco Bay and elsewhere represented deposits accumulated over a relatively long period of time and that many of "the questions as to their antiquity, and as to the development of culture which the implements contained in them may show, depend for a satisfactory answer on the accumulation of a large mass of material. While something has been done, it has served to show how problems much more fundamental may be solved if a greater quantity of data can be amassed" (1909:39). The shell midden excavations and analyses during the first two decades of the twentieth century (Uhle 1907; Nelson 1909, 1910; Loud 1918; Gifford 1916) began to provide the data called for by Kroeber.

Although there were some disagreements among the archaeologists of the day, they generally agreed that the shell mounds of San Francisco Bay and elsewhere demonstrated little or no change over a considerable period of time. Nelson's (1910:402) final paragraph is a clear statement of this interpretation for the Ellis Landing shell mound:

> . . . it may be pointed out that the same general types of implements prevail from the bottom of the refuse heap to the top. Certain notable additions were made in later times, and the progress towards perfection of manufacture is gen-

erally marked; but aside from the normal changes there are no important breaks in the culture represented. This means that if more than one people have lived on the mound, whether these were friendly migrants or disputing enemies, they were all essentially of the same type of culture, and the last occupants of the shell mound at Ellis Landing were probably Indians similar to those that have lived in Middle California within historic times.

Dixon (1913:550), in his presidential address delivered at the annual meeting of the American Anthropological Association, observed that there was great cultural uniformity within the mounds of California. In addition to the uniformity represented by the cultural remains in the San Francisco Bay shell mounds, he noted that in Southern California, "Many of these shell heaps seem, by virtue of their relation to raised beaches, to be of very respectable antiquity," while on the other hand European items were found in graves of other sites. However, "The character of the objects as a whole . . . is quite uniform, and except for the things of European origin, there is little or no evidence in this region of any other type of culture from the earliest period down to that of the establishment of the missions."

In the *Handbook of the Indians of California,* actually written before World War I, Kroeber stated (1923: 925–26):

> Exploration of prehistoric sites anywhere in the state rarely reveals anything of moment that is not apparent in the life of the recent natives of the same locality. This rule applies even to limited districts. The consequence is that until now the archaeology of California has but rarely added anything to the determinations of ethnology beyond a dim vista of time and some vague hint toward a recognition of the development of culture. But as regards endeavors in this direction, practically nothing has been achieved.

> Nor do the local varieties of culture seem to have advanced or receded or replaced one another to any extent. . . .

In other words, the upshot of the correlations of the findings of archaeology and ethnology is that not only the general California culture area, but even its subdivisions or provinces, were determined a long time ago and have ever since maintained themselves with relatively little change.

This interpretation of California prehistory was to influence the direction of research for a number of decades. However, it would appear that there was some confusion regarding cultural uniformity within the shell middens. Kroeber (1909), as cited above, felt that changes in certain specialized types were relatively unimportant, that it was a "change of degree only," and that it did not equal a fundamental change as that from Paleolithic to Neolithic. Nelson (1910) noted cultural developments at Ellis Landing of a similar scale to that noted earlier by Uhle (1907) for Emeryville. Nelson recognized that the occupations throughout the mound were of the "same type of culture," while Uhle implied that the Emeryville occupations were of a single stage of development.

In 1926 Loud noted differences in the Stege mounds at Richmond. Though he did not work out a chronology, he did state that: "The probability of chronological differences, however, emphasizes the need for further intensive exploration of small as well as large mounds. The problem of prehistory in this area, especially the gradual development of its culture, can be solved only with further and more exact data" (1926:369).

Within a matter of a few years there was a shift of emphasis, as the Old World taxonomy of Neolithic and Paleolithic dropped from use in California, and "cultural uniformity" became "cultural continuity." Until 1929 the accepted doctrine was that California shell middens showed little cultural change of significance throughout their deposits. No cultural sequence was worked out. However, in 1929 three separate studies from three different areas of the state offered chronologies to the prehistorians. In the north, Schenck and Dawson (1929) devised a rather tentative chronology for sites in the Lodi region of the northern San Joaquin Valley. This chronology was based on the presence or absence of historic material on one hand, and the seriation of several types of aboriginal artifacts on the other.

In the southern part of the state, M. J. Rogers (1929a) had developed a sequence of three "cultures" (Shell Midden, Scraper Maker, and Historic Yuman) based on seriation of artifact types and an assumption of typological evolution of certain artifacts. This sequence later proved to be inaccurate, in that the two older cultures were reversed.

The most widely recognized of the sequences developed in 1929 has been D. B. Rogers' Oak Grove, Hunting, and Canalino Cultures of the Santa Barbara coastal area. In this case the sequence was based on stratification at key sites; differences of artifact assemblages; and different economic practices, as reflected by tools and refuse in middens.

Olson (1930), working in the same area, published a preliminary report in 1930 that confirmed D. B. Rogers' sequence in part. Olson never published the full results of his Santa Barbara excavations.

These chronologies wrought a change in California archaeology. No longer would California prehistory be viewed as timeless and unchanging. However, evidence for cultural sequences was not the only development of importance. Gifford's (1916) study of the composition of California shell mounds marked the beginning of a long development of shell midden analyses that have continued throughout the subsequent history of California archaeology. The shell midden analysis led to some disagreement between Gifford, Nelson, and Schenck regarding the changes in the environment of the Bay region. However, in the long run, the analysis resulted in a better understanding of shell midden accumulation and the prehistoric population and its relationship to its surroundings.

The earlier studies of the shell mounds were concerned primarily with establishing a date, hopefully early, for their initial occupation. Both Uhle and Nelson were under pressure from geologists to ascertain the maximum age of the human remains. They therefore concerned themselves with problems of "paleolithic affiliations" in the case of Uhle and problems of stratigraphy (which was just beginning to be recognized for its great significance to archaeology) in the case of Nelson. Both men were concerned with the subsidence of the shell mounds below sea level.

Schenck undertook the salvage archaeology at Emeryville shell mound at the time that the upper twenty-two feet were removed in 1924. Schenck excavated a series of trenches into the lower eight feet and published his results in 1926. As noted by Kroeber (1936:112), "Conditions were not of the best for culture change determinations, and Schenck evidently was considerably preoccupied with showing that previous estimates of absolute age of the mound were unprovable and probably excessive." Nevertheless, one of Schenck's contributions to California archaeology can be noted in this paper (1926: 151):

> It is in an endeavor to make such regional comparisons easier in the future that we have developed and described so fully as many types as possible, that we have sometimes used materials inadequate in quantity, and have indulged in conjecture based thereon. A *casual* survey would establish the shellmound culture as ranking very low in the cultural scale. Hence the value of its study seems to lie in the possibility of tracing relationships through regional comparisons.

Schenck presented a formal typology for the Emeryville material and collaborated with Gifford on a typology for materials collected in the survey of the southern San Joaquin Valley (Schenck 1926, Gifford and Schenck 1926). This work marked the beginning of the development of modern typological studies and of the use of the comparative method in California archaeology.

By 1930, California archaeology had developed: 1. cultural chronologies that demonstrated culture change; 2. the beginnings of shell midden analysis; 3. initial studies in artifact typology; 4. an awareness of some of the problems in comparative studies.

In 1936 Kroeber, contrasting contemporary work with the earlier work of Nelson and Uhle, wrote: "Recent work tends to center around the problem of cultural change, and by starting with native remains with which post-contact artifacts are associated, work back first to a pre-contact Late culture, and then, if possible, to a differentiated one which is presumably Early, or at least Earlier" (1936:111).

Although this approach is apparent in Schenck and Dawson (1929) and M. J. Rogers' works (1929a), among others, it is explicitly and expertly stated by Heizer (1941). Heizer is also in large part responsible for its fine development and utilization in central California. Heizer, working with colleagues first at Sacramento Junior College and later at Berkeley, developed the methodology that was to make considerable gains toward the understanding of central California prehistory. As the possibility of a cultural sequence became apparent in the early thirties, archaeologists digging in the central valley sought out small sites in order to isolate single components of each culture, as well as larger sites in which the cultural manifestations were stratified but often mixed due to disturbance within the mounds (Lillard, Heizer, and Fenenga 1939).

Also of major importance was the analytical technique used in the treatment of the numerous burials of central California mounds. The artifacts associated with a single burial were treated as a unit of analysis. Certain artifact forms were often associated with historic materials while others were not, and through stratigraphic studies and seriation, the burial associations could be arranged to form a sequence of burial complexes that provided the basic artifact sequence for the cultural manifestation of the mounds.

This kind of analysis obviously required finer typological analysis than had occurred earlier. Studies of typology in California, which began to develop under the influence of Schenck (1926, 1929; Gifford and Schenck 1926) in his studies at Emeryville and in the southern and northern San Joaquin Valley, later were influenced by Gifford (1939, 1940, 1947). But here again Heizer and his colleagues in the work on central California were first to recognize shell beads and ornaments as classes of artifacts that were frequent enough in occurrence and variable enough in form to be sensitive indicators of chronology. This methodology culminated in the chronology of the central valley sequence first indicated by Lillard and Purves (1936) and further elaborated by Lillard, Heizer, and Fenenga (1939) and Heizer (1941).

During 1933–34, the Civil Works Administration undertook archaeological excavation in the southern San Joaquin Valley in order to reduce unemployment. Under the direction of W. D. Strong and W. M. Walker, several sites were excavated in the region of Buena Vista Lake. These were published in 1941 and formed another cultural sequence for the central valley (Wedel 1941).

On a broader scale, Kroeber suggested a wider correlation based on changes in frequency and types of charmstones. He stated (1936:114):

Our one thin guiding thread backward into the prehistory of most of California is, then, to date, the much-debated plummet-shaped stone which the historic Indians did not make but did use as a charm. On the story of its relative frequency, or perhaps changes in form, there can be strung other facts of more local distribution, such as the development of circular fishhooks and the metate-mortar displacement on the Santa Barbara Coast, the appearance of pipes, clay balls, bone incising and delicate chipping in the heart of the Great Valley, with which in turn other distinctive phenomena may be expected to correlate.

In 1939 Heizer and Fenenga attempted a broad chronological synthesis tying in the Southern California Coast with the Central Valley, and a cursory examination of the San Francisco Bay area. While their correlations of horizons have not stood the test of time in all instances, "two facts" that appeared as a result of their analysis are still valid (1939:397):

> . . . First, cultural development in certain California areas has apparently not been autochthonous, but in at least the three areas outlined above there has been a parallel succession, thus making it a general California phenomenon, further evidence of which we may expect when additional areas are investigated carefully. Second, the traditional uniformity and essential stability of California culture of the past is no longer a tenable interpretation; culture change has been definite and pronounced.

The anthropology of central California was largely shaped by A. L. Kroeber, and his priority clearly placed salvage of the fast-vanishing ethnographic data before excavation of archaeological sites. This does not imply that Kroeber placed no value in archaeology. He had clearly stated as early as 1909 (pp. 3–4) that the subject matter of archaeology and ethnology was the same, that the two fields moved toward the same goals, "differing only in their methods," and that the ethnologist is dependent upon the archaeologist if he wishes to give "his results historical reality, introduce the element of time, and consider the factor of development." It was presumably this interest that influenced the archaeology of central California and led to the development and use of the direct historical approach and the detailed typological studies.

Although these interests were clearly furthering archaeology in central California, a different approach was being used in Southern California. Both M. J. Rogers and Elizabeth W. C. Campbell were working in the California deserts during the late twenties and thirties. Rogers published *Survey of the Mohave Sinks* (1929b) and *Early Lithic Industries of the Colorado Basin and Adjacent Desert Regions* (1939), while Campbell and colleagues' more important publications were: *An Archaeological Survey of Twenty-nine Palms* (1931), *The Pinto Basin Site—An Ancient Aboriginal Camping Ground in the California Desert* (1935), *The Archaeology of Pleistocene Lake Mohave* (1937), and the article, "Archaeological Problems in the Southern California Deserts" (1936).

The deserts of California presented archaeological problems entirely different from those of central California. Desert sites were often open-surface sites, where erosion had removed the finer material to leave the artifacts incorporated in or resting on a desert pavement. There was no stratigraphy; in fact, there was no midden in these sites. Rogers combined the direct historical approach with studies of geology and ethnology, but nowhere is his approach explicitly stated.

Elizabeth Campbell developed an approach that is interesting because of its problem orientation and sophistication. She clearly sets forth her objectives (1936:295):

> . . . one to cover all likely areas where sites might be found, the other to try to discover if cultural groups follow certain geologic formations and if so, to place these types in their proper sequence, all of which is no very simple task. With these two main objectives in view, it is proposed to scour the more arid region of Southern California, with the idea that any solution of the problem connected with this territory may prove a possible clue towards unravelling the story of prehistoric man in wider portions of the Great Basin, which we hope to explore in the future.

> . . . It is to be hoped that a thorough study of their flint and stone objects' relation to their topographic situation will ultimately throw light on placing types in their proper order, and possibly on their approximate antiquity. That it is difficult to bring forward convincing proof of antiquity where there is no stratification, we are well aware . . . and it is expected

that a conscientious recording of conditions connected with
all sites which appear to be old will ultimately speak for
itself and tell a clear story. . . . We are satisfied that the
very nature of sites in our desert terrain will eventually cause
forms found thereon to be placed where they rightfully be-
long, be it old or young. . . .

Campbell notes association of artifact assemblage with
different topographic features, and ends with a statement:
"While we are conscious of the need of being extremely
conservative in any arbitrary placing or segregating of
definite cultures in the time scale until further evidence is
in hand, nevertheless, it becomes apparent that already
certain objects fall more or less into a chronologic sequence" (1936:300), and she presents a tentative
chronology for the California desert.

There has been some debate as to the nature of Campbell's approach and the validity of her conclusions
(Warren 1970, Heizer 1970). Some critical errors of fact
in Rogers' 1939 report and Roberts' 1940 summary of
early man in California remained unchallenged until the
1950s, by which time Campbell's work had been to a considerable extent discredited. Nonetheless, Campbell's studies represent both the beginnings of a chronology for the
California deserts and of early man studies in that area.

Rogers' 1939 paper on early lithic industries outlined
a cultural sequence for the desert in more detail and
clarity than Campbell's. Rogers identified cultural manifestations and discussed their dates and their distribution.
Although his relative sequence for the desert has proven
to be essentially correct, his absolute dates were in error.

Other investigations dealing with the antiquity of man
being undertaken during the thirties and early forties included: 1. the accidental find of "Los Angeles Man," a
skeleton located some twelve to thirteen feet below the
surface, by workmen digging a storm drain along the Los
Angeles River. A few weeks later bones of a mammoth in

the same strata were discovered (Lopatin 1939). At a later date fluorine tests were run on the bone, which indicated that the mammoth and the human skeleton were of approximately the same age (Heizer and Cook 1952). 2. M. J. Rogers' excavation of the San Dieguito type site, which was not published until 1966 (Warren 1966), but which served as a basis for crucial statements published by Rogers or attributed to him. The type site, known as the C. W. Harris site, is an important stratified site, which provides the basic cultural sequence for San Diego County, placing the San Dieguito (Scraper Maker culture of Rogers' 1929a paper) in its proper chronological position. 3. In 1938, M. R. Harrington also began his excavations at the Borax Lake site, which were to be carried on sporadically until 1946.

During the period of the late thirties and early forties, a number of excavations were made in both Southern and central California; the results of many of these excavations would not be published until after World War II. In the south, Walker (1951) was excavating a series of sites, Phil Orr (1943) had begun his excavations in the Santa Barbara area for the Santa Barbara Natural History Museum, and George Carter (1941) reported on excavations of a stratified site at Point Sal. At Berkeley, numerous excavations were being undertaken throughout the surrounding area (Heizer 1949). Basic cultural sequences were worked out for major areas of California during the period 1935–45 and were being extended gradually to surrounding areas when the war interrupted. It was also a period when problems of methodology involving typology and comparative method were first dealt with adequately. The direct historical approach was developed in the north to a very fine degree, while in the south the environmental-geological approach seems to have dominated many of the studies that were directed toward the California deserts, the locus of early man studies.

After World War II, archaeological activity again increased. Many sites were excavated, and important papers were published. Beardsley (1948, 1954) developed a sequence for the San Francisco Bay area and presented what was to become the Central California Taxonomic System, representing agreement reached among Heizer, Fenenga, and Beardsley (Beardsley 1948:3). The cultural horizons outlined for the lower Sacramento Valley formed the basic framework. Then "Each horizon of the sequence is split into provinces, which are areas of cultural similarity that also show a certain geographic consistence . . . separate province names have been used for each horizon. The cultural units in each province are called facies, and are groups of intimately related settlements or components." This sequence of culture horizons embraced the archaeology of the littoral zone as well as the interior zone of central California.

In 1948 the University of California Archaeological Survey was established at Berkeley under the direction of R. F. Heizer. The decade of the fifties was a period of data accumulation and further developments in methodology and techniques. In 1958 the second branch of the Archaeological Survey was established at UCLA under the direction of C. W. Meighan.

Since the end of World War II, local sequences have been established for the North Coast Range (Harrington 1948; Heizer 1953; Meighan 1955; Meighan and Haynes 1970), northeastern California (Fenenga and Riddell 1949; Riddell 1956, 1960; Baumhoff and Olmsted 1963), the Sierras (Heizer and Elsasser 1953; Elsasser 1960; Bennyhoff 1956; Fitzwater 1962, 1968), Owens Valley (Lanning 1963), California desert (Harner 1958; Hunt 1960; Wallace 1962; Rogers 1945) and South Coast (Wallace 1955).

A few general papers on California archaeology have been attempted. Meighan (1959b) characterized the California cultures as Archaic in that they represented the persistence of a basic tool type. However, the subsistence pattern allowed for elaboration "of ornaments, art, and other leisure-time activities." All of these elaborations were taking place within the framework of an Archaic cultural stage. Heizer, on the other hand, would rank some late prehistoric cultures as formative. The different interpretation here is more apparent than real. While Meighan has defined Archaic on the basis of technology and subsistence, Heizer has emphasized social features, population density, and nonmaterial elaborations.

Other general studies, relating California cultures to non-California cultures, and/or a comparative study statewide, have also been attempted (Bennyhoff 1958, Meighan 1959b, 1965). Typological studies continue, with application of cross dating and recognition of outside influences on California. The California-Nevada relationships were noted by Heizer, Baumhoff, and Bennyhoff (Baumhoff and Heizer 1958, Bennyhoff and Heizer 1958) and southwestern influence in California by Heizer (1946), Lathrop (1950), and Treganza (1942). Other typological studies led to the definition of the widespread desert side notch point (Baumhoff and Byre 1959) and the description of various types of bone artifacts (Gifford 1947, Bennyhoff 1950).

Still a different direction in California archaeology is the attempt to correlate prehistoric culture with language. Gerow (1968) noted possible relationships, while Baumhoff and Olmsted (1963) and Taylor (1961) presented some interesting arguments for relating certain languages to specific prehistoric cultures. Similar studies in the Great Basin have also involved the eastern edge of California and the California desert (Hopkins 1965, Goss 1968).

In 1968 two papers questioned the traditional sequence of cultural horizons in both central California and the Southern California coast. Gerow (1968) postulated the coexistence of two distinct cultures or traditions in central California at 1500 to 1000 B.C., after which time they gradually converged. These two traditions are early Bay, which had widespread relationships to other early cultures, and early Delta, which was more localized. He would further relate the early Bay to Hokan speakers and the Delta culture to the Penutian speakers.

Warren (1968) has presented a model for the prehistory of the South Coast area that replaces the horizons of Wallace's (1955) chronology with several cultural traditions, which allow for more cultural variation at one time. Warren, for example, would have the Encinitas tradition persist in San Diego County until recent times (ca. A.D. 1000), while in Santa Barbara County, the Campbell tradition would replace the Encinitas tradition at ca. 3000 B.C., so that the Encinitas tradition and Campbell tradition would coexist for some time after 3000 B.C. Significantly, these papers do not question the data but rather their interpretation. It would appear that the horizon concept functioned well when the basic problem was one of chronology. The problem of chronology in California now appears relatively easy to solve, and attention is being directed toward problems of process and interrelationships between culture and environment.

In the later forties and early fifties, S. F. Cook revived midden analysis with a series of papers by himself and with colleagues (Cook 1946, 1950; Cook and Treganza 1947, 1950; Treganza and Cook 1948; Cook and Heizer 1951; Heizer and Cook 1956). A series of publications dealing with the analysis of midden constituents followed, and for over two decades this has been an important aspect of California archaeology. Meighan and others (1958:1) have suggested that this "ecological approach" was developed and was important because "the archaeology here lacks elaborate remains, making ecology one of the more fruitful lines of investigation." That its development largely corresponds to the period following the establishment of a basic chronology and that new problems could be approached within a chronological framework seem to substantiate Meighan and others' views of the matter.

The investigations dealt with problems of sampling, describing the constituents, and extrapolating the volume or mass of the deposit from the sample. Treganza and Cook (1948) went so far as to screen and weigh an entire midden in an attempt to develop criteria for a minimal sample. Cook and Treganza (1950) also attempted to correlate bone and shell remains with the quantity of edible food they furnished. The major aim of much of the midden analysis has been to develop correlations of midden constituents, food consumption, and population. The publications dealing with these problems are rather numerous, with major contributions being made by Cook, Heizer, Treganza, Greengo, Meighan, and Ascher, among others. Recently the methodology has been criticized for lack of control and accuracy (Glassow 1967, Koloseike 1969). Other studies have utilized the analysis of midden components to show relationship of man to his environment and suggest changes in environment and/or culture. As early as 1916 Gifford utilized midden constituents to reconstruct the environment of archaeological sites around San Francisco Bay. Changes in shell species found in California shell middens have been interpreted to reflect changes in sea level and resultant changes in the coastal ecology. Greengo (1951:16) reports the silting in of portions of San Francisco Bay reflected in the Bay shell mounds, while the development of a sandy beach and silting in of lagoons along the San Diego coast is recorded in change in shellfish species in sites of that area (Warren and Pavesic 1963; Shumway, Hubbs, and Moriarty 1961). Midden analysis has also been used to interpret cultural remains and to contribute to reconstruction of the prehistoric culture. Meighan, in his study of the Little Harbor site, noted:

It is apparent that in a region of simple technology and slow change, real understanding of cultural development and cultural relationships cannot be obtained from the study of artifacts alone, nor from trait list comparisons. Only an environmental-functional study which considers the available nonartifactual evidence can provide a basis for systematizing the many variants of the simpler cultures. Thus, a comparison of the artifact assemblage from Little Harbor with 20 other artifact assemblages described for California yield no particular understanding of Little Harbor. . . . The distinctive features of the Little Harbor culture, its maritime adaptations, are only dimly reflected in a mere artifact inventory (1959a: 404).

As early as 1929, Howard (1929:380–83) suggested year-round occupation for the Emeryville shell mound on the basis of both summer and winter birds. Baumhoff (1955:64) inferred that the occupation of Kingsley Cave occurred during the winter and spring from the absence of bones of juvenile deer. McGeein and Mueller (1955:59) interpreted Mrn-20, a small site in the northern Bay area, as having been occupied primarily during the fall and winter because of the large percentage of bones from species that populated the area only during the fall.

Leonard (1966) utilized the presence of pelagic fish bones in determining the seasonal occupation at Ven-70. Weide (1969) was able to postulate that the occupation of site Ora-82 occurred most heavily during the late winter and early spring on the basis of seasonal growth rings of Pismo clam.

EARLY MAN

Early man studies during the late forties were limited primarily to Hewes' (1946) problematical early man site at Tranquility and M. R. Harrington's (1948) report of the Borax Lake site. Neither was the ideal site for demonstrating antiquity of man in California. The Borax Lake site was considerably disturbed by rodent activity, with fluted points on the surface as well as deeply buried and in apparent association with artifacts typical of late sites in the region. The Tranquility site appears ancient on the basis of fossilization of animal and human bone, but the artifacts appeared to be typologically relatively late.

Consequently, neither of these sites were accepted as being ancient by the leading California archaeologists. Roberts' (1940) criticism of Campbell's early man studies and M. J. Rogers' (1939) dating of Lake Mohave at the Little Pluvial seem to have placed most "early man finds" late in time or highly questionable as to date, even though Brainerd (1952, 1953), Antevs (1952), and Campbell (1949) believed that a longer chronology was called for in the desert region. The argument for a longer chronology was not improved by the claims of Carter (1957) for Pleistocene man at San Diego, Clements' (1953) Pleistocene man in Death Valley, Orr's Pleistocene man on Santa Rosa, nor Simpson's (1961) "Paleolithic like" tools at Manix Lake.

Haury's (1950) discussion of San Dieguito in the Ventana Cave report further obscured an already confusing terminology for San Dieguito (for amplification see Warren 1967, Hayden 1966). Meighan as late as 1959 not only rejected the Carter finds, but also placed the Borax Lake material at slightly before the time of Christ and rejected any "paleolithic like" or "pre-projectile point" assemblages. Furthermore, there was clearly confusion of San Dieguito and assemblages of the later "Milling Stone Horizon" due to inadequate definition of the San Dieguito Complex.

In central California, Treganza was investigating the Farmington Complex, thought to be of early postglacial date (Treganza 1952, Treganza and Heizer 1953). However, radiocarbon dates from the gravels in which the assemblage was enclosed were much younger than expected. Heizer and McCown (1950) reported what is "probably early man" in their discussion of the Stanford skull, but by the late 1950s little progress had been made in early man studies.

By 1960 Hunt described the sequence for Death Valley, which she dated back to the Early Recent period, but it lacked radiocarbon dates.

In 1961 the San Dieguito component of the C. W.

Harris site was placed in a chronological framework, with radiocarbon dates indicating an age older than seventy-five hundred years (Warren and True 1961). Warren and True also found comparable material reported in Campbell, et al. (1937), in Rogers' (1939) work at Lake Mohave, and Hunt's Death Valley I. They suggested that an early non-desert culture existed throughout a wide area of Southern California prior to seventy-five hundred years ago.

In 1962 Orr (1962a, 1962b) reported the finding of Arlington Springs man, which consisted of fragmentary human remains with one date 10,390 years ago on associated charcoal and another 9950 years ago from charcoal about a foot from the remains.

Wallace (1962) reported a chronology for the California deserts that supported the conclusions reached by Warren and True.

By 1965 Meighan had accepted many of the early man finds and made some positive suggestions regarding Simpson's Lake Manix Complex (1965:715):

Lake Manix, California. All surface finds; inadequately described at present. This is the best contender for a tradition of great age that is not a projectile point tradition; the assemblages merit the most careful study and description.

Meighan and Haynes (1970) undertook a reanalysis of the geology and artifacts at the Borax Lake site, which led to the tentative reconstruction of the Borax Lake site, with fluted points and crescents dated at ten thousand years ago or earlier.

By 1967 three radiocarbon dates had been obtained for the San Dieguito Complex that ranged from 6540 to 7080 B.C., and a review and reanalysis of Lake Mohave materials was begun, which has resulted in an ongoing controversy (Warren and True 1961; Warren and DeCosta 1964; Heizer 1965, 1970; Davis 1967; Warren 1967, 1970). However, recently a geomorphic history of Lake

Mohave has been developed in which some cultural remains consisting of flakes and a possible artifact have been found enclosed in beach deposits at Lake Mohave and dated at 10,260 years (Ore and Warren, 1971).

By 1969 Davis had postulated a western lithic cotradition based primarily on California desert material (Davis, Brott, and Weide 1969).

Riddell and Olson (1969) have reported what is apparently another early surface site on the shore of Tulare Lake in the San Joaquin Valley. This site contains a number of artifacts, including a variety of projectile point types, scrapers, crescents, and some milling tools. The most significant finds are fluted points, which suggest that the site was occupied at an early date.

Early man research, which had moved slowly for a number of years in a state plagued by erroneous if not fraudulent claims for early man, has in recent years established beyond doubt the presence of man in California about ten thousand years ago. This area of study has suffered from conceptual bias as well as a paucity of stratified sites.

NEW DIRECTIONS

The problem of chronology was solved largely by the development of radiocarbon dating, several seriational techniques, obsidian dating, and analysis of chemical changes in the fossilization of bone, among other standard techniques.

With absolute and relative dating techniques, regional chronologies were produced with relative ease, and a knotty problem that had plagued California archaeologists for over fifty years was essentially laid to rest. Archaeologists turned their attention to other problems. Midden analysis led to problems of demography, population, settlement pattern, and ultimately to social organization. Heizer's (1958) paper dealt with this question, although it was written in terms of Willey and Phillips' formative and preformative stages. From midden analysis and the general interest in ecology during the fifties and sixties, evolved studies concerned with various cultural processes. Problems of adaptation, and interrelation of culture and environment were of primary concern (Warren, True, and Eudey 1961; Warren and Pavesic 1963; Crabtree, Warren, and True 1963; Davis 1963; Shumway, Hubbs, and Moriarty 1961; Reinman 1964; Fredrickson 1969; Kowta 1969).

Still another influence with significant impact on California archaeology has been the "new archaeology" of Lewis Binford, James Hill, and James Deetz. There has been an increasing concern with scientific methodology, the deductive approach and use of statistics. Ethnographic analogy has played an important role in constructing hypotheses. Many insightful studies have resulted from this approach. There have been attempts to infer social organization from mortuary practices (Stickel 1968, L. King 1969) and from the distribution of artifacts (Deetz 1968). Papers have also dealt with sampling procedures and field strategy for the "new archaeology" (Chartkoff and Chartkoff 1968). Although the approach is exciting and fertile, the papers have not always been as stimulating nor especially well thought out. Though this is not the place for extended criticism, we might note that argument based on ethnographic analogy ought to include an evaluation of the points of similarity and differences between the two analogs before one puts too much stock in the analogy.

The "new archaeology" is in many ways complementary to the ecological approach of California. At times when the ethnographic analogy may break down, the ecological approach can provide the needed empirical data regarding settlement pattern or seasonal round of activities (Leonard 1966, Weide 1969). Certainly the "new archaeology" has given new direction, greater emphasis on theory, and renewed vitality to California archaeology.

Archaeology in California appears to be on the threshold of a new, exciting, and productive era.

REFERENCES

ANTEVS, ERNST
   1952   "Climatic History and the Antiquity of Man in California." *Univ. Cal. Arch. Survey Reports* 16:23–31.

ASCHER, ROBERT
   1959   "A Prehistoric Population Estimate Using Midden Analysis and Two Population Models." *Southwestern Jour. Anthro.* 15:168–78.

BAUMHOFF, MARTIN A.
   1955   "Excavation of Teh-1 (Kingsley Cave)." *Cal. Arch. Pap.* 33:40–73.

——— and OLMSTED, D.
   1963   "Palaihnihan: Radiocarbon Support for Glottochronology." *Am. Anthro.* 65:278–84.

——— and HEIZER, ROBERT
   1958   "Outland Coiled Basketry From the Caves of West Central Nevada." *Univ. Cal. Arch. Survey Report* 42:49–59.

BEARDSLEY, RICHARD K.
   1948   "Culture Sequence in Central California Archaeology." *Am. Ant.* 14:1–29.
   1954   "Temporal and Areal Relationships in Central California Archaeology," Parts I and II. *Univ. Cal. Arch. Survey Report* 24–25.

BELOUS, RUSSELL E.
   1953   "The Central California Chronological Sequence Re-examined." *Am. Ant.* 18:341–53.

BENNYHOFF, JAMES A.
   1950   "California Fish Spears and Harpoons." *Univ. Cal. Anthro. Records* 9:295–337.
   1956   "An Appraisal of the Archaeological Resources of Yosemite National Park." *Univ. Cal. Arch. Survey Report* 34.
   1958   "The Desert West: A Trial Correlation of Culture and Chronology," in "Current Views on Great Basin Archaeology." *Univ. Cal. Arch. Survey Report* 42:98–112.

———, and HEIZER, ROBERT F.
   1958   "Cross-dating Great Basin Sites by California Shell Beads," in "Current Views on Great Basin Archaeology." *Univ. Cal. Arch. Survey Report* 42:113–92.

BRAINERD, G. W.
   1951   "The Place of Chronological Ordering in Archaeological Analysis." *Am. Ant.* 16:301–13.

1952 "On the Study of Early Man in Southern California." *Univ. Cal. Arch. Survey Report* 16:18–22.

1953 "A Re-examination of the Dating Evidence for the Lake Mohave Artifact Assemblage." *Am. Ant.* 18:270–71.

CAMPBELL, ELIZABETH W. C.

1931 "An Archaeological Survey of the Twenty Nine Palms Region." *Southwest Mus. Pap.* 7.

1936 "Archaeological Problems in the Southern California Deserts." *Am. Ant.* 1:295–300.

1949 "Two Ancient Archaeological Sites in The Great Basin." *Science* 109:340.

——— and CAMPBELL, WILLIAM H.

1935 "The Pinto Basin Site." *Southwest Mus. Pap.* 9.

———; CAMPBELL, W. H.; ANTEVS, ERNST; AMSDEN, CHARLES A.; BORDIERI, JOSEPH A.; and BODE, FRANCIS D.

1937 "The Archaeology of Pleistocene Lake Mohave: A Symposium." *Southwest Mus. Pap.* 11.

CARTER, GEORGE F.

1941 "Archaeological Notes on a Midden at Point Sal." *Am. Ant.* 6:214–26.

1957 *Pleistocene Man at San Diego.* Baltimore: Johns Hopkins Press.

CHARTKOFF, JOSEPH, and CHARTKOFF, KERRY

1968 "1967 Excavations at the Finch Site: Research Strategy and Procedures." *Univ. Cal. Arch. Survey Annual Report 1967*:315–70.

CLEMENTS, THOMAS, and CLEMENTS, LYDIA

1953 "Evidence of Pleistocene Man in Death Valley, California." *Geolog. Soc. Am. Bull.* 64:1189–1204.

COOK, S. F.

1946 "A Reconsideration of Shellmounds with Respect to Population and Nutrition." *Am. Ant.* 12:50–53.

1950 "Physical Analysis as a Method for Investigating Prehistoric Habitation Sites." *Univ. Cal. Arch. Survey Report* 7(1):1–22.

——— and HEIZER, ROBERT F.

1951 "The Physical Analysis of Nine Indian Mounds of the Lower Sacramento Valley." *Univ. Cal. Pub. Am. Arch. Eth.* 40(7):281–312.

——— and TREGANZA, ADAM E.

1947 "The Quantitative Investigation of Aboriginal Sites: Comparative Physical and Chemical Analysis of Two California Indian Mounds." *Am. Ant.* 23:135–41.

1950 "The Quantitative Investigation of Indian Mounds." *Univ. Cal. Pub. Am. Arch. Eth.* 40(5):223–62.

CRABTREE, ROBERT H.; WARREN, CLAUDE N.; and TRUE, D. L.

1963 "Archaeological Investigations at Botiquitos Lagoon, San

Diego County, California." *Univ. Cal. Arch. Survey Annual Report 1962–63*:319–406.

DAVIS, E. L.
1963   "The Desert Culture of the Western Great Basin: A Lifeway of Seasonal Transhumance." *Am. Ant.* 29:202–12.
1967   "Man and Water at Pleistocene Lake Mohave." *Am. Ant.* 32:345–53.

———; BROTT, C. W.; and WEIDE, D. L.
1969   "The Western Lithic Co-Tradition." *San Diego Mus. Pap.* 6.

DEETZ, JAMES
1968   "The Inference of Residence and Descent Rules from Archaeological Data," *New Perspective in Archaeology*, S. R. Binford and L. R. Binford (eds.). 41–48. Chicago: Aldine Publishing Co.

DIXON, ROLAND B.
1913   "Some Aspects of North American Archaeology." *Am. Anthro.* 15:549–66.

ELSASSER, ALBERT
1960   "The Archaeology of the Sierra Nevada in California and Nevada." *Univ. Cal. Arch. Survey Report* 51.

FENENGA, FRANKLIN, and RIDDELL, FRANCES
1949   "Excavation of Tommy Tucker Cave, Lassen County, California." *Am. Ant.* 14:203–14.

FITZWATER, R. J.
1962   "Final Report of Two Seasons Excavation at El Portal, Mariposa County." *Univ. Cal. Arch. Survey Annual Report 1961–62*:235–82.
1968   "Big Oak Flat; Two Archaeological Sites in Yosemite National Park." *Univ. Cal. Arch. Survey Annual Report 1968*:275–314.

FREDRICKSON, DAVID A.
1969   "Technological Change, Population Movement, Environmental Adaptation, and the Emergence of Trade: Influences on Culture Change Suggested by Midden Constituent Analysis." *Univ. Cal. Arch. Survey Annual Report 1969*:101–26.

GEROW, BERT
1968   *An Analysis of the University Village Complex.* Stanford: Stanford University.

GIFFORD, EDWARD WINSLOW
1916   "Composition of California Shellmounds." *Univ. Cal. Pub. Am. Arch. Eth.* 12(1):1–29.
1939   "Typology for Archaeology." *Vigesmoseptimo Congreso Internacional de Americanistas, Actas de la Primera Sesion, Celebrada en la Ciudad de Mexico en 1939.* 2:7–11.
1940   "California Bone Artifacts." *Univ. Cal. Anthro. Records* 3(2):153–237.

1947 "California Shell Artifacts." *Univ. Cal. Anthro. Records* 9(1):1–32.

——— and SCHENCK, W. EGBERT
1926 "Archaeology of the Southern San Joaquin Valley, California." *Univ. Cal. Pub. Am. Arch. Eth.* 23(1):1–122.

GLASSOW, MICHAEL A.
1967 "Consideration in Estimating Prehistoric California Coastal Population." *Am. Ant.* 32:354–59.

GOSS, JAMES
1968 "Culture-Historical Inference from Utaztekan Linguistic Evidence." *Occas. Pap. Idaho State Univ. Mus.* 22:1–42.

GREENGO, ROBERT E.
1951 "Molluscan Species in California Shell Middens." *Univ. Cal. Arch. Survey Report* 13.

HARNER, M. J.
1958 "Lowland Patayan Phases in the Lower Colorado River Valley and Colorado Desert." *Univ. Cal. Arch. Survey Report* 42:93–97.

HARRINGTON, M. R.
1948 "An Ancient Site at Borax Lake, California." *Southwest Mus. Pap.* 16.

HAURY, EMIL W.
1950 *The Stratigraphy and Archaeology of Ventana Cave, Arizona.* Albuquerque and Tucson: University of New Mexico Press and University of Arizona Press.

HAYDEN, JULIAN D.
1966 "Restoration of the San Dieguito Type Site to Its Proper Place in the San Dieguito Sequence." *Am. Ant.* 31:439–40.

HEIZER, ROBERT F.
1941 "The Direct Historical Approach in California Archaeology." *Am. Ant.* 7:98–122.
1946 "The Occurrence and Significance of Southwestern Grooved Axes in California." *Am. Ant.* 11:187–93.
1949 "The Archaeology of Central California, Part I, The Early Horizon." *Univ. Cal. Anthro. Records* 12(1).
1953 "Archaeology of the Napa Region" (ed.). *Univ. Cal. Anthro. Records* 12(6):225–358.
1958 "Prehistoric Central California: A Problem of Historical-Developmental Classification." *Univ. Cal. Arch. Survey Report* 41:19–26.
1965 "Problems of Dating Lake Mojave Artifacts." *The Masterkey* 39:125–34.
1970 "Environment and Culture: The Lake Mojave Case." *The Masterkey* 44:68–72.

——— and COOK, S. F.
1952 "Fluorine and Other Chemical Lists of Some North Ameri-

244　　　　　　　　　CLAUDE N. WARREN

can Human and Fossil Bones." *Am. Jour. Physical Anthro.* 10:289–304.

1956　"Some Aspects of the Quantitative Approach in Archaeology." *Southwestern Jour. Anthro.* 12:229–48.

——— and ELSASSER, ALBERT B.
1953　"Some Archaeological Sites and Cultures of the Central Sierra Nevada." *Univ. Cal. Arch. Survey Report* 21.

——— and FENENGA, FRANKLIN
1939　"Archaeological Horizons in Central California." *Am. Anthro.* 41:378–99.

——— and McCOWN, THEODORE D.
1950　"The Stanford Skull, A Probable Early Man from Santa Clara County, California." *Univ. Cal. Arch. Survey Report* 6:1–9.

HEWES, G. W.
1946　"Early Man in California and the Tranquility Site." *Am. Ant.* 11:209–15.

HOLMES, WILLIAM H.
1901　"Review of the Evidence Relating to Auriferous Gravel Man in California." *Smith. Instit. Annual Report 1899:*419–72.

HOPKINS, NICHOLAS
1965　"Great Basin Prehistory and Uto-Aztekan." *Am. Ant.* 31:48–60.

HOWARD, HILDEGARDE
1929　"The Avifauna of Emeryville Shellmound." *Univ. Cal. Pub. Zoology* 32(2):378–83.

HUNT, ALICE
1960　"Archaeology of the Death Valley Salt Pan." *Univ. Utah Anthro. Pap.* 47.

JONES, PHILLIP MILLS
1923　"Mound Excavation near Stockton." *Univ. Cal. Pub. Am. Arch. Eth.* 20(2):113–24.

KING, LINDA
1969　"The Medea Creek Cemetery (LAn-243): An Investigation of Social Organization from Mortuary Practices." *Univ. Cal. Arch. Survey Annual Report 1969:*23–68.

KOLOSEIKE, ALAN
1969　"On Calculating the Prehistoric Food Resource Value of Molluscs." *Univ. Cal. Arch. Survey Annual Report 1969:*143–60.

KOWTA, MAKOTO
1969　"The Sayles Complex: A Late Milling Stone Assemblage from Cajon Pass and the Ecological Implications of its Scraper Planes." *Univ. Cal. Pub. in Anthro.* 6.

KROEBER, A. L.
  1909   "The Archaeology of California." *Putnam Anniversary Volume.* The Torch Press, Cedar Rapids, Iowa: 1–42.
  1923   "The Handbook of the Indians of California." *Bureau of Am. Eth. Bull.* 78.
  1936   "Prospects in California Prehistory." *Am. Ant.* 2:108–16.

LANNING, EDWARD P.
  1963   "Archaeology of the Rose Spring Site, Iny-372." *Univ. Cal. Pub. Am. Arch. Eth.* 49(3):237–336.

LATHROP, DONALD W.
  1950   "A Distinctive Pictograph from Carrizo Plains, San Luis Obispo County." *Univ. Cal. Arch. Survey Report* 9:20–26.

LEONARD, NELSON, III
  1966   "Ven-70 and Its Place in the Late Period of the Western Santa Monica Mountains." *Univ. Cal. Arch. Survey Annual Report 1966:*215–42.

LILLARD, J. B. and PURVES, W. K.
  1936   "The Archaeology of the Deer Creek-Cosumnes Area, Sacramento County, California." *Bull. Sacramento Junior Coll.* 1.

LILLARD, J. B.; HEIZER, ROBERT F.; and FENENGA, FRANKLIN
  1939   "An Introduction to the Archaeology of Central California." *Bull. Sacramento Junior Coll.* 2.

LOPATIN, IVAN A.
  1939   "Fossil Man in the Vicinity of Los Angeles, California." *Proc. Sixth Pacific Science Cong.* 4:177–81.

LOUD, LLEWELLYN L.
  1918   "Ethnogeography and Archaeology of the Wiyot Territory." *Univ. Cal. Pub. Am. Arch. Eth.* 14(3):221–436.
  1926   "The Stege Mounds at Richmond, California." *Univ. Cal. Pub. Am. Arch. Eth.* 17(4):355–72.

MCGEEIN, D. J., and MUELLER, W. C.
  1955   "A Shellmound in Marin County, California." *Am. Ant.* 21:52–62.

MEIGHAN, C. W.
  1955   "Archaeology of the North Coast Ranges, California." *Univ. Cal. Arch. Survey Report* 30:1–39.
  1959a "The Little Harbor Site, Catalina Island: An Example of Ecological Interpretation in Archaeology." *Am. Ant.* 24:383–405.
  1959b "California Cultures and the Concept of an Archaic Stage." *Am. Ant.* 24:289–305.
  1965   "Pacific Coast Archaeology." *The Quaternary of the United States: a review volume for the VII Congress of the International Association for Quaternary Research.* H. E. Wright, Jr., and David G. Frey (eds.). Princeton, New Jersey: Princeton University Press: 709–22.

——— and HAYNES, C. VANCE
   1968   "New Studies on the Age of the Borax Lake Site." *The Mas-
          terkey* 42:4–9.
   1970   "The Borax Lake Site Revisited." *Science* 167:1213–21.

———; PENDERGAST, D M.; SWARTZ, B. K., JR.; and WISSLER, M. D.
   1958   "Ecological Interpretation in Archaeology, Part I." *Am.
          Ant.* 24:1–23.

MEREDITH, H. C.
   1900   "Archaeology of California: Central and Northern Cali-
          fornia." *Prehistoric Implements: A Reference Book,* War-
          ren K. Moorehead (ed.). Cincinnati: The Robert Clarke
          Co.: 258–94.

MERRIAM, JOHN C.
   1906   "Recent Cave Exploration in California." *Am. Anthro.*
          8:221–28.

MICHELS, JOSEPH
   1965   "A Progress Report on the UCLA Obsidian Hydration Dat-
          ing Laboratory." *Univ. Cal. Arch. Survey Annual Report
          1965:*377–88.

NELSON, NELS C.
   1909   "Shellmounds of the San Francisco Bay Region." *Univ. Cal.
          Pub. Am. Arch. Eth.* 7(4):309–56.
   1910   "The Ellis Landing Shellmound." *Univ. Cal. Pub. Am. Arch.
          Eth.* 7(5):357–426.

OLSON, RONALD L.
   1930   "Chumash Prehistory." *Univ. Cal. Pub. Am. Arch. Eth.*
          28(1):1–21.

ORE, H. THOMAS, and WARREN, CLAUDE N.
   1971   "Late Pleistocene-Early Holocene Geomorphic History of
          Lake Mohave, California." *Geolog. Soc. Am. Bull.*
          82:2553–62.

ORR, PHIL C.
   1943   "Archaeology of Mescalitan Island and Customs of the
          Canalino." *Santa Barbara Mus. Nat. Hist. Occas. Pap.* 3.
   1962a "The Arlington Springs Site, Santa Rosa Island, California."
          Am. Ant. 27:417–19.
   1962b "Arlington Springs Man." *Science* 135:219.
   1962c "On New Radiocarbon Dates from the California Channel
          Islands." *Santa Barbara Mus. Nat. Hist. Depart. Anthro.
          Bull.* 8.

PUTNAM, F. W.
   1879   "The Southern Californians: Introduction." *Report upon
          United States Geographical Survey of the Territory of the
          United States West of the One Hundredth Meridian.* Vol.
          VII Archaeology. George M. Wheeler (ed.) Engineer
          Dept., U. S. Army, Washington, Government Printing Of-
          fice: 1–31.

1906   "Evidence of the Work of Man on Objects from Quaternary Caves in California." *Am. Anthro.* 8:229–35.

REINMAN, FRED M.
1964   "Maritime Adaptation on San Nicholas Island, California." *Univ. Cal. Arch. Survey Annual Report 1964:*47–80.

RIDDELL, FRANCES
1956   "Final Report on the Archaeology of Tommy Tucker Cave." *Univ. Cal. Arch. Survey Report* 35:1–25.
1960   "The Archaeology of the Karlo Site (Las-7) California." *Univ. Cal. Arch. Survey Report* 53.

——— and OLSON, WILLIAM H.
1969   "An Early Man Site in the San Joaquin Valley, California." *Am. Ant.* 34:121–30.

ROBERTS, FRANK H. H.
1940   "Developments in the Problem of the North American Paleo-Indian." *Smith. Misc. Coll.* 100:51–116.

ROGERS, D. B.
1929   *Prehistoric Man of the Santa Barbara Coast.* Santa Barbara: Santa Barbara Museum of Natural History.

ROGERS, M. J.
1929a   "Stone Art of the San Dieguito Plateau." *Am. Anthro.* 31:454–67.
1929b   "Report of an Archaeological Reconnaissance in the Mohave Sink Region." *San Diego Mus. Pap.* 1(1).
1939   "Early Lithic Industries of the Lower Basin of the Colorado River and Adjacent Desert Areas." *San Diego Mus. Pap.* 3.
1945   "An Outline of Yuman Prehistory." *Southwestern Jour. Anth.* 1:167–98.

SCHENCK, W. EGBERT
1926   "The Emeryville Shellmound (Final Report)." *Univ. Cal. Pub. Am. Arch. Eth.* 23(3):147–282.

——— and DAWSON, ELMER J.
1929   "Archaeology of the Northern San Joaquin Valley." *Univ. Cal. Pub. Am. Arch. Eth.* 25(4):289–413.

SCHUMACHER, PAUL
1875   "The Manufacture of Shell Fishhooks by the Early Inhabitants of the Santa Barbara Channel Islands." *Archiv. fur Anthropologie,* 8:223–24. Translated in *Univ. Cal. Arch. Survey Report* 50:23–25, 1960.
1877   "Researches in the Kjokkenmoddings and Graves of a Former Population of the Santa Barbara Islands and the Adjacent Mainland." *Bull. United States Geolog. and Geograph. Survey of the Territories* 3.

SHUMWAY, GEORGE; HUBBS, CARL L.; and MORIARTY, JAMES R.
1961   "Scripps Estates Site, San Diego, California: A La Jolla Site Dated 5460 to 7370 Years before the Present." *New York Acad. of Sci. Annals* 93:37–132.

SIMPSON, RUTH D.
1961 "Coyote Gulch." *Arch. Survey Assoc. of Southern Cal. Pap.* 5.

SINCLAIR, W. J.
1904 "The Exploration of the Patten Creek Cave." *Univ. Cal. Pub. Am. Arch. Eth.* 2(1):1–28.
1908 "Recent Investigation Bearing on the Question of the Occurrence of Neocene Man in the Auriferous Gravels of the Sierra Nevada." *Univ. Cal. Pub. Am. Arch. Eth.* 7(2):107–31.

STICKEL, E. GARY
1968 "Status Differentiations at the Rincon Site." *Univ. Cal. Arch. Survey Annual Report 1968:*209–61.

TAYLOR, WALTER W.
1961 "Archaeology and Language in Western North America." *Am. Ant.* 27:71–81.

TREGANZA, ADAN
1942 "An Archaeological Reconnaissance of Northeastern Baja California and Southwestern California." *Am. Ant.* 7:152–63.
1952 "Archaeological Investigations in the Farmington Reservoir Area, Stanislaus County, California." *Univ. Cal. Arch. Survey Report* 14.

——— and BIERMAN, ANGUS
1958 "The Topanga Culture: Final Report on Excavations, 1948." *Univ. Cal. Anthro. Records* 20:45–86.

——— and COOK, S. F.
1948 "The Quantitative Investigation of Aboriginal Sites: Complete Excavation with Physical and Archaeological Analysis of a Single Mound." *Am. Ant.* 23:287–97.

——— and HEIZER, ROBERT F.
1953 "Additional Data on the Farmington Complex, a Stone Implement Assemblage of Probable Early Postglacial Date from Central California." *Univ. Cal. Arch. Survey Report* 22:28–41.

——— and MALAMUD, C. G.
1950 "The Topanga Culture: First Season's Excavation of the Tank Site, 1947." *Univ. Cal. Anthro. Records* 12(4).

TRUE, D. L.
1958 "An Early Complex in San Diego County, California." *Am. Ant.* 23:255–63.

UHLE, MAX
1907 "The Emeryville Shellmound." *Univ. Cal. Pub. Am. Arch. Eth.* 7(1):1–106.

WALKER, EDWIN F.
1951 *Five Prehistoric Archaeological Sites in Los Angeles County, California.* Publications of the F. W. Hodge Anniversary Publication Fund, Los Angeles, Southwest Museum.

WALLACE, WILLIAM J.
  1955 "Suggested Chronology for Southern California Coastal Ar-
         chaeology." *Southwestern Jour. Anth.* 11:214–30.
  1960 "Archaeological Resources of the Buena Vista Watershed,
         San Diego County, California." *Univ. Cal. Arch. Survey
         Annual Report 1959–60:*277–306.
  1962 "Prehistoric Cultural Developments in the Southern Cali-
         fornia Deserts." *Am. Ant.* 28:172–80.

WARREN, CLAUDE N.
  1966 "The San Dieguito Type Site: M. J. Rogers' 1938 Excava-
         tion on the San Dieguito River" (ed.). *San Diego Mus. Pap.* 5.
  1967 "The San Dieguito Complex: A Review and Hypothesis."
         Am. Ant. 32:168–85.
  1968 "Cultural Tradition and Ecological Adaptation on the South-
         ern California Coast." *Eastern New Mexico Univ. Cont.
         Anthro.* 1(3):1–14.
  1970 "Time and Topography: Elizabeth W. C. Campbell's Ap-
         proach to the Prehistory of the California Desert." *The
         Masterkey* 44:4–14.

——— and DeCOSTA, JOHN
  1964 "Dating Lake Mohave Artifacts and Beaches." *Am. Ant.*
         30:206–9.

——— and PAVESIC, MAX G.
  1963 "Shell Midden Analysis of Site SDi-603 and Ecological Im-
         plications for Cultural Development of Batiquitos Lagoon,
         San Diego County, California." *Univ. Cal. Arch. Survey
         Annual Report 1962–63:*407–38.

——— and TRUE, D. L.
  1961 "The San Dieguito Complex and its place in California
         Prehistory." *Univ. Cal. Arch. Survey Annual Report
         1960–61:*246–338.

———; TRUE, D. L.; and EUDEY, A. A.
  1961 "Early Gathering Complexes of Western San Diego County."
         *Univ. Cal. Arch. Survey Annual Report 1960–61:*1–106.

WEDEL, WALDO R.
  1941 "Archaeological Investigations at Buena Vista Lake, Kern
         County, California." *Bur. of Am. Eth. Bull.* 130.

WEIDE, MARGARET L.
  1969 "Seasonality of Pismo Clam Collecting at Ora-82." *Univ.
         Cal. Arch. Survey Annual Report 1969:*127–42.

WHITNEY, J. D.
  1879 "The Auriferous Gravels of the Sierra Nevada of California."
         Mem. Mus. Comp. Zoology Harvard Coll. 3(1).

YATES, LORENZO G.
  1900 "Archaeology of California: Southern California." *Prehis-
         toric Implements: A Reference Book,* Warren K. Moore-
         head (ed.). Cincinnati: The Robert Clarke Co.: 230–52.

KEY

1. Ozette
2. San Juan Islands
3. Fraser Canyon
4. The Dalles, Wakemap Mound, Five Mile Rapids
5. McNary Reservoir
6. Lind Coulee
7. Lake Roosevelt
8. Marmes Rockshelter
9. Weis Rockshelter
10. Klamath Basin

The Pacific Northwest

9 THE PACIFIC NORTHWEST

Roderick Sprague

INTRODUCTION

The Pacific Northwest, an area of vastly varied climatological and physiographic regions, includes the political
units of British Columbia, Washington, Oregon, Idaho,
and by some definitions parts of Alberta, Montana, and
California. The Northwest Coast includes rugged mountains reaching to the sea and forming islands north of
Puget Sound with more sloping beaches south to northern
California. The Japanese Current accounts for the mild,
generally moist climate, with rainfall reaching as high
as 140 inches annually in the Olympic Peninsula. The
ethnographic Northwest Coast is an area of tribal and
linguistic diversity, in contrast to a fairly constant complex
of cultural traits, including a marine-oriented economy,
well-developed wood technology, a stratified society, and
a well-developed and unique art style. Drucker (1943)
provides the best definition and subdivisions for both the
ethnographic and archaeological Northwest Coast.

Beyond the Coast Range, the Cascade Mountains separate the climatological and ethnographic Northwest Coast
from the interior or ethnographic Plateau. The Interior
Plateau, often divided into the Canadian Plateau and the
Columbia Plateau, is a noticeably drier area, with less
than eighteen inches' annual rainfall in parts of central
Washington and Oregon. Also in contrast to the Northwest Coast, it has less tribal and linguistic diversity. The
Salish- and Sahaptian-speaking groups occupy more than
80 percent of the area. Some, especially Malouf, quite

properly extend the ethnographic Plateau into the mountainous regions of Montana, while others with equally good reason include the Carrier, Sekani, and other Athabaskan-speaking peoples to the north and the Klamath-Modoc to the south. An area of forests in the north giving way to rolling grasslands in the south, the archaeological Plateau has only recently been clearly defined (Nelson 1969: 2–3), in contrast to the physiographic and ethnographic definitions.

Those academic institutions situated within the political boundaries of the Pacific Northwest do not necessarily restrict their archaeological activities to that region. Archaeological work in Alaska has been carried out by several Northwest schools; the University of Oregon and Idaho State University have a strong interest in the Great Basin; the several Montana schools, and at one time the University of Idaho, worked in the Plains region. However, the emphasis has been and probably will continue to be largely one of local archaeology.

The references cited for the Pacific Northwest will in no way be a complete or even representative bibliography for the region. Such bibliographic material can be found in Fladmark (1970) for British Columbia, Butler (1968) for Idaho, Johnson and Cole (1969) for Oregon, Swartz (1967) for the Klamath Basin portion of Oregon and northern California, and Sprague (1967) for Washington.

The only recent summaries of archaeological history in the Northwest are Butler (1968) for Idaho, and Carlson (1970) for British Columbia. David G. Rice is preparing a history of amateur societies in the Pacific Northwest.

No attempt will be made to summarize the various theoretical contributions to the Northwest because this has been done most recently by Leonhardy (1968), Nelson (1969), and especially Rice (1967) for the Plateau and for both the Plateau and the Northwest Coast by Jeanine Anderson (1967).

THE PERIOD OF EXPLORATION

The explorations of Lewis and Clark in 1804–6 constituted the first well-documented contact by Euroamericans with the Indians of the Plateau and in many cases with the Northwest Coast. Although not engaging in any archaeological excavations, Lewis and Clark often made ethnographic observations without parallel in the later record. For example, we have only archaeological evidence plus the observations of Lewis and Clark for subterranean sweat lodges among the Nez Perce. Also, many of the burial practices observed by Lewis and Clark on the Snake and Columbia rivers are known only through their observations or through archaeological work.

The first "archaeological excavations" in the Pacific Northwest involved three ethnographic grave-robbing incidents at the mouth of the Columbia River: in 1811 by Ross Cox, in 1825 by John Scouler, and in 1835 by John K. Townsend. As a result of these or other raids upon the deformed skulls of the Chinook region, Samuel G. Morton in 1846 was able to describe several of the typical flattened skulls in his Boston collection.

The work of Henry R. Schoolcraft involved descriptions of burial practices in Oregon and antiquities on the coast of Oregon, plus a section concerning antiquities in Oregon by George Gibbs, an ethnographer with the railroad surveys in the Pacific Northwest. Much of Gibbs' work was later assembled as a *Contribution to North American Ethnology* in 1877, which contained several sections that were more archaeological than ethnographic in nature.

The work of John K. Lord in 1866 described a long expedition through British Columbia and Washington and involved frequent reference to surface finds plus descriptions of Indian burial grounds. The first periodical article to be concerned with the archaeology of the Pacific

Northwest comes from work in Oregon by H. A. Chase entitled "Indian Mounds and Relics on the Coast of Oregon" in the 1873 *American Journal of Science and Arts*. This work on the coast of Oregon was followed by two brief articles in U. S. government publications in the 1870s by Paul Schumacher (no relation to former Chief, Archeological Investigations, Western Service Center, National Park Service).

Two early adversaries in fossil hunting, Cope and Marsh, both became involved in early man discoveries in the Pacific Northwest during the 1870s and 1880s. A later early man authority was Charles H. Sternberg, writing on Pleistocene man and fossil elephants during the 1890s and 1900s in Washington and Oregon. The review of Daugherty (1956) on early man studies in the Intermontane Region presents a summary of these early beginnings. Another early name in the Pacific Northwest was that of Rev. Myron Eells, who published generally in the *American Antiquarian and Oriental Journal* and *The Archaeologist* on relics and mounds in Oregon and Washington during the last quarter of the nineteenth century. The publication of Bancroft's *Works* in 1883 was basically the first summary to be presented on antiquities of the Pacific Northwest. His "The Native Races" presents an excellent summary of every published source available at that time. The following year a collection by Captain C. Bendire from the John Day River, Oregon, was described in the *Third Annual Report of the Bureau of* [American] *Ethnology*. Garrick Mallery provided the first reports of the rich pictographic inventory to be found in the Pacific Northwest, also published by the Bureau of American Ethnology near the end of the century.

An anonymous article in the *American Antiquarian and Oriental Journal* in 1889 describing historic artifacts from an Indian burial in eastern Washington could be interpreted as the first historical archaeology to be published in the region. An obscure work by James Terry (1891) concerning sculptured anthropoid ape heads near the John Day River created profound interest in sculpture of the Columbia River, an interest that has continued unabated for some eighty years. In the same year in Albany, Oregon, a local schoolteacher, George L. Howe, began publication of a journal entitled *The Antiquarian* (not to be confused with the journal of the same title published later in Columbus, Ohio), in which Howe wrote articles himself on such topics as Egyptian mummies but included many interesting tidbits on Pacific Northwest archaeology and ethnology. Familiar names such as Rev. Eells, James Wickersham, and James Deans were to be found in the three numbers of *The Antiquarian* that were published.

THE EARLY PIONEER PERIOD AND THE JESUP EXPEDITION

The Jesup North Pacific Expedition, financed largely by Morris K. Jesup, president of The American Museum of Natural History, was directed by Franz Boas and constituted the first major effort in Pacific Northwest archaeology. Virtually all of the archaeology was under the personal direction of Harlan I. Smith. Smith, a prolific writer often publishing the same article in three or four places, published on Northwest prehistory from 1898 to 1936 long after he had ceased active field work in the region. Even considering the time period, his field work left much to be desired. On the other hand, much of his work is invaluable because it represents the only reported excavations in much of British Columbia and Washington. The major portion of Smith's better reports are contained in *The American Museum of Natural History Memoirs*, or, as it is better known in the Northwest, by its subseries title, *Publications of the Jesup North Pacific Expedition*. These works were issued at irregular intervals between 1900 and 1907.

Minor archaeological excavations were carried out in

1901 by Merton L. Miller in connection with the Field
Columbian Museum expedition to the Plateau. It was also
during the close of the nineteenth and the beginning of
the twentieth century that Charles Hill-Tout began his long
but rather unspectacular work in British Columbia and
Washington. Carlson (1970:11) sees Hill-Tout's 1895 report as the beginning of scientific archaeology in British
Columbia. In 1907, the Peabody Museum at Harvard
University sent Herbert Joseph Spinden to conduct ethnographic research among the Nez Perce Indians of Idaho.
While the work of Spinden (1908) is generally thought
of as the basic ethnographic work concerning the Nez
Perce, it is also a very valuable and useful archaeological
record of the same region. One of the most useful works
of Harlan I. Smith was published in 1910, representing a
survey in the Yakima Valley under the auspices of The
American Museum of Natural History. The extreme detail of Smith's descriptions of artifacts and collections he
visited make this an invaluable source for the archaeology of the central Plateau.

The first systematic archaeological survey in northern
Idaho is to be found in the 1912 work of H. J. Rust in the
Lake Coeur d'Alene region. Albert B. Reagan, a part-
time Northwest archaeologist, conducted archaeological
investigations in western Washington and western British
Columbia during the second decade of the twentieth
century.

A strange chapter in Pacific Northwest archaeology occurred in the Spokane region, probably beginning in 1919
and reaching its climax in the summer of 1924 with the
almost daily newspaper reports on the work of a local
would-be runic expert, Oluf L. Opsjon. Opsjon was convinced that the pictographs in the Spokane region were
Norse runes left by early Norsemen of the Norse Sagas.
A recent revival of this particular view has been published
by Karl H. Isselstein (1965) of Spokane under the title,
Ancient Cataclysms which Changed Earth's Surface.

THE LATE PIONEER PERIOD
AND WORK ON THE COLUMBIA RIVER

The modern period of Northwest archaeology begins with the first really theoretical work in 1923 by A. L. Kroeber entitled, "American Culture and the Northwest Coast." This work outlined many of the problems of Northwest Coast-Interior relationships that are only now being investigated enough for us to begin testing hypotheses of the type Kroeber was suggesting.

Virtually all major work following Smith and until after the Second World War was done on the Columbia River below the Canadian border. Schenck and Strong initiated a long period of Lower Columbia work with a study of petroglyphs near the Dalles, followed shortly thereafter by two articles in the *American Anthropologist* by Julian H. Steward on artifacts from the Lower Columbia. These three men combined efforts (Strong, Schenck, and Steward 1930) to produce the first comprehensive site survey and excavation report in the Pacific Northwest. This publication, "Archaeology of The Dalles-Deschutes Region," issued by the University of California in their *Publications in American Archaeology and Ethnology,* set a precedent for careful and detailed work. Even by modern standards it is a well-written, well-organized report with sufficient photographs, illustrations, maps, profiles, tables, and all of the other traits we have come to accept in good archaeological reporting. Also extremely important and long affecting Plateau archaeology is a diagram of forms for the classification of "arrowheads, spearpoints, or knives" (1930:78). While no longer an acceptable taxonomic system, the chart and its labels were utilized by professional archaeologists well into the 1950s and are still commonly utilized by amateurs within the region.

A second major contribution to the Columbia River archaeology of the late pioneer period from 1926 through

1934 was the work of Herbert W. Krieger, Curator of Ethnology, U. S. National Museum. Krieger worked largely within the Middle Columbia River, doing extensive surveying and testing in both burial and housepit sites. Krieger was also responsible for the only work that was done in the Bonneville Dam Reservoir prior to its flooding, work that is only now being prepared for publication by George Phebus, Jr., of the Department of Anthropology, Smithsonian Institution. Krieger gives us what little information we have on the earliest amateur group in the Northwest, the Columbia River Archaeological Society. The major contribution of this society is the collection of R. T. Congdon, M.D., Wenatchee, Washington, housed in the Chelan County Historical Museum, Cashmere, Washington. There is a current move in the Wenatchee area to reorganize this society.

Two publications from the late 1930s also give some indication of the activities of amateur archaeologists in the Pacific Northwest during this time period. A work by Harold C. Cundy entitled *Petrographs of North Central Washington* was a voluminous, privately printed, colorplate book illustrating pictographs in the Wenatchee area. A work by another amateur, Jay Perry (1939), on cedar cist burials on the Middle Columbia, was so far ahead of its time in content and observations that it had to be reprinted in 1959 by the Oregon Archaeological Society. Another well-known amateur, N. G. Seaman, published his recollections and ramblings in the *Oregon Historical Quarterly* as a further indication of the state of amateur archaeology just prior to the Second World War. His later book (1946) became a favorite with amateurs but has never been widely accepted by the professionals.

During this time period, what little work was going on in Idaho was largely within the Great Basin rather than the Plateau, with the exception of some recording of pictographs in the *Idaho State Historical Society, Annual Reports.*

The Great Fraser Midden in Vancouver was the subject of frequent newspaper articles in the Vancouver area.

Charles Hill-Tout published a description of the mound in 1930 in *Museum and Art Notes,* the publication of The Art, Historical and Scientific Association of Vancouver. This series has never been a strong source in archaeology, with no outstanding works until Charles E. Borden's Tweedsmuir Park Survey in 1952.

The long and prolific career of L. S. Cressman in the Northwest began in 1933, shortly after arriving at the University of Oregon, with the publication of a burial site report from southwestern Oregon. The first university-based archaeological program in the Pacific Northwest was started by Cressman, and if one man can be singled out as making the greatest contribution to Pacific Northwest archaeology it is indeed L. S. Cressman, with his four decades of continual and devoted work. His work on the petroglyphs of Oregon, published in 1937, was the first statewide petroglyph study in the Pacific Northwest. An honors thesis by Robin A. Drews in 1938 was apparently the first thesis on archaeology to be written in the Pacific Northwest and was directed by Cressman. Likewise the first master's thesis in Northwest archaeology was written in 1939 by Alex D. Krieger, also under the direction of L. S. Cressman.

A third major project of the late pioneer period was the effort on the part of many, including Cressman, to conduct salvage archaeological excavations behind Grand Coulee Dam in Lake Roosevelt from July 1939 through September 1940. The published results of this work by Collier, Hudson, and Ford (1942), while not up to the standards of the work of Strong, Schenck, and Steward, is still one of the best pre-World War II publications to be produced in the Pacific Northwest. Much of the local support of the project in Spokane was through the efforts of Joel E. Ferris, working through the Eastern Washington State Historical Society. The labor for the project was provided by the National Youth Administration, while the actual work was directed from the Department of Anthropology of the University of Washington and the Department of Sociology and Anthropology of the State College

of Washington. The work of Donald Collier while at the
State College of Washington (Washington State University) marks the introduction of this institution into the field
of Northwest archaeology. In addition to the authors of
the report, the field notes still on file at the Eastern Washington State Historical Society, Spokane, reveal such well-
known names as Alex D. Krieger (no relation to Herbert
W. Krieger), Philip Drucker, and Robert L. Stephenson.
Often in direct competition with the archaeological project was the disinterment of "historic" graves by the Ball
& Dodd Funeral Home of Spokane. Very little is known of
this operation except through interviews with Howard T.
Ball and one brief article on the project (Ball 1941).

The war years were a time of meager archaeological
activity in the Pacific Northwest, as was typical for most of
the United States and Canada. It was a time of limited
activity at the University of Oregon, with Cressman and
Laughlin working largely within the Willamette Valley.
It was also a period of stock taking, with Heizer (1941)
publishing a review of Oregon prehistory and with the
publication of "Pacific Northwest Anthropological Research" by Melville Jacobs in 1941 in *Pacific Northwest
Quarterly*.

Philip Drucker's (1943) survey of the northern Northwest Coast conducted in the late 1930s was the first really
systematic work in the region, and only in the late 1960s
was any research begun to verify many of his original
observations. The work of Joel V. Berreman (1944) on
Chetco archaeology is the only work on the Northwest to
be found in the short-lived *General Series in Anthropology* in the 1940s. A master's thesis from the University of
Arizona by H. Thomas Cain written in 1946 was eventually published in 1950 by the University of Washington
Press. It was another in a long series of efforts to understand the rock art of the Pacific Northwest, and it still
remains as one of the basic works.

The first article in twenty-five years of archaeological
reporting by Lucile McDonald, a feature story writer for
the *Seattle Times,* was published in 1946. Lucile's stamina

in seeking out archaeological stories when and where they were happening overshadows that of the stronger sex in Pacific Northwest newspaper circles. Her loyalty to the field and her efforts to promote Northwest archaeology have resulted in over forty feature articles published in the *Seattle Times*.

THE RIVER BASIN SURVEY ERA

The year 1947 saw the first publication of some thirty-five different mimeographed works of the Columbia Basin Project, River Basin Surveys, the Smithsonian Institution. The earliest report, dating from October 1947, lists Philip Drucker as field director. The early reports were authored by the actual surveyors, including such names as Richard D. Daugherty, Francis A. Riddell, and Franklin Fenenga. The later reports have traditionally been listed as authored by the field director. In October of 1948, Douglas Osborne was listed as acting field director. By May of 1950 Osborne was at the Department of Anthropology, University of Washington, and Joel L. Shiner was acting field director. The more lengthy site excavation reports were issued by Osborne and Shiner until June of 1951. The archaeological survey work from September 1949 until the closing of the Columbia Basin Project office in June of 1952 was conducted by Shiner as acting field director. Publications in this series continued until December of 1953. The office was maintained in cooperation with the University of Oregon in Eugene.

During the approximate six years of operation, the Columbia Basin Project produced over forty surveys and reconnaissances of reservoirs and nine substantial reports of archaeological excavations. Frequent articles in *American Antiquity;* regional journals; and the *Bureau of American Ethnology, River Basin Survey Papers,* including one lengthy volume by Osborne (1957) on excavations in the McNary Reservoir, were also published. This last work, while poorly organized and extremely difficult to utilize for comparative purposes, is a landmark in the River Basin Survey work, since it is a complete inventory of the work accomplished in McNary Reservoir and shows exhaustive historical background research. It has also served as a point of origin for theoretical constructs in Plateau prehistory and the relationship between the Plateau and the Northwest Coast. It deserves a greater acknowledgment in the more recent theoretical schemes.

The contribution of the River Basin Survey work to later archaeological investigations in the Plateau cannot be denied. It was here that such extensive programs as the University of Washington work in McNary and Chief Joseph reservoirs, University of Oregon excavations in The Dalles and John Day reservoirs, Washington State University excavations in the Lower Snake River region, and later University of Washington excavations in Priest Rapids, Wanapum, and Wells reservoirs received their starts. On the other hand, the failure of the surveys to record the sites adequately (for example, in Lower Granite Reservoir the initial survey found seven sites, while a later survey reported almost one hundred sites) and a lack of imagination in preparing budgets combined with subsequent inflation have resulted in an almost catastrophic lack of funds for excavation in the Columbia Basin region in the past fifteen years.

After the Columbia Basin Project became administered by the National Park Service, the program prospered under the able direction of Paul J. F. Schumacher, former Chief, Archeological Investigations, Western Service Center, San Francisco. Although largely an administrator, Schumacher has also conducted several historical archaeological excavations at National Park Service sites in the Northwest.

At the same time that increased activities were being financed by the River Basin Surveys, the area of historical archaeology in the Pacific Northwest was receiving its first important financing. Louis R. Caywood, beginning in 1947 and continuing through 1955, conducted excavations at Fort Vancouver, Fort Clatsop, Spokane House, and Fort Okanogan. Also in the late 1940s and early 1950s, Thomas R. Garth, Jr., excavated at Waiilatpu Mission and Fort Walla Walla. The only archaeological work to be reported by Whitman College, Walla Walla, was in cooperation with Garth from 1948 through 1950. Work on the Northwest Coast and interior British Columbia was coming of age by the 1940s with a survey by A. E. Pickford and the work of Marian W. Smith (1950) in the Fraser region, the work of Arden R. King (1950) in the San Juan Islands, and a survey of the Lower Puget Sound by Winterhouse. The first annual archaeological field school in the Northwest was set up by the University of Washington in 1947 in the San Juan Islands with direction during the next five years from Arden King, Carroll Burroughs, and Aden Treganza.

Charles E. Borden began work in the Fraser Delta from the University of British Columbia in 1946, and soon (Borden 1950) was bringing the archaeological picture of British Columbia into focus. Borden, a diligent field archaeologist, also enjoys setting up straw men for his colleagues to demolish. More often than not, Borden has beaten his colleagues to the punch by demolishing his own schemes and erecting new ones. Salvage archaeology in British Columbia also began under Borden with his survey of Tweedsmuir Park. The Canadian site designation system is likewise the work of Borden (1952). During the same time period Douglas Leechman published several items on British Columbia archaeology in regional journals.

As a direct result of a survey by Riddell and Daugherty in the summer of 1947, an important early man site was found in the Lind Coulee of central Washington. This site was investigated in a preliminary way during the summers of 1948 to 1950 and was extensively excavated in the summers of 1951 and 1952. Daugherty utilized this work for a doctoral dissertation at the University of Washington in 1953. The descriptive material was published separately from the extensive comparative data (Daugherty 1956), and this same material was also to become the basis for the first popularization of archaeological investigations in the

state of Washington (Daugherty 1959). This circular,
put out by the Division of Mines and Geology in Olympia,
was one of two such circulars that became instrumental
in popularizing and gaining public support for the archaeology program at the State College of Washington
(Washington State University).

The Lind Coulee material was unquestionably the
earliest material in the Northwest at the time of its discovery. Along with material of Cressman's from southern
Oregon, it was among the first materials to be dated by
the radiocarbon technique by Libby. The age determinations assigned the Lind Coulee material have been exceeded in other sites, but because they were solid carbon
determinations the general consensus today is that they
are too late.

The arrival of Richard D. Daugherty at the State College of Washington in 1949 was to signal the end of the
domination of Northwest archaeology by the coastal
schools. Daugherty, with the active support of Allan H.
Smith, has built a large and impressive archaeology program, including extensive laboratory facilities. The school
at Pullman has dominated the archaeology scene in
Washington with excursions into Idaho, Oregon, and
British Columbia for the past twenty years. Daugherty set
up the first archaeological field school at Washington
State in the summer of 1953, with five students excavating at McGregor Cave in eastern Washington.

PROBLEM-ORIENTED ARCHAEOLOGY IN AND OUT OF THE RESERVOIRS

While excavations were continuing, there were also
important surveys being conducted during the early
1950s. Among these were the work of Collins on the
Oregon coast, Herbert C. Taylor, Jr., in the San Juan
Islands, Warren W. Caldwell in central British Columbia,
Alan L. Bryan on Puget Sound, Bruce Stallard and Clay-
ton Denman on the Washington coast, Charles E. Borden

in the Kootenay (Kutenai) region, and Richard V. Emmons in the Nooksack River Valley.

Work in northern Idaho experienced a short-lived flourish under Tom O. Miller, Jr., while he was briefly situated in the Coeur d'Alene region. On the Coast, Roy L. Carlson (1960) utilized excavations in the San Juan Islands for a master's thesis from the University of Washington, which gave one of the first chronological sequences on the Northwest Coast. The year 1955 was important in terms of new theoretical contributions to the Pacific Northwest archaeology. This was the year that Willey and Phillips produced their "method and theory" articles in the *American Anthropologist* and made minor reference to situations in the Northwest. Philip Drucker (1955) published "New Interpretations of Aboriginal American Culture History," while the year before Borden (1954) had fired the first salvo in a long, involved, but friendly exchange with practically everyone in the Pacific Northwest. Borden's concern was mainly with the question of Coastal-Interior relationships and the direction of flow of cultural innovations found in the two regions. Osborne took up the challenge the following year, and with the aid of two students, Warren W. Caldwell and Robert H. Crabtree (1956), issued a reply with the provincial title, "The Problem of Northwest Coastal-Interior Relationships as Seen from Seattle." Fuel was added to the fire from outside the region by Chester S. Chard, with his work in the same year, "Northwest Coast-Northeast Asiatic Similarities: A New Hypothesis."

Prior to 1950 publication in the Pacific Northwest was limited almost entirely to national journals or to the two regional publication series, *University of Oregon Monographs, Studies in Anthropology,* largely dominated by the work of Cressman, and an occasional work in the *University of Washington Publications in Anthropology,* by this time a dead series. As is typical of the Pacific Northwest, the archaeological work has been tightly integrated in the over-all anthropological programs of the various academic institutions. In 1955 a new journal entitled the *Davidson Journal of Anthropology,* named in honor of D. S. Davidson, one of the 1948 founders of the Seattle Anthropological Society, began publication from the University of Washington. This was an ambitious and highly professional journal in spite of its mimeograph format, but, unfortunately, it was to survive for only 3½ years. Another excellent but short-lived journal was *Anthropology in British Columbia,* an annual series beginning in 1950 and lasting through No. 5 in 1956. Accompanying this was a *Memoir* series beginning in 1952 and struggling on through No. 5 in 1964. Carling Malouf, Montana State University, Missoula (University of Montana) served as editor for *Anthropology and Sociology Papers,* a series devoted mainly to the Plains but with obvious connections to the mountainous regions of the Plateau.

From its inception on May 8, 1948, in Portland, Oregon, the Northwest Anthropological Conference has been meeting yearly at various institutions throughout the Pacific Northwest. By 1955 the Northwest Anthropological Conference had largely supplanted the essentially defunct Western States Branch, American Anthropological Association, which had briefly published a *Newsletter* and *News Bulletin* in 1951 and a series known as *Western Anthropology* under the editorship of Carling Malouf. The Northwest Anthropological Conference is almost unique in American anthropology as an organization with no dues, no officers, and no formal constitution. Meetings are set up by an *ad hoc* committee from the institution that has agreed to host the meetings the next year. The content of the meetings over the years has been surprisingly well-balanced, with virtually all of the important archaeological excavations reported, and with theoretical constructs presented in a preliminary form during this series of meetings (Sprague 1968).

Amateur activity during the 1950s also increased, with the formation of the Oregon Archaeological Society (OAS) in 1951. This society began publication of a newsletter entitled *Screenings* in March of 1952. In the early, formative years, this society was largely under the influence of a devoted amateur, Emory Strong. As Strong became more and more professional in his outlook, his influence upon the society progressively decreased. Strong is best known for his popular books on archaeology (1959) and studies in trade items, especially beads and Phoenix buttons. Of all of the amateur societies, probably the OAS is the most openly antagonistic to the objectives of the professional and scientific archaeologists. It is a society apparently directed at the collection and display of fine artifacts and seems to have little or no interest in culture history or the broader aspects of anthropological theory.

In direct opposition to the activities of the Oregon Archaeological Society, the Washington Archaeological Society (WAS) was formed in Seattle in 1955 as a result of an evening class in Northwest archaeology taught by Douglas Osborne. The WAS, in contrast to the OAS, has long been a rather small but devoted group of amateurs operating on scientific principles. The early direction was in the capable hands of Douglas Osborne. Also instrumental in the success of the society over the years was the devoted work of Mr. and Mrs. Charles G. Nelson, formerly of Seattle. However, cooperation between the University of Washington and the Washington Archaeological Society was seriously injured when Osborne was discharged by the university and the WAS demanded but never received an explanation for this dismissal (Nelson 1957). This rupture of relations was to have a serious effect on the initial success of Osborne's successor at the University of Washington, Robert Greengo. In the late 1950s satellite chapters of the Seattle group were formed at Pullman under the title of Palus Chapter, with direction from Daugherty, and at Ephrata (entitled Columbia Basin Chapter), largely with guidance from State Senator Nat Washington. Because of a lack of local interest and certain changes in the incorporation of the Seattle society, these two chapters shortly folded. The Society began publication of *The Washington Archaeologist* in 1957.

Another new but short-lived society, entitled the Columbia Archaeological Society, was formed in the late 1950s in Seattle and undertook excavations on Fishhook Jim Island in the Snake River.

Although not generally thought of as an archaeological publication series, the *Research Studies of the State College of Washington* issued a single Northwest archaeology number in March of 1956 under the editorship of Richard D. Daugherty. This was a highly successful venture involving articles by Daugherty, Warren A. Snyder, Osborne, Malouf, Taylor, Duff, and Borden, including both Plateau and Northwest Coast sites in Washington, British Columbia, and Montana. Especially significant from this volume are the works of Malouf describing cultural connections between the upper Missouri and the Columbia River systems, and the strong entry of Wilson Duff of the British Columbia Provincial Museum into the archaeology of British Columbia. It was also here that Daugherty first expanded the Krieger typological concept with the terms "form" and "style."

During the middle 1950s, extensive excavations on a crash basis were being undertaken by the University of Washington at Wakemap Mound on the Lower Columbia River (Butler 1958, Caldwell 1956). The importance of this site to the understanding of Lower Columbia archaeology cannot be overemphasized. Unfortunately, at this site Northwest archaeology reached an all-time low in terms of interpersonal relationships between professional archaeologists, between sponsoring agencies and professional archaeologists, and between amateur and professional archaeologists.

The Klamath Basin, the ethnographic territory of the Klamath and Modoc, is considered by most Pacific Northwest anthropologists as not only within the ethnographic Plateau but also as a part of the archaeological Plateau. However, the work within the Klamath Basin has been almost a subunit of the greater Plateau, with its own professionals, amateurs, museums, publications, and bibliography.

The one point of continuity has been the work of L. S. Cressman, as might be expected, since the major portion of the region is situated in Oregon. Cressman was the first worker to enter the region, and he has published two major works on Klamath Basin prehistory (1942, 1956). Attacking the area from the south, largely through work financed by the National Park Service in Lava Beds National Monument, R. J. Squier and Gordon L. Grosscup conducted surveys and archaeological excavations in the early 1950s. Thomas M. Newman and Cressman conducted excavations in connection with the Big Bend power development in the late 1950s.

The Klamath County Museum in Klamath Falls, Oregon, became actively involved in the archaeology of the region largely through the efforts of two curators with archaeological training. Roy L. Carlson in the late 1950s conducted surveys from the museum and also established the short-lived journal, *Klamath County Museum, Clearing House for News,* in 1957. Following Carlson was Benjamin K. Swartz, Jr., who continued the survey work, especially the survey and recording of pictographs. Swartz also founded the *Klamath County Museum, Research Papers,* a scholarly monograph series including not only archaeology but all phases of anthropology and history. Swartz left the museum in the late 1950s but returned to the area in the early 1960s to conduct archaeological surveys and excavations in the Lava Beds National Monument; his work was to form the basis for a doctoral dissertation at the University of Arizona in 1964. The pictography study by Swartz (1963) was the only work from the Pacific Northwest to be published in the *Archives of Archaeology* series. In 1968, Carrol B. Howe (nephew of George L. Howe), an amateur in the area, produced a work entitled *Ancient Tribes of the Klamath Country,* in the tradition of N. G. Seaman and Emory Strong.

Highway salvage archaeology in the State of Washington received the first of two starts in 1957 under the direction of Daugherty and Bruce Stallard. As a by-product of Stallard's work, a second circular was issued by the Division of Mines and Geology in the State of Washington, entitled *Archeology in Washington,* in 1958. This was the first over-all review to be presented on the archaeology of the entire state and was also the first organized bibliography to be published. This brief bibliography served as the basis for the more extensive bibliography of Sprague (1967). The first issue of the *Washington State University, Laboratory of Anthropology, Report of Investigations* was issued under Stallard's authorship in 1957; however, this series was not formally established nor numbers assigned until 1962, at which time the first nineteen issues were numbered retroactively.

While the University of Washington was working on the Washington side of the Columbia River in The Dalles Reservoir, the University of Oregon was covering its side of the river in field seasons from 1952 through 1956. Two major sites at either end of Five Mile Rapids are described in the extensive report by Cressman and four of his students: David L. Cole, Wilbur A. Davis, Thomas M. Newman, and Daniel J. Scheans (1960). All have continued to work in Oregon: Cole and Scheans in the Natural History Museum, University of Oregon, Davis at Oregon State University, and Newman at Portland State University. The report has been important in Northwest prehistory because it was one of the first stratigraphic sequences dating from the post-Pleistocene to the historic period. Like so much of Cressman's work, it was ahead of its time in the use of the ecological approach. It is also important in understanding the relationships between the Plateau and Northwest Coast because of the strategic location at the major point of contact between these two culture areas.

Following the work in The Dalles Dam Reservoir, the University of Oregon, initially under the direction of Cressman and increasingly under the direction of David L. Cole, began excavations in the John Day Reservoir area in 1958 and continued on an annual basis until the spring of 1968. Cole has followed a policy of not publishing his material until the total project is completed. However, he has made concise, well-written annual reports available to other workers in the Pacific Northwest, thus avoiding the common complaint in salvage archaeology that the lag between research and publication is often measured in decades rather than years. During the late 1950s the University of Washington salvage operations were largely within the Priest Rapids Reservoir under the direction of Robert E. Greengo.

The first historic archaeology in northern Idaho was conducted by Donald R. Tuohy at Sacred Heart Mission as part of a pipeline survey in 1956. The following year, Alfred W. Bowers, of the University of Idaho, commenced work on the Dean Site at Brown's Bench in central Idaho. Previous to this, most of Bowers' work had been conducted in the Great Plains. This was the same year that Earl H. Swanson, Jr., arrived at Idaho State College (Idaho State University); the following year he began publication of *Tebiwa,* a journal of the Idaho State University Museum, and a monograph series entitled *Occasional Papers of Idaho State University Museum.* Shortly thereafter, Swanson brought B. Robert Butler to Pocatello, thus creating one of the strongest archaeological programs in the Pacific Northwest.

In 1958, B. Robert Butler first stunned the Northwest archaeological circles with his Northwest Anthropological Conference paper entitled "Indian Wells I, A Speculation on a Possible Old Pan-Cordilleran Culture Tradition." Butler, an often controversial figure in Pacific Northwest archaeology, was a former student of Osborne's at the University of Washington. With a strong background in sociological theory and one of the best over-all knowledges of Plateau prehistory, he has served as devil's advocate and a thorn in the bed of roses of the more conventional Plateau archaeologists. The basic scheme of Butler's Old Cordilleran culture is best expressed in his 1961 work, while the theoretical basis for such a scheme is presented in an *American Anthropologist* article, "The Structure and Function of the Old Cordilleran Culture Concept," in 1965.

During the early 1960s amateur activities progressed on a more professional level, with the Washington Archaeological Society continuing its high-level activity at the Fish Town site, while the Oregon Archaeological Society cooperated more closely with professional archaeologists, especially at Wakemap Mound and in the Portland area. The Oregon Archaeological Society also initiated an *Occasional Publication* series of higher standards than their *Screenings*.

As a new source of funds, Washington State University, again under the direction of Daugherty, pressed for state allocations and through the cooperation of an interested amateur, State Senator Nat Washington, funds were made available for archaeology in the Sun Lakes State Park, with excavations conducted from 1958 through 1961 involving Osborne, Sprague, Steven S. Clinehens, and Oscar L. Mallory. Historical archaeological excavations from Washington State University were handled during this period by John D. Combes at Spokane House and military Fort Spokane. Olympic Peninsula archaeology by Washington State University was conducted by T. Stell Newman and Stanley J. Guinn.

Archaeological explorations in south-central and southwestern Washington were receiving their first emphasis in the late 1950s through the work of several former University of Washington students, including Claude N. Warren, Alan L. Bryan, and Donald R. Tuohy. Warren conducted the first important archaeological excavations in the Yakima region since the work of Harlan I. Smith shortly after the turn of the century. The publication of this work (1968) contained one of several contrasting views of Plateau culture history produced during this period. During the late 1950s and early 1960s, the major emphasis at Washington State University was on the Lower Snake River, beginning with Ice Harbor Reservoir and moving up through Lower Monumental and Little Goose reservoirs. By this time the University of Washington had moved to the Wanapum Reservoir. The publication of salvage work at both of these Washington schools suffered because virtually all of the research was tied up in student theses and dissertations. Frequently it was several years before reports were published, and in some cases whole sites and seasons have never been published.

In 1961 the results of the archaeological excavations in Rocky Reach Reservoir were published by Alexander Gunkel (1961) in a new series from Washington State University entitled *Theses in Anthropology*. Unfortunately, this rather ambitious series aborted with the first volume.

A popularization of Oregon archaeology was published in 1962 by Cressman under the title *The Scandal and the Cave, the Indians of Oregon*. The same year, Daugherty (1962) published his theoretical contribution to Pacific Northwest archaeology under the title "The Intermontane Western Tradition," in *American Antiquity*. Eight years later, Leonhardy and Rice (1970) made the following comment concerning Daugherty's work: "Based on what is now considered to have been exceedingly limited data, Daugherty's scheme was remarkably accurate." An equally important theoretical paper was also published in 1962 by Earl H. Swanson, Jr. His work, "The Emergence of Plateau Culture," was a revision of the theoretical portion of his doctoral dissertation at the University of Washington and has been a basic part of any subsequent study of Plateau culture history.

The first color film concerned with Pacific Northwest archaeology was produced in 1963 by E. Mott Davis as one of a series of salvage archaeology films from all over the United States funded by the National Science Foundation. This particular film, entitled *Spade Work for History: Plateau and Pacific,* is an interesting record of archaeological techniques in the early 1960s, but it has largely been replaced by more modern films as a teaching tool. Two years later, in 1965, Louis Huber produced a film entitled *Digging up the Past* through his own company, Northern Films of Seattle. This film, involving digs from the University of Washington and Washington State University, is a classic in unfortunate film work. The bad quality of the photography and splicing is exceeded only by the incredible dialogue that accompanies it.

Work at the University of Washington in the early 1960s continued with surveys of state parks and salvage in reservoirs, generally under the field direction of advanced students, including Brian G. Holmes, Sonja O. Solland, and Robert S. Kidd. The University of Washington also began excavations in the Wells Reservoir area, largely under the direction of Garland F. Grabert. Activities at Idaho State University were centered mainly on Weis Rockshelter near Cottonwood in north-central Idaho and at Birch Creek in eastern Idaho. Survey work continued from the University of Idaho under Bowers, while Cole at the University of Oregon continued work in the John Day Reservoir on the Columbia River.

Borden's work at the University of British Columbia in the early 1960s was concentrated largely on the Fraser Canyon, especially at cobble tool sites of somewhat controversial antiquity. In addition to Borden, Donald H. Mitchell, David Sanger, Derek G. Smith, Donald N. Abbott, Duff, and Kidd were also working and publishing on British Columbia archaeology during the 1960s. The passage in 1960 of the British Columbia Archaeological and Historic Sites Protection Act further protected and encouraged scientific excavations in the province.

Biological studies as an adjunct to archaeology were increasing, with special emphasis on birds by Loye Miller, on molluscs by Robert J. Drake and James J. Landye, and on mammals by C. E. Gustafson. Drake began publication of a small journal, *Molluscs in Archaeology and the Recent,* in 1960.

In the mid-1960s, archaeological programs in Oregon outside of Eugene became established, with Wilbur A. Davis at Oregon State University and with the active entry of Portland State University into the picture through the work of Thomas M. Newman at Cascadia Cave. Important work reported in 1965 included the cultural sequence of Windust Cave by Harvey S. Rice (no relation to David

G. Rice), a chronology involving Lind Coulee-related projectile points; the work of David Sanger in the Lochnore-Nesikep Creek area of British Columbia; and a description of 260 historic Palus burials excavated at the mouth of the Palouse River by Sprague. By 1966 the highway salvage program in Washington was revived, with the two major institutions dividing the state. The University of Washington was also involved in the Marymore site near Seattle (Greengo & Houston 1970) and was utilizing the services of David L. Browman, David A. Munsell, and William S. Dancey for most of their archaeological work. Washington State University by this time had moved up to Lower Granite Reservoir and had produced reports by several graduate students, including Barbara A. Grater, Charles R. Nance, and Monte R. Kenaston. Archaeological salvage operations at Washington State University were transferred to Roderick Sprague in 1965 and to Frank C. Leonhardy in 1968. This change in administration left Daugherty to pursue his original archaeological interests in Washington Coast archaeology on the Olympic Peninsula. A large program financed by the National Science Foundation was begun at Ozette in 1966. This program utilized the ecological approach with a plant ecologist, a zoologist, and a Pleistocene geologist.

With the construction of new powerhouse facilities in Grand Coulee Dam, the water level in Lake Roosevelt was lowered beyond the normal levels of the past thirty years. This permitted the first archaeological investigation in the region since the work of 1939–40. Survey work and excavation were first carried out from Washington State University and later from the University of Idaho.

Several theoretical and review articles were published in 1967. "Hells Canyon Archaeology" by Warren W. Caldwell and Oscar L. Mallory (1967) was the only Northwest item in *Publications in Salvage Archaeology*. In this summary Caldwell and Mallory presented their views on Plateau archaeology as viewed from the Upper Snake River, or perhaps to follow Osborne's terminology, this is the "view from Lincoln." In keeping with Osborne's title, David Sanger (1967) published an article in *American Antiquity* entitled "Prehistory of the Pacific Northwest as Seen from the Interior of British Columbia." In a doctoral dissertation from the University of Arizona in 1967, Sprague presented a summary of archaeological and ethnographic evidence for burial practices in the Plateau region. This was the first basic summary of the Plateau burial practices and the first cultural-historical suggestions on the topic since the pioneering work of Osborne in 1957. Also in 1967, a new journal was initiated, originally under the title, *Northwestern Anthropological Research Notes,* with the second issue changed to *Northwest Anthropological Research Notes* (NARN). The first issue of this new journal consisted of a ninety-page bibliography of Washington archaeology by Sprague (1967). In keeping with the objective of publishing bibliographies and other stimuli to research, the second issue was a revised edition of the anthropological bibliography of the Klamath Basin region by B. K. Swartz, Jr. (1967).

The University of Oregon, *Museum of Natural History, Bulletin 4,* was the first archaeological report in that new series, with a report by Frank Leonhardy (1967) on the Iron Gate site in northern California. As a special publication of the Idaho State University Museum, B. Robert Butler published *A Guide to Understanding Idaho Archaeology* (1968) as the first popular work in that state in the tradition of Stallard for Washington and Cressman for Oregon. In addition to the archaeology, this work presents a summary of the history of archaeology in Idaho, including both the Plateau and the Great Basin.

Three new publication series were initiated in 1968. The first of these, from the University of Washington, was entitled *Reports in Archaeology,* the first two numbers of which were utilized to report the work of Grabert in the Wells Reservoir, both historic and prehistoric. The second publication was an *Occasional Paper* series issued by the Washington Archaeological Society as a supplement to the *Washington Archaeologist*. The third series, *Syesis*, published by the British Columbia Provincial Museum, included archaeology among several subject areas.

Still another theoretical construct for the Plateau was added to the already long list by David L. Browman and David A. Munsell in 1969 under the title, "Columbia Plateau Prehistory: Cultural Development and Impinging Influences." Of all the constructs so far presented, this one has been the most poorly received, probably because it was admittedly hurriedly prepared and published. Although published in 1969, a work by Charles M. Nelson (son of Charles G. Nelson) records his theoretical point of view as of 1962, with minor revisions in 1967. To date this is the most thorough analysis of Plateau culture history and related theory to be published.

A new and interesting development in 1968 was the publication of a report by David H. Chance, *Survey of Antiquities Management on Bureau of Land Management Land in Oregon, 1968*. This work established a new precedent in the Northwest for the direct hiring of professional archaeologists by the Bureau of Land Management. Chance was headquartered at the University of Oregon during his work. During the late 1960s, Washington State University continued work largely in Lower Granite Reservoir under the direction of Frank Leonhardy, while David G. Rice conducted extensive survey work and frequent excavations all over the state of Washington, including Lower Granite Reservoir, Asotin Reservoir, Lake Roosevelt, the Cascade Mountains, and several highway salvage operations. Highway salvage archaeology in Washington was conducted on the eastern terminus by Harvey S. Rice and from the western side of the state by David A. Munsell. Max G. Pavesic replaced Dan Morse as Idaho Highway Archaeologist in 1967, with the site at Lenore on the Clearwater River the most significant highway salvage work. The archaeological picture at the University of Idaho changed in 1967 with the retirement of Alfred W. Bowers and the subsequent hiring of Roderick

Sprague, with an emphasis on historical archaeology. The addition of David G. Rice in 1969 rounded out the archaeological program at Moscow. Work was concentrated at Fort Colvile in Lake Roosevelt and at English Camp and American Camp on San Juan Island. The latter work was in cooperation with the University of Washington.

In the late 1960s, the archaeological picture in British Columbia flourished with the University of Calgary fielding Knut R. Fladmark, Jason W. Smith, A. H. Stryd, and Christopher Turnbull, plus James Baker from Vancouver City College and Paul G. Sneed from the University of British Columbia; the University of Colorado conducted archaeological excavations in the Bella Bella region of British Columbia under James J. Hester; the Centennial Museum at Vancouver sent out Gay Calvert; Simon Fraser University began working in 1966 with several ongoing archaeological projects under both Philip M. Hobler and Roy L. Carlson; the University of Victoria and the Archaeological Sites Advisory Board of the Province of British Columbia had a crew in the Gulf Islands under the direction of Donald H. Mitchell and surveys under the direction of Bjorn O. Simonsen; the National Museum of Man under the direction of Roscoe Wilmeth had a large project in the Carrier-speaking portions of British Columbia involving Paul Donahue and Kenneth M. Ames; and George F. MacDonald of the National Museum of Canada was on the lower Skeena and in the Queen Charlotte Islands. Historical archaeology in British Columbia also received a boost with the work of William J. Folan and John Dewhirst of the National Historic Sites Service at the site of Yuquot.

A similar expansion developed in Washington in the state colleges and community colleges in the late 1960s, especially at Seattle Community College under the direction of Astrida R. Onat, Central Washington State College under William C. Smith, and Western Washington State College under Garland F. Grabert.

In 1966 the Archaeological Society of British Columbia

was founded in Vancouver. The Mid-Columbia Archaeological Society was formed in 1967, largely through the efforts of David G. Rice in the Tri-Cities area of Washington. In 1968 the Vancouver Island Archaeological Society was founded in Victoria, British Columbia. An additional amateur group was formed in Oregon under the title of Northwest Archaeological Research Association. The organization of a group including both professional and amateurs, The Archaeological Association, University of Calgary, has resulted in a series of annual archaeological meetings held in Calgary and the publication of proceedings since 1969.

The Marmes (mar-muss) Rockshelter in eastern Washington was first reported by a survey party in connection with the McGregor Cave excavations of 1953. At that time Daugherty felt that the rockshelter was too close to the Palouse River and had probably been scoured out frequently by floods and thus contained no early material. In retrospect, Daugherty feels that this was probably a fortunate conclusion, because in 1953 the techniques necessary for a full interpretation of the Marmes Rockshelter simply were not available. Excavation was begun in 1962 by Washington State University when operations at the Palus Village site proved to be less than rewarding. Excavations were carried out during the full season in 1963 and again in 1964. A brief two-week excavation by a small crew was conducted in 1965 in an effort to establish that sterile levels had indeed been reached in the rear portion of the rockshelter. In the summer of 1965, Pleistocene geologist Roald Fryxell was directing the cutting of a bulldozer trench from the rockshelter to the flood plain below when skeletal material was exposed. All material was collected and passed on to C. E. Gustafson, zoologist in the Department of Anthropology, Washington State University. In 1967, Gustafson became the discoverer of Marmes Man when he identified human bone in a tray of material collected from the cut of 1965. A graduate class discovered additional skeletal material in the trench in April of 1968. Following this, efforts were made by Daugherty through U. S. Senator Warren G. Magnuson of Washington for a special federal appropriation to recover the remains apparently on the flood plain in front of the rockshelter. The result was the recovery of additional skeletal material, some of which probably had spilled over from a higher level in the rockshelter, and several bone and stone tools. An attempt was then made to protect the site from the flood waters of Lower Monumental Reservoir with an earthen dike; however, this structure failed, and the site was flooded. The initial claims of an antiquity of twelve to thirteen thousand years received far more publicity than the later final evidence of ten to eleven thousand, and tends to cast some doubt on the journalistic claim of the oldest human remains in North America. Although certainly not the oldest site in the Pacific Northwest, Marmes Rockshelter will undoubtedly remain for a long time as the most expensive and best-publicized archaeological site in the region (Washington Archaeological Society 1969).

In 1969, the Washington State Archaeological Council was formed, not as a group of individuals but as a group of institutions within the state involved in archaeological excavation. The objective of the group was to create a more equitable distribution of available research funds and to coordinate research activities on a statewide basis.

Another film was added to the regional inventory with the preview at the twenty-fifth annual meeting of the Society for American Archaeology of Astrida Onat's *The Dig*. This film, directed at the beginner, is one of the most realistic training films to be produced in archaeology.

Work on the Oregon Coast was renewed after several years of inactivity through the efforts of George Phebus, Jr., of the Department of Anthropology, Smithsonian Institution, with field direction by Robert M. Drucker.

The most recent theoretical work in the Plateau is a cultural sequence for the Lower Snake River region by Leonhardy and Rice (1970). This is not another revision of previous schemes but rather a new and refreshing analysis based on evidence from only one *region,* in the Willey and Phillips sense of the word. Two special publications from British Columbia in 1970 have dramatically increased the archaeological knowledge of the region. A special number in *BC Studies,* edited by Roy L. Carlson, included a review of British Columbia archaeology by the editor, a bibliography of the same area by Knut R. Fladmark, and six regional reports by Baker, Borden, Calvert, Carlson, Fladmark, and Hobler. A special issue of *Syesis* by David Sanger presented a summary of interior British Columbia archaeology. The publication in *NARN* of two archaeological symposia from the 1969 Northwest Anthropological Conference in Victoria (MacDonald 1969, Swanson 1970) further increased the diffusion of archaeological knowledge on a regional basis.

REFERENCES

ANDERSON, JEANINE
1967 "Northwest Coast Culture: The Problem of Origins." *Tebiwa* 10:1–12.

BALL, HOWARD T.
1941 "Disinterments at Grand Coulee." *Casket and Sunnyside* 71:35–38.

BERREMAN, JOEL V.
1944 "Chetco Archaeology." *General Series in Anthro.* 11.

BORDEN, CHARLES E.
1950 "Preliminary Report on Archaeological Investigations in the Fraser Delta Region." *Anthro. in British Columbia* 1:13–26.
1952 "A Uniform Site Designation Scheme for Canada." *Anthro. in British Columbia* 3:44–48.
1954 "Some Aspects of Prehistoric Coastal-Interior Relations in the Pacific Northwest." *Anthro. in British Columbia* 4:26–32.

BROWMAN, DAVID L., and MUNSELL, DAVID A.
1969 "Columbia Plateau Prehistory: Cultural Development and Impinging Influences." *Am. Ant.* 34:249–64.

BUTLER, B. ROBERT
1958 "Archaeological Investigations on the Washington Shore of The Dalles Reservoir, 1955–1957." Report submitted to the National Park Service.

1961   "The Old Cordilleran Culture in the Pacific Northwest."
        Occas. Pap. of the Idaho State Coll. Mus. 5.
1965   "The Structure and Function of the Old Cordilleran Culture
        Concept." *Am. Anthro.* 67:1120–31.
1968   *A Guide to Understanding Idaho Archaeology.* Pocatello:
        Idaho State University Museum.

CAIN, H. THOMAS
1950   *Petroglyphs of Central Washington.* Seattle: University of
        Washington Press.

CALDWELL, WARREN W.
1956   "The Archaeology of Wakemap: A Stratified Site near The
        Dalles of the Columbia." Ph.D. dissertation, University of
        Washington.

——— and MALLORY, OSCAR L.
1967   "Hells Canyon Archaeology." *River Basin Surveys Pub. in
        Salvage Arch.* 6.

CARLSON, ROY L.
1960   "Chronology and Culture Change in the San Juan Islands,
        Washington." *Am. Ant.* 25:562–86.
1970   "Archaeology of British Columbia." *BC Studies* 6–7:7–17.

CHANCE, DAVID H.
1968   "Survey of Antiquities Management on Bureau of Land
        Management Lands in Oregon, 1968." Report submitted to
        the Bureau of Land Management.

COLLIER, DONALD; HUDSON, A. E.; and FORD, ARLO
1942   "Archaeology of the Upper Columbia Region." *Univ. Wash.
        Pub. in Anthro.* 9(1).

CRESSMAN, L. S.
1942   "Archaeological Researches in the Northern Great Basin."
        Carnegie Inst. of Wash. Pub. 538.
1956   "Klamath Prehistory." *Trans. Am. Phil. Soc.* 46(4).
1962   *The Scandal and the Cave; The Indians of Oregon.* Portland:
        Beaver Books.

———; COLE, DAVID L.; DAVIS, WILBUR A.; NEWMAN, THOMAS M.;
        and SCHEANS, DANIEL J.
1960   "Cultural Sequences in The Dalles, Oregon: A Contribution
        to Pacific Northwest Prehistory." *Trans. Am. Phil. Soc.*
        50(10).

DAUGHERTY, RICHARD D.
1956a   "Archaeology of the Lind Coulee Site, Washington." *Proc.
        Am. Phil. Soc.* 100(3):223–78.
1956b   "Early Man in the Columbia Intermontane Province." *Univ.
        Utah Anthro. Pap.* 24.
1959   *Early Man in Washington.* State of Washington, Department
        of Conservation, Division of Mines and Geology, Informa.
        Circ. 32.
1962   "The Intermontane Western Tradition." *Am. Ant.* 28(2):
        144–50.

DRUCKER, PHILIP
1943 "Archaeological Survey on the Northern Northwest Coast."
    Bureau of Am. Ethn. Bull. 133:17–132.
1955 "Sources of Northwest Culture," *New Interpretations of
    Aboriginal American Culture History; 75th Anniversary
    Volume of the Anthropological Society of Washington*, 59–81.
    Washington, D.C.: Anthropological Society of Washington.

FLADMARK, KNUT R.
1970 "Bibliography of the Archaeology of British Columbia."
    BC Studies 6–7:126–51.

GREENGO, ROBERT E., and HOUSTON, ROBERT
1970 "Excavations at the Marymoor Site." *Reports in Arch.* 4.

GUNKEL, ALEXANDER
1961 "A Comparative Cultural Analysis of Four Archaeological
    Sites in the Rocky Beach Reservoir Region, Washington."
    Theses in Anthro. 1.

HEIZER, ROBERT F.
1941 "Oregon Prehistory—Retrospect and Prospect." *Common-
    wealth Review* 23:30–40.

HOWE, CARROL B.
1968 *Ancient Tribes of the Klamath Country.* Portland: Binfords
    and Mort.

ISSELSTEIN, KARL H.
1965 "Ancient Cataclysms which Changed Earth's Surface."
    Mokelumne Hill, Calif.: Health Research.

JOHNSON, LEROY, JR., and COLE, DAVID L.
1969 *A Bibliographic Guide to the Archaeology of Oregon and
    Adjacent Regions.* Special Pub. Mus. Nat. Hist. Univ.
    Oregon.

KING, ARDEN R.
1950 "Cattle Point, a Stratified Site in the Southern Northwest
    Coast Region." *Soc. Am. Arch. Mem.* 7.

KROEBER, A. L.
1923 "American Culture and the Northwest Coast." *Am. Anthro.*
    25:1–20.

LEONHARDY, FRANK C.
1967 "The Archaeology of a Late Prehistoric Village in North-
    western California." *Mus. Nat. Hist. Univ. Oregon Bull.* 4.
1968 "An Opinion on Archaeological Interpretation in the Pla-
    teau." *Eastern New Mexico Univ. Contrib. in Anthro.*
    1(3):27–31.

——— and RICE, DAVID G.
1970 "A Proposed Culture Typology for the Lower Snake River
    Region, Southeastern Washington." *Northwest Anthro. Re-
    search Notes* 4:1–29.

MacDonald, George F. (ed.)
   1969   "Current Archaeological Research on the Northwest Coast, Symposium Presented at the 22nd Annual Northwest Anthropological Conference." *Northwest Anthro. Research Notes* 3:193–263.

Nelson, Charles G.
   1957   "The Osborne Case—A Report by the President." *Washington Arch.* 1(7):4–5.

Nelson, Charles M.
   1969   "The Sunset Creek Site (45-KT-28) and Its Place in Plateau Prehistory." *Washington State Univ. Lab. of Anthro., Report of Investigations* 47.

Osborne, Douglas
   1957   "Excavations in the McNary Reservoir Basin near Umatilla, Oregon." *Bureau of Am. Eth. Bull.* 166.

———; Caldwell, Warren W.; and Crabtree, Robert H.
   1956   "The Problem of Northwest Coastal-Interior Relationships as Seen from Seattle." *Am. Ant.* 22:117–28.

Perry, Jay
   1939   "Notes on a Type of Indian Burial Found in the Mid-Columbia River District of Central Washington." *New Mexico Anthro.* 3:80–82.

Rice, David G.
   1967   "A Commentary on the Derivation of Plateau Culture." Master's special problem paper, Washington State University.

Rust, H. J.
   1912   "A Brief Historical and Archaeological Sketch of Lake Coeur d'Alene, Kootenai County, Idaho." *Arch. Bull.* 3:46–48.

Sanger, David
   1967   "Prehistory of the Pacific Northwest as Seen from the Interior of British Columbia." *Am. Ant.* 32:186–97.

Seaman, N. G.
   1946   *Indian Relics of the Pacific Northwest.* Portland: Binfords and Mort.

Smith, Harlan I.
   1910   "Archaeology of the Yakima Valley." *Anthro. Pap. Am. Mus. Nat. Hist.* 6(1).

Smith, Marian W.
   1950   "Archaeology of the Columbia-Fraser Region." *Soc. Am. Arch. Mem.* 6.

Spinden, Herbert J.
   1908   "The Nez Perce Indians." *Am. Anthro. Mem.* 9.

Sprague, Roderick
   1967   "A Preliminary Bibliography of Washington Archaeology." *Northwest Anthro. Research Notes* 1(1).

1968   "Papers Presented at the First Twenty Annual Meetings of the Northwest Anthropological Conference, 1948–1967." *Northwest Anthro. Research Notes* 2(1):123–39.

STALLARD, BRUCE
1958   *Archaeology in Washington.* State of Washington, Department of Conservation, Division of Mines and Geology, Information Circular 30.

STRONG, EMORY
1959   *Stone Age on the Columbia River.* Portland: Binfords and Mort.

STRONG, WILLIAM DUNCAN; SCHENCK, W. EGBERT; and STEWARD, JULIAN H.
1930   "Archaeology of The Dalles-Deschutes Region." *Univ. Cal. Pub. Am. Arch. and Eth.* 24(1).

SWANSON, EARL H., JR.
1962   "The Emergence of Plateau Culture." *Occas. Pap. Idaho State Univ. Mus.* 8.

——— (ed.)
1970   "Cultural Relations between the Plateau and Great Basin, Symposium Presented at the 22nd Annual Northwest Anthropological Conference." *Northwest Anthro. Research Notes* 4(1):65–125.

SWARTZ, B. K., JR.
1963   "Klamath Basin Petroglyphs." *Archives of Arch.* 21.
1967   "A Bibliography of Klamath Basin Anthropology with Excerpts and Annotations," Revised Edition. *Northwest Anthro. Research Notes* 1(2).

TERRY, JAMES
1891   *Sculptured Anthropoid Ape Heads Found in or Near the Valley of the John Day River, a Tributary of the Columbia River, Oregon.* New York: J. J. Little.

WARREN, CLAUDE N.
1968   "The View from Wenas: A Study in Plateau Prehistory." *Occas. Pap. Idaho State Univ. Mus.* 24.

WASHINGTON ARCHAEOLOGICAL SOCIETY
1969   "The Marmes Year, April 1968–April 1969." *Washington Arch.* 13(2–3).

10 PLUMBING, PHILOSOPHY, AND POETRY

James E. Fitting

In spite of the strong regional traditions in North American archaeology, it is clear that there are common trends in many areas. It is not surprising that archaeological investigations began earlier in the East than in the West, and for that reason, the earliest developmental stages are lacking in the latter area. It is also clear that with the development of even more efficient systems of communication and with the increasing mobility of archaeologists themselves, there has been a concomitant acceleration in the rates of archaeological change and the rapidity with which new analytical concepts are spread.

There has been an overwhelming increase in the number of both professional and amateur archaeologists within the past few decades. Public support of archaeology has also increased. The role of the WPA in the Southeast and the River Basin Survey in the Plains has been explained in detail in particular chapters of this volume.

Since the 1950s, the National Science Foundation has (until recently, at least) given even-handed and equitable support to archaeology around the country. As of the early 1970s, it would appear that government support for archaeology will continue, but on a diminished basis. Some archaeologists have demonstrated that the private sector is strongly interested in supporting archaeology. Only time will tell whether this type of support will be developed in other areas and what changes it will bring in archaeology. Archaeology supported by the general public conjures up the image of a scientific Disneyland, but it certainly will require archaeologists to talk to nonarchaeologists for a change—something that could not help but be beneficial.

It would be a fairly simple task to typologize North American archaeology beyond the regional level. Archaeology in the late eighteenth and early nineteenth centuries was isolated, whimsical, and certainly preparadigmatic, although its practitioners, like Thomas Jefferson, could proceed by rules that we would now call scientific. During the second half of the nineteenth century, data collecting began on a large scale throughout North America, and for the first time standardized comparative studies were undertaken. I still see no standardization of theory in this area, with geographical, direct historical and, to a much lesser extent, chronological problems being dominant.

With the appearance of formal training in anthropology around the turn of the century, archaeology became a subdivision within that discipline and participated, usually with a slight time lag, in the development of anthropology. When anthropology was descriptive and its modes of integration cultural-historical, so was archaeology. When American anthropology became analytical, archaeology, with noticeable reluctance, followed suit, but still maintained a dependent status (Willey and Phillips 1958:1).

Among anthropologists, archaeologists have always been viewed as an odd lot. Although they tended to follow theoretical bandwagons like dutiful puppy dogs, their other habits were less endearing. Much of their peculiar theory seemed little more than field technique, and they often talked to historians, geologists, and paleontologists and even plain folks who did not have an -ologist to their name.

After World War II there was certainly a technological revolution in archaeology. Radiocarbon dating was most significant but was only one aspect of this technological revolution. Archaeology put its plumbing in order, and although at that time its theory must still be found in its technique, its techniques were in the process of elaboration. Individuals who worked with scientists using computers and differential equations would soon adapt these items to their own work. In the late 1950s and early 1960s, many archaeologists wondered if the complicated crafts of their field were compatible with the traditional training patterns in anthropology. At least one separate department of archaeology was formed at that time, and others were contemplated.

But plumbing does not exist by itself. To paraphrase John Gardner, the archaeology that supports its plumbers and neglects its philosophers will have neither good plumbing nor good philosophy. And neither will hold water.

After the plumbers came the philosophers. There was no question about their logic and, initially, their premises were taken from the traditional paradigms of archaeological interpretation—ones dependent on anthropology. The result was "anthropological archaeology." It was realized that the deductive potentials of archaeology are considerable and largely unrealized. Like Thomas Browne in his *Hydriotaphia* (1658), it was stated, "What songs the Syrens sang, or what name Achilles assumed when he hid himself among women, though puzzling questions are not beyond all conjecture."

The epistomology of archaeology became important, and its origins were found in positivism. Its goals, like those of anthropology, were nomothetic, but with a noble past, its relationship to anthropology changed. Its paradigm was changing, and there are some recent hints of a new independent relationship, at least symbiotic if not contributory, with general anthropology. Archaeology has moved, in Edmund Leach's (1961) terms, from "butterfly collecting" to "inspired guesswork," and possibly beyond, if all things are open to the deductive potentials, the axiomatic corollaries, of its theories. It has reached a point where both its plumbing and its philosophy can hold water.

It may have also reached a point where it can do more than hold water. If its plumbing led to its philosophy, its philosophy takes it into the realm of literature. The quotation from *Hydriotaphia* was used as the introductory note for a classic deductive model, Edgar Allan Poe's "The Murders in the Rue Morgue." The subject matter of that short story is not too distant from the Sunday supplement archaeology of today. Unfortunately, too much of today's archaeology, while possessing elegant logic, lacks the style of "The Murders in the Rue Morgue." It lacks the style to live beyond the boundaries that it imposes on itself. It is, of course, a science and, as such, rapidly becomes immune from the taint of intelligibility. It has a reality, truth, and paradigm, and is accountable only to itself. However, there is another disturbing aspect of scientific truth. It is never really absolute. The King of Siam could complain of not being sure of things that he knew were absolutely certain. There are times, particularly in scientific crises, where the logically absurd becomes absurdly logical, when questions too obvious to be asked are answered in the negative, and when the only times we are really sure we are wrong are in those instances when there is no question about our being correct. General systems theory can generate its own answers, and when our interpretations take on a reality of their own, our evaluation of them passes from scientific to aesthetic. With the spiral of interpretive statements elegantly based on suspect or self-serving data, who could fail to see archaeology as more than a divine comedy, robbed of the seriousness of a Poe story by the seriousness with which it takes itself? We need to ask, "Where is the locus of archaeological reality?" Will its reliance on science, mathematics, and logic bring it closer to reality? Years ago, Leslie White (1949:285) demonstrated that there is no contradiction in the statements, "Mathematical truths have an existence and a validity independent of the human mind" and "Mathematical truths have no existence and validity apart from the human mind." The same thing can be said for archaeology. The plumbing and the philosophy of archaeology are so perfected that their excellence exists apart from, and often in spite of, individual ignorance of them and resistance to them. The second statement is also true in a nomothetic sense, although it damns such nomothetic interpretations. Truth is determined by the cultural context in which it exists. Prerevolutionary science is neither more nor less scientific than postrevolutionary science. No matter how elegant the theory or how absolute its predictions, it is still evaluated on a chessboard, a place where an infinite number of moves take place on a finite series of squares.

Archaeologists, through a series of internal developments, have learned to talk to themselves. They do not have all of the answers, but they now feel that this fault will inevitably be cured, given enough time. They still talk to other "ologists" but with a superior air that they may have lacked before, and the plain folk are left far behind.

As a science, archaeology may have matured, but as a people, archaeologists have not. The "inspired guesswork" is too certain in their minds, and it is only when, with the inspirer of the inspired guesswork, they can analyze three hundred myths and realize that they have reached no conclusion that they will again be human, inspiring, and fun. If we take the statement, "Archaeology is anthropology or it is nothing" at face value, we have two interesting alternatives. The *a priori* assumption of agreement has led to a series of logical conclusions that in turn indicate that the very statement might not be true. If archaeology is either more, or less, than anthropology, it is nothing, and if it is nothing, it is in an even better position to be yet something more.

> And instead, during the brief intervals in which humanity can bear to interrupt its hive-like labors, let us grasp the essence of what our species has been and still is, beyond thought and beneath society: an essence that may be vouchsafed to us in a mineral more beautiful than any work of man; in the scent, more subtly involved than our books, that lingers in the heart of a lily; or the wink of an eye, heavy with patience, serenity and mutual forgiveness, that sometimes, through an involuntary understanding, one can exchange with a cat [Levi-Strauss 1964:398].

REFERENCES

LEACH, EDMUND
  1961 "Rethinking Anthropology." *London School of Economics Monographs on Social Anthropology* 22.

LEVI-STRAUSS, CLAUDE
  1964 *Tristes Tropiques.* New York: Antheneum.

WHITE, LESLIE A.
  1949 *The Science of Culture.* Farrar, Straus & Cudahy.

CONTRIBUTORS

DAVID S. BROSE is an Associate Professor at Case Western Reserve University and Associate Curator at the Cleveland Museum of Natural History. He received his Ph.D. from the University of Michigan in 1968. He has done field work in the Great Lakes, the Southeast, the Canadian Maritimes, and Europe, and has published numerous monographs and articles on historic and prehistoric archaeology.

ALBERT A. DEKIN, JR., is an Assistant Professor of Anthropology at the State University of New York at Potsdam. He received his archaeological training at Dartmouth, UCLA, and Michigan State University, where he is completing his doctoral studies. He has done archaeological field work in the Canadian Arctic, the Great Lakes region, and northern New York.

JAMES E. FITTING has held academic positions at Wayne State University, the University of Michigan, and Case Western Reserve University. He is a Research Associate at Southern Methodist University and State Archaeologist of Michigan. He received his Ph.D. from the University of Michigan in 1964 and has done field work in the Great Lakes, the Southwest, the Caribbean, and Central America. He is author of *The Archaeology of Michigan* and other monographs and papers.

GEORGE C. FRISON is head of the Department of Anthropology at the University of Wyoming. He received his Ph.D. from the University of Michigan in 1967 and has done field work on the Plains. He has published numerous papers and monographs on Plains archaeology.

WILLIAM C. NOBLE is an Assistant Professor in the Department of Sociology and Anthropology at McMaster University. He received his Ph.D. from the University of Calgary in 1968 and has carried out field work in Ontario, Manitoba, Saskatchewan, Alberta, and the Northwest Territories.

ARTHUR H. ROHN is Associate Professor of Anthropology and Chairman of the Department at Wichita State University. He received his Ph.D. from Harvard in 1966 and has done field work in the Southwest for many years. He is author of *Mug House* and other monographs and articles.

RODERICK SPRAGUE is Professor of Anthropology and head of the Department of Sociology and Anthropology at the University of Idaho. He received his Ph.D. from the University of Arizona in 1967 and has done field work in the Pacific Northwest and the Canadian Maritimes. He has numerous publications on burial practices of the Northwest and the Southwest, Plateau ethnohistory, and historic archaeology.

JAMES B. STOLTMAN is Associate Professor of Anthropology at the University of Wisconsin, Madison. He received his Ph.D. from Harvard in 1967 and has done field work in the Southeast, the Great Lakes, and Europe. He is author of *Groton Plantation* and other monographs and articles.

CLAUDE N. WARREN is Professor of Anthropology and Chairman of the Department at the University of Nevada–Las Vegas. He received his Ph.D. from UCLA in 1964 and has done field work in California, the Great Basin, the Columbia Plateau, and Nevada. He is author of *The View from Wenas* and other publications.

INDEX